PEN IN HAND

Pen in Hand

Reading, Rereading
and Other Mysteries

TIM PARKS

ALMA BOOKS

ALMA BOOKS LTD

3 Castle Yard
Richmond
Surrey TW10 6TF
United Kingdom
www.almabooks.com

This collection first published by Alma Books Limited in 2019
© Tim Parks, 2019

Cover design: Leo Nickolls

Tim Parks asserts his moral right to be identified as the author of this work
in accordance with the Copyright, Designs and Patents Act 1988

Printed and bound by CPI Group (UK) Ltd, Croydon, CR0 4YY

ISBN : 978-1-84688-457-3

Contents

Foreword:
A Weapon for Readers

Imagine you are asked what single alteration in people's behaviour might best improve the lot of mankind. How foolish would you have to be to reply: have them learn to read with a pen in their hands? But I firmly believe such a simple development would bring huge benefits.

We have too much respect for the printed word, too little awareness of the power words hold over us. We allow worlds to be conjured up for us with very little concern for the implications. We overlook glaring incongruities. We are suckers for alliteration, assonance and rhythm. We rejoice over stories, whether fiction or "documentary", whose outcomes are flagrantly manipulative, self-serving or both. Usually both. If a piece of writing manifests the stigmata of literature – symbols, metaphors, unreliable narrators, multiple points of view, structural ambiguities – we afford it unlimited credit. With occasional exceptions, the only "criticism" brought to such writing is the kind that seeks to elaborate its brilliance, its cleverness, its creativity. What surprised me most when I first began publishing fiction myself was how much at every level a novelist is allowed to *get away with*.

This extravagant regard, which seemed to reach a peak in the second half of the twentieth century as the modernists of a generation before were canonized as performers of the ever more arduous miracle of conferring a little meaning on life, is reflected

1

in the treatment of the book itself. The spine must not be bent back and broken, the pages must not be marked with dog ears, there must be no underlining, no writing in the margins. Obviously, for those of us brought up on library books and school-owned textbooks (my copy of Browning bore the name of a dozen pupils who had used the text before me), there were simple and sensible reasons supporting this behaviour. But the reverence went beyond a proper respect for those who would be reading the pages after you. Even when I bought a book myself, if my parents caught me breaking its spine so that it would lay open on the desk, they were shocked. Writing was sacred. In the beginning was the Word, the word written down, hopefully on quality paper. Much of the resistance to e-books, notably from the literati, has to do with a loss of this sense of sacredness, of the vulnerable paper vessel that thrives on our protective devotion.

But the absolute need to read with a pen in one's hand became evident to me watching my students as we studied the art of translation together. I would give them the same text in English and Italian and ask them to tell me which was the original text. Or I would give them a text without saying whether it was a translation or not and ask them to comment on it. Again and again, the authority conveyed by the printed word and an aura of literariness, or the excitement of dramatic action, or the persuasive drift of an argument, would prevent them from noticing the most obvious absurdities. They would read a sentence like "For a little while in his arms Maria was like a doll, she allowed herself to be undressed and turned in the bed without taking a breath" (from William Weaver's translation of Rosetta Loy's *Le strade di polvere*) and be so captivated by the romantic context as to miss the fact that one cannot be undressed and turned in a bed without taking a breath; it takes rather longer to undress someone and have your way with them than most people can survive without breathing. This is a poor translation of an Italian mix of idiom and invention – *senza emettere un fiato* – which might best have been translated "without so much as a sigh".

Or they would read, "Then came the train. It began by looking like a horse, a horse with its cart raised up on the rough stones" (from Isabel Quigley's translation of Pavese's *The Moon and the Bonfires*), and amid the drama of the action they wouldn't see how incongruous this image of a cart "raised up on rough stones" was, how unlikely it would be to raise up a cart on rough stones. It was just a poor translation of a horse and cart on cobbles (*un cavallo col carretto su dei ciottoli*).

But beyond these small technicalities, the kind of internal inconsistencies that someone like Beckett actually introduced into his work deliberately in order to wake the reader up (and again many students do not notice such deliberate inconsistencies), I would find that we had read a page of Virginia Woolf together without the students appreciating that we were being encouraged to think positively about suicide, or we would read D.H. Lawrence without their being aware that the writer was insisting that some lives were definitely worth more than others. I even remember a class reading this passage from Henry Green (admittedly as part of a larger scene) without any student being aware of its sexual content:

> But in spite of Mrs Middleton's appeal, the girl, with a "here you are" leant over to the husband and opened wide the pearly gates. Her wet teeth were long and sharp, of an almost transparent whiteness. The tongue was pointed also and lay curled to a red tip against her lower jaw, to which the gums were a sterile pink. Way back behind, cavernous, in a deeper red, her uvula seemed to shrink from him.

Aside from simply insisting, as I already had for years, that they be more alert, I began to wonder what was the most practical way I could lead my students to a greater attentiveness, teach them to protect themselves from all those underlying messages that can shift one's attitude without one's being aware of it? I began to think about the way I read myself, about the activity of reading, what you put into it rather than what was simply on the page. Try this experiment, I eventually told them: from now on always read with a pen in your hands, not beside you on the table, but actually in your hand, ready, armed. And always make three or four comments on every page, at least one critical, even aggressive. Put a question mark by everything you find suspect. Underline anything you really appreciate. Feel free to write "splendid", but also, "I don't believe a word of it". And even "bullshit".

A pen is not a magic wand. The critical faculty is not conjured from nothing. But it was remarkable how many students improved their performance with this simple stratagem. There is something predatory, cruel even, about a pen suspended over a text. Like a hawk over a field, it is on the lookout for something vulnerable. Then it is a pleasure to swoop and skewer the victim with the nib's sharp point. The mere fact of holding the hand poised for action changes our attitude to the text. We are no longer passive consumers of a monologue but active participants in a dialogue. Students would report that their reading slowed down when they had a pen in their hand, but at the same time the text became more dense, more interesting, if only because a certain pleasure could now be taken in their own response to the writing when they didn't feel it was up to scratch, or worthy only of being scratched.

Looking back over a book we have just read and scribbled on, or coming back to the same book months and maybe years later, we get a strong sense of our own position in relation to the writer's position. Where he said this kind of thing, I responded with that, where he touched this nerve, my knee jerked thus.

Hence a vehicle for self-knowledge is created, for what is the self if not the position one habitually assumes in relation to other selves? These days, going back to reading the novels and poetry that have been on my shelves since university days, I see three or four layers of comments, perhaps in different-coloured pens. And I sense how my position has changed, how I have changed.

In this regard, you might say that the opportunity to comment on articles published online is an excellent thing. And it is. I do not share the view of some fellow writers that those commenting, criticizing and protesting are beyond the pale. Often I will find comments below an article (on occasion, alas, below my own articles) that are more intelligent, even better informed, than the article itself. This is exciting, even when it is mortifying.

Nevertheless, commenting on articles online is not the same thing as writing in the margins of the novels one has bought. Online one is expressing one's opinion for other readers. There is a risk of falling back on partisan positions, of using the space to ride old hobby horses, of showing off. Often the debate moves far away from the article itself. And once the comments are made it is unlikely one will go back to look at them, certainly not in the way one is more or less bound to go back, over the years, to Hemingway or Svevo, or Katherine Mansfield, or Elsa Morante; and then it is fascinating to see what you did and didn't see in the past. You criticized an opinion that makes perfect sense now; you applauded a detail that now looks suspiciously fake. What will I feel about today's comments on my next reading?

Some readers will fear that the pen-in-hand approach denies us those wonderful moments when we fall under a writer's spell, the moments when we succumb to a style, and are happy to succumb to it, when suddenly it seems to us that this approach to the world – be it Proust's or Woolf's or Beckett's or Bernhard's – is really, at least for the moment, the only approach we

5

are interested in, moments that are no doubt among the most exciting in our reading experience.

No, I wouldn't want to miss out on that. But if writers are to entice us into their vision, let us make them work for it. Let us resist enchantment for a while, or at least for long enough to have some idea of what we are being drawn into. For the mindless, passive acceptance of other people's representations of the world can only enchain us and hamper our personal growth, hamper the possibility of positive action. Sometimes it seems the whole of society languishes in the stupor of the fictions it has swallowed. Wasn't this what Cervantes was complaining about when he began *Don Quixote*? Better to read a poor book with alert resistance than devour a good one in mindless adoration.

And so, dear reader, before going on to read the following pages, where I try to speak intelligently about the arts and mysteries of reading and writing and translation, please by all means pick up a pen, a sharp pen, keep it tightly gripped between your fingers and be ready to use it whenever and however seems appropriate, viciously, generously, above all judiciously.

Pen in Hand

How Could You Like that Book?

How Could You Like that Book?

I rarely spend much time wondering why others do not enjoy the books I like. Henry Green, an old favourite, almost a fetish, is never an easy read and never offers a plot that is immediate or direct. "There's not much straight shootin'," he admitted, in the one interview he gave. Elsa Morante is so lush and fantastical, so extravaganty rhetorical, she must seem way over the top to some. Thomas Bernhard offers one nightmare after another in cascades of challenging rhetoric; it's natural to suspect he's overdoing it. Christina Stead is so wayward, so gloriously tangled and disorganized, it's inevitable that some readers will grow weary. And so on.

Perhaps it's easy for me to understand why so many are not on board with these writers, because I occasionally feel the same way myself. In fact, it may be that the most seductive novelists are also the ones most willing to risk irritating you. Faulkner comes to mind, so often on the edge between brilliant and garrulous. Italy's Carlo Emilio Gadda was another. Muriel Spark. Sometimes even Kafka. Resistance to these writers is never a surprise to me.

On the other hand, I do spend endless hours mulling over the mystery of what others like. Again and again the question arises: how *can* they?

I am not talking about genre fiction, where the pleasures are obvious enough. Reviewing duties over the last few years have had me reading Stieg Larsson, E.L. James and a score of Georges Simenon's Maigrets. Once you accept the premise that you are reading for entertainment, their plots and brightly drawn dramatis personae quickly pull you in. However "adult" the material, one is reminded of the way one read as a child: to know what happens. You turn the pages quickly, even voraciously, and when something galls – the ugly exploitation of sexual violence in Larsson, the cartoon silliness of James, the monotonous presentation of Maigret as the dour, long-suffering winner – you simply skip and hurry on, because the story has you on its hook. You can see why people love these books and, above all, love reading lots of them. They encourage addiction, the repetition of a comforting process: identification, anxiety/ suspense, reassurance. Supposedly realistic, they actually take us far away from our own world and generally leave us feeling pleased that our lives are spared the sort of melodrama we love to read about.

But what are we to say of the likes of Haruki Murakami? Or Salman Rushdie? Or Jonathan Franzen? Or Jennifer Egan, or recent prize-winners like Andrés Neuman and Eleanor Catton or, most monumentally, Karl Ove Knausgaard? They are all immensely successful writers. They are clearly very competent. Knausgaard is the great new thing, I am told. I pick up Knausgaard. I read a hundred pages or so and put it down. I cannot understand the attraction. No, that's not true, I do get a certain attraction, but cannot understand why one would commit to its extension over so many pages. It doesn't seem attractive *enough* for what it is asking of me.

Take Elena Ferrante. Again and again I pick up her novels, and again and again I give up around page fifty. My impression is of something wearisomely concocted, determinedly melodramatic, forever playing on Neapolitan stereotype. Here, in *My Brilliant Friend*, the narrator is remembering a quarrel between neighbours:

As their vindictiveness increased, the two women began to insult each other if they met on the street or the stairs: harsh, fierce sounds. It was then that they began to frighten me. One of the many terrible scenes of my childhood begins with the shouts of Melina and Lidia, with the insults they hurl from the windows and then on the stairs; it continues with my mother rushing to our door, opening it and looking out, followed by us children; and ends with the image, for me still unbearable, of the two neighbours rolling down the stairs, entwined, and Melina's head hitting the floor of the landing, a few inches from my shoes, like a white melon that has slipped from your hand.

What can one say? Making no effort of the imagination, Ferrante simply announces melodrama: "Harsh, fierce sounds"; "One of the many terrible scenes of my childhood"; insults are "hurled". The memory is "for me still unbearable", though in the following pages the incident is entirely forgotten. Is "entwined" really the right word for two people locked in struggle on the stairs? As in a B-movie, a head hits the floor a few inches from our hero's shoes. Then comes the half-hearted attempt to transform cartoon reportage into literature: "like a white melon that has slipped from your hand".

I can't recall dropping a melon myself, but if the aim of a metaphor is to bring intensity and clarity to an image, this one goes in quite a different direction. The dull slap of the soft white melon hitting the ground and rolling away from you would surely be a very different thing from the hard crack of a skull and the sight of a bloody face. I'm astonished that, having tossed the metaphor in, out of mechanical habit one presumes, the author didn't pull it right out again. And even more I'm astonished that other people are not irritated by this lazy writing.

It's not only fiction that does this to me. I am told, for example, that Stephen Grosz's book *The Examined Life* – a psychoanalyst giving us his most interesting case histories – is a work of genius and is selling like hotcakes. I buy a copy, and halfway through I toss it away, literally, at the wall, in intense irritation. How can people like these stories, with their over-easy packaging of what are no doubt extremely complex personal problems, their evident and decidedly unexamined complacency about the rightness of the analyst's intervention?

There. I live under the constant impression that other people, other readers, are allowing themselves to be hoodwinked. They are falling for charms they shouldn't fall for. Or imagining charms that aren't there. They should be making it a little harder for their authors. Reading Neuman's *Traveller of the Century*, I appreciate that he is brilliant, that he effortlessly churns out page after page of complex prose, but I feel the whole thing is an ambition-driven exercise in literariness. Same with so many who flaunt their fancy prose. Even when I read an author I recognize as a very serious and accomplished artist – Alice Munro, Colm Tóibín – I begin to wonder how people can be so wholehearted in their enthusiasm. Both writers, it seems to me, equate fiction with the manufacture of a certain rather predictable pathos, an unspoken celebration of our capacity for compassion and the supposed redemption of suffering in the pleasure of fine prose and good storytelling. No doubt these things do have their worth – I acknowledge that – it is the growing impression that they are merely being rehearsed that is wearisome. Toni Morrison is another. The writer has learnt how to concoct our sophisticated drug for us. How can readers feel at ease with that?

No sooner have I articulated my amazement, my sense of betrayal almost, than I begin to feel insecure. Is it really possible that so many people I respect have got it wrong? Close friends as well. Am I an inveterate elitist? A puritan? Or resentful of other people's success? Shouldn't I perhaps relax and enjoy my reading a little more, rather than approaching books with constant suspicion?

On the other hand, there are those moments when a work overcomes my suspicion, and persuades me that what I'm reading really is something more than a carefully calculated literary operation. I remember my first encounters with W.G. Sebald or J.M. Coetzee or Natalia Ginzburg – and those moments give me great pleasure and make me feel happy with how I read. Then I'm glad I didn't waste too much time with the white melons.

Where to go with this uncertainty? Perhaps rather than questioning other readers' credulity, or worrying about my own presumption, what might really be worth addressing here is the whole issue of incomprehension: mutual and apparently insuperable incomprehension between well-meaning and intelligent people, all brought up in the same cultural tradition, more or less. It's curious, for example, that the pious rhetoric gusting around literature always promotes the writing and reading habit as a powerful communication tool, an instrument for breaking down barriers, promoting understanding – and yet it is exactly over my reaction to books that I tend to discover how completely out of sync with others I am.

I have often argued not just over whether *Disgrace* is a good novel, but over what it means. How can you suppose (I grow heated) that Coetzee is too austere, that he lacks a sense of humour? How can you imagine that he is claiming a direct moral equivalence between a professor sleeping with one of his students and a band of young men raping a woman in her isolated farmhouse? Yet people do suppose Coetzee has no humour, and they do imagine he means that equivalence. And perhaps he does. Certainly I have no way of proving he doesn't.

Could this be the function, then, or at least one important function of fiction: to make us aware of our differences? To have our contrasting positions emerge in response to these highly complex cultural artefacts? Not that superficial togetherness in celebration that the publishing industry, the literary festivals and the interminable literary prizes are forever seeking to generate, the happy conviction that we have found a new literary hero and can all bask together in his or her achievement – but all the heated debate that actually preceded the prize-giving: the shifting alliances as each book was discussed, the times you just couldn't believe that the fellow juror who supported you over book A is now seriously proposing to ditch book B, and so on.

In this view, our reaction to literature becomes a repeated act of self-discovery. Our contrasting reactions to the books we read tell us who we are. We are our position in relation to each other as understood in the reaction to these books. Reading other people's takes on Primo Levi, Murakami or David Eggers and comparing them to my own, I get some sense of who we all are and what we're up to. Sometimes this turns out to be far more interesting than reading the book itself.

If this is the case, then, the important thing would be, first, really to understand one's own reaction, to observe it with great care; and, second, to articulate it honestly, without any fudging for fear that others might disagree. Though even a fudge is a declaration of identity. And nothing could be more common among the community of book reviewers than fudging.

Reading Is Forgetting

There are moments when quite separate fragments of information or opinion come together and something hitherto only vaguely intuited becomes clear. Opening a new book called *Forgetting* by the Dutch writer Douwe Draaisma, I am told almost at once that our immediate visual memories "can hold on to stimuli for no more than a fraction of a second". This fact – our inevitable forgetting, or simply barely registering most of the visual input we receive – is acknowledged with some regret, since we are generally encouraged, Draaisma reflects, "to imagine memory as the ability to preserve something, preferably everything, wholly intact".

The same day, I ran across a quotation from Vladimir Nabokov on the Internet: "Curiously enough," the author of *Lolita* tells us, "one cannot read a book: one can only reread it." Intrigued by this paradox, I checked out the essay it came from. "When we read a book for the first time," Nabokov complains, "the very process of laboriously moving our eyes from left to right, line after line, page after page, this complicated physical work upon the book, the very process of learning in terms of space and time what the book is about, this stands between us and artistic appreciation." Only on a third or fourth reading, he claims, do we start behaving towards a book as we would towards a painting, holding it all in the mind at once.

Nabokov does not mention forgetting, but it's clear that this is what he is largely talking about. The physical effort of moving the eyes back and forth remains exactly the same on every reading of a book, nor have I ever found it particularly laborious. What is different on a second and subsequent readings is our growing capacity for retention, for putting things in relation to one another. We know the end of the story now and can see how it is foreshadowed at the beginning, how the strands are spun and gathered together. Rereading *Mrs Dalloway*, for example, we are struck on the first page to find the comment "What a lark, what a plunge", of Clarissa's sallying forth from her house into the street, aware as we now are that later in the book one of the characters will plunge to his death from an upper window. At once we feel we know the novel better, or at least are more aware of its careful construction. It is gratifying.

Nabokov continues his essay, quoting Flaubert: "*Comme l'on serait savant si l'on connaissait bien seulement cinq ou six livres.*" ("What a scholar one might be if one knew well only five or six books.") The ideal here, it seems, is total knowledge of the book, total and simultaneous awareness of all its contents, total recall. Knowledge, wisdom even, lies in depth, not extension. The book, at once complex and endlessly available for revisits, allows the mind to achieve an act of prodigious control. Rather than submitting ourselves to a stream of information, in thrall to each precarious moment of a single reading, we can gradually come to possess, indeed to memorize, the work outside time.

Since a reader could only achieve such mastery with an extremely limited number of books, it will be essential to establish that very few works are worth this kind of attention. We are pushed, that is, towards an elitist vision of literature, in which aesthetic appreciation requires exhaustive knowledge only of the best. It is the view of writing and reading that was taught in English departments forty years ago: the dominance of the canon, the assumption of endless nuance and ambiguity, the need for close textual analysis.

Needless to say, it's also an approach that consoles professors for having to reread the same texts year in year out. (Indeed, if I frequently quote from Lawrence and Joyce and Beckett and Woolf in this space, it is because these are authors whose works I regularly teach and have reread more times than I care to think.) And of course it is precisely the kind of text that is wilfully complex and difficult – *Ulysses*, *In Search of Lost Time*, *The Magic Mountain*, Gadda's *That Awful Mess on the Via Merulana*, Faulkner's *Absalom, Absalom!* – that allows the professor, who has read it ten times, to stay safely ahead of his bewildered students.

Meanwhile, our reactions to a book on first reading are irrelevant, except in so far as they do or don't encourage us to go back to the beginning and start again. But since this whole approach assumes that no book worth its salt will yield its best first time around, and that we can't know what might come up on further readings – an idea that is easy to sell to a young and inexperienced reader approaching Musil or Svevo or Kafka – the decision to reread is more or less taken for us by our teachers, or by critics. In short, our betters will tell us from their experience which books we should be reading – rereading, that is – since our first reading is hardly reading at all. Once the canon is established, then, it is unlikely to change, since who has time to check out the stuff that didn't make it? If, that is, on Flaubert's recommendation, my half-dozen books are still yielding new depths, why should I look elsewhere?

So, is this an ideal attitude to literature? Is Nabokov right that there is only rereading? Does the whole posture, both Nabokov's and that of critical orthodoxy, bear any relation to the reality of our reading habits, particularly in a contemporary environment that offers us more and more books and less and less time to read them?

Let's go back to Douwe Draaisma. Why does he describe our inability to recall the sense impressions of a few seconds before as "forgetting"? That would imply that I had "possessed" those impressions or wanted to possess them. The underlying implication is that life has less worth, less *dignity*, if it just, as it were, slips by. Yet even as I write now I am aware of scores of sense impressions. The position of papers, teacups, pens, phone and books on the glass surface of my living-room table, which is also reflecting the opposite wall with its shelves and bric-a-brac and, as it happens, fresh white paint; the hum of the fridge and a distant siren, a dog barking and the sunlight bouncing off the façade across the street, yellowing the cream colour of my curtains. I will never be able to recall a fraction of all this tomorrow, or a year hence. Yet such perceptions are very much part of the pleasure of being here in the present as I write, and without them life would be poor indeed.

Of course, one reason I won't be able to recall all my impressions is that they will have been substituted by others, equally rich, plus the fact that, having written down a few elements of the here and now, any memory of it I might have mustered will be coloured if not hijacked by that account. In dismissing the myth of total recall, Draaisma reminds us that the memories we do retain are largely fabrications, reworkings, shifting narratives, simplifications, distortions, photos replacing faces and so on; what's more, that there is no reason to suppose that the original impression is intact somewhere in our heads. We do not possess the past, even that of a few moments ago, and this is hardly a cause for regret, since to do so would severely obstruct our experience of the present.

Does this throw any light on the business of reading? Well, one has to wonder about Nabokov's enthusiasm for rereading. Is it really a gradual and always positive accumulation of greater and greater control and retention, or is it rather a precarious process in which each new engagement with the text cancels and alters earlier ones? I will never recover my first excitement on reading, say, Coleridge's *The Rime of the Ancient Mariner*, or Browning's *Men and Women*, or Beckett's *Molloy*. Often I have a sense of disappointment when I reread: Graham Greene, E.M. Forster, Calvino, Antonio Tabucchi do not seem as exhilarating now as when I first tackled them. But why should that diminish the pleasure I once experienced? Why should I not rejoice that I am enjoying a new book today, rather than worry what the verdict of some future rereading might be? The purpose of reading is not to pass some final judgement on the text, but to engage with what it has to offer to me now.

Nabokov of course was an obsessive collector of butterflies; the most elusive of creatures were to be pinned down. Many of his characters exhibit the qualities, perversions and insecurities of the collector. Humbert Humbert opens his story with an attempt to possess Lolita through the pronunciation of her name: "Lo-lee-ta: the tip of the tongue taking a trip of three steps down the palate to tap, at three, on the teeth." Words in general have a vocation for rearranging and fixing experience in a way that can be communicated across space and time. Yet often it seems that our experience of the words once written down is as volatile and precarious as our other sense impressions. No reader ever really takes complete control of a book – it's an illusion – and perhaps to expend vast quantities of energy seeking to do so is a form of impoverishment. Couldn't there be a hint of irony in Flaubert's "*Comme l'on serait savant...*"? Is it really wise to renounce all the impressions that a thousand books could bring, all that living, for the wisdom of five or six?

The Key to Rereading

Let's reread Nabokov on rereading. On our first approach to a novel, Nabokov claimed, we are overwhelmed with too much information and fatigued by the effort of scanning the lines. Only later, on successive encounters with the text, will we begin to see and appreciate it as a whole, as we do with a painting. So, paradoxically, then, "there is no reading, only rereading".

This attitude, as I suggested in the previous piece, amounts to an elitist agenda, an unhappy obsession with control, a desire to possess the text (with always the implication that there are very few texts worth possessing) rather than accept the contingency of each reading moment by moment.

"Wrong!" a reader objects. "Isn't it true," he says, inviting an analogy with music, "that the first time we hear a new song we can't really enjoy it? Only after two or three hearings will it really begin to give us pleasure." He then adds this intriguing formulation:

When we perceive something new for the first time, we cannot really perceive it, because we lack the appropriate structure that allows us to perceive it. Our brain is like a lock-maker that makes a lock whenever a key is deemed interesting enough. But when a key – for example, a new poem, or a new species of animal – is first met, there is no lock yet ready for such a key. Or, to be precise, the key is not even a key, since it does not open anything yet. It is a potential key. However, the encounter between the brain and this potential key triggers the making of a lock. The next time we meet or perceive the object/key, it will open the lock prepared for it in the brain.

It's an elaborate theory, and in fact the reader turns out to be the philosopher and psychologist Riccardo Manzotti. Intriguing above all is the reversal of the usual key/lock analogy. The mind is not devising a key to decipher the text, it is disposing itself in such a way as to allow the text to become a key that unlocks sensation and "meaning" in the mind.

Is Manzotti right? And if so, what does it tell us about reading?

Certainly we have all had the experience he describes on first encounter with difficult texts, poetry in particular. My first reading of *The Waste Land*, in a school English lesson at age sixteen, was hardly a reading at all. It would take many lessons and cribs and further readings before suddenly Eliot's approach could begin to awaken recognition and appreciation, before "April is the cruellest month", that is, genuinely reminded me how difficult life and change could be in contrast to hibernation. The mind had conjured a lock that allowed the poem to function as a key; it fitted into my mind, and something turned and swung open.

Two reflections. This *Waste Land* lock also seemed well suited to or easily adapted for a range of other keys. My mind could now be opened by other modernist poems far more quickly. Eliot's other poems, in particular, all activated the senses smoothly enough. And while one would never perhaps reach the point of satisfying all one's curiosity for a new poem in a single reading, still the lock-making process was now infinitely faster, to the point that there would sometimes be a sense of déjà vu: "Oh, it's this sort of lock the key wants to open." Or even: "Oh, not this again, how disappointing!" Which perhaps explained why poets now no longer wrote in this way and had moved on.

This prompts a second reflection. With a certain kind of reading, the pleasure lies in the lock-making process, the progressive meshing of mind and text. Once we are familiar with the kind of experience the text opens up in our minds, we will be less excited. Or at least, the pleasure will be of a different kind, offering the reassurance of the known, or simply a happy reminder of that more strenuous lock-making period. Such a distinction might help us tackle the old chestnut of the difference between genre fiction and literary work. There is no continuing learning process with genre fiction. We know how to read a Maigret and would never dream of rereading one. It always prompts the same reactions. But with a literary novel, we would expect the pleasure of an effort of adjustment, of new vistas being opened in the mind.

So Nabokov was right perhaps, or at least for complex novels, which for him were probably the only ones he was interested in. We have to reread.

Of course the poem can afford to be impenetrable, at least initially, because it is brief. You can read *The Waste Land* in twenty minutes. Not so *Finnegans Wake*. My feeling is that a novel that is really novel will generally get us through, or fairly far along in the lock-making process in the opening pages, where we may very well find ourselves rereading a paragraph or two in order to get our bearings. This one on the opening page of *Mrs Dalloway* for example. Curiously enough, in the preceding paragraph Woolf has used an analogy, if not of locks, then of hinges; Clarissa Dalloway is expecting some workmen to come and remove the doors from their hinges in the ground floor of her house to facilitate the party she's planning later that day. Then, as she goes out into the street, we have:

What a lark! What a plunge! For so it had always seemed to her when, with a little squeak of the hinges, which she could hear now, she had burst open the French windows and plunged at Bourton into the open air. How fresh, how calm, stiller than this of course, the air was in the early morning; like the flap of a wave; the kiss of a wave; chill and sharp and yet (for a girl of eighteen as she then was) solemn, feeling as she did, standing there at the open window, that something awful was about to happen; looking at the flowers, at the trees with the smoke winding off them and the rooks rising, falling; standing and looking until Peter Walsh said, "Musing among the vegetables?" – was that it? – "I prefer men to cauliflowers" – was that it?

What is the experience, or disposition, that this text is seeking to unlock in us? One where past and present are co-present as thoughts of various kinds are allowed to spread out in extended syntactical convolutions, until someone comes along to interrupt them, with a cynical quip and a pocket knife. The formula will be repeated a hundred times in the book, the mind reaching out in reverie and then being abruptly brought back to the present by some intrusion. Uninitiated readers may indeed need to read this a number of times before the text awakens and opens a freshly made lock in their minds.

But not all readers are the same. Not all are the same age. As Gregory Bateson observed, in his *Steps to an Ecology of Mind*, humans distinguish themselves not so much by their ability to learn, but their ability to learn how to learn, to recognize that a new situation requires a learning process and to facilitate that process in every way. So the experienced reader coming to Woolf senses at once that the reference to removing hinges and plunging out of doors is telling them something about how the book is to be read. By the time we get to this paragraph twenty pages in, where a man distributing sectarian pamphlets feels the seduction of the mother church, at least this aspect of the method will now be so obvious as to be risking mannerism:

> Then, while a seedy-looking nondescript man carrying a leather bag stood on the steps of St Paul's Cathedral, and hesitated, for within was what balm, how great a welcome, how many tombs with banners waving over them, tokens of victories not over armies, but over, he thought, that plaguy spirit of truth-seeking which leaves me at present without a situation, and more than that, the cathedral offers company, he thought, invites you to membership of a society; great men belong to it; martyrs have died for it; why not enter in, he thought, put this leather bag stuffed with pamphlets before an altar, a cross, the symbol of something which has soared beyond seeking and questing and knocking of words together and has become all spirit, disembodied, ghostly – why not enter in? he thought and while he hesitated out flew the aeroplane over Ludgate Circus.

Certainly, by the end of *Mrs Dalloway*, this play between the individual mind's wanderings and the world's intrusions, between the isolated human being and the community, is all too clear. You hardly need to go back and reread except for the pleasure of seeing the Ts crossed. Which can be a great pleasure. Or perhaps, years later, with the lock now rusty, you might want to go back and dip in, to clean it up, to remember, in fast replay, the experience that Woolf's writing evokes. "Ah yes," you say after a couple of pages, "those are the cogs and wheels *Mrs Dalloway* turns."

This is my own experience of rereading. I don't go back and read a whole novel in the Nabokovian project of feeling I have to possess it all and pin down every butterfly nuance. I dip in again, read a chapter or two, or even just a page here and there, quite at random. To remember the excitement of feeling that particular lock turn in my mind.

So, recently, I opened my old copy of Beckett's *Watt* and found a passage I couldn't remember having read at all, but which recalled all of the techniques that make this particular lock-in-the-head one of the most baroque and splendidly complicated to turn of all. If it does turn. For, funnily enough, the passage talks, precisely, about the problem of perception, and of objects that, in Watt's case, never quite manage to make sense:

Watt was beginning to tire of running his eyes up and down this highway, when a figure, human apparently, advancing along its crown, arrested, and revived, his attention. Watt's first thought was that this creature had risen up out of the ground, or fallen from the sky. And his second, some fifteen or twenty minutes later, that it had perhaps gained its present position by way of first a hedge, and then a ditch. Watt was unable to say whether this figure was that of a man, or that of a woman, or that of a priest, or that of a nun. That it was not that of a boy, nor that of a girl, was shown, in Watt's opinion, by its dimensions. But to decide whether it was that of a man, or that of a woman, or that of a priest, or that of a nun, was more than Watt could do, strain as he might his eyes. If it was that of a woman, or that of a nun, it was that of a woman, or that of a nun, of unusual size, even for this part of the country, remarkable for the unusual size of its women and its nuns. But Watt knew too well, too too well, of what dimensions certain women, and certain nuns, were capable, to conclude, from those of this night-wanderer, that this night-wanderer was not a woman, nor a nun, but a man, or a priest...

What so agitated Watt was this, that in the ten minutes or half an hour that had elapsed, since he first became aware of this figure, striding along, on the crest of the road, towards the station, the figure had gained nothing in height, in breadth or in distinctness. Pressing forward all this time, with no abatement of its foundered precipitation, towards the station, it had made no more headway, than if it had been a millstone.

Watt was puzzling over this, when the figure, without any interruption of its motions, grew fainter and fainter and finally disappeared.

The whole of *Watt* might be described as a sadistic savouring of key and lock never quite meeting, as if Beckett were discouraging his readers from ever imagining that any text of his might ever result in a smooth clunk in their literary brains.

Why Read New Books?

Hasn't it all been done before? Perhaps better than anyone today could ever do it? If so, why read contemporary novels, especially when so many of the classics are available at knockdown prices and for the most part absolutely free as e-books? I just downloaded for free the original Italian of Ippolito Nievo's *Confessions of an Italian*. It's beautifully written. I'm learning a lot about eighteenth- and nineteenth-century Italy. It's 860 pages long. A few more finds like that and my reading time will all be accounted for. Why go search out the untested contemporary author?

As a reviewer of books she would often pan, Virginia Woolf thought one of the pleasures of reading contemporary novels was that they forced you to exercise your judgement. There was no received opinion about a book. You had to decide for yourself whether it was good. The reflection immediately poses an intriguing semantic puzzle: if, on reading a book, you enjoy it, then presumably it is good, at least as far as you are concerned. This is not something you have to "decide". If you have to decide whether a book is good, does that mean you don't know whether you enjoyed it or not, an odd state of affairs, or you don't know whether your enjoyment or lack of enjoyment is an appropriate response?

This sounds rather complicated, yet we know perfectly well what Woolf is talking about. A new kind of book might offer pleasures we haven't yet learnt to enjoy and deny us pleasures we were expecting. Rather than fitting in with something we are long familiar with, it is asking us to change. And how many people are genuinely open to changing their taste? Why should they be? One of the curiosities of Joyce's *Ulysses* is how many reviewers and intellectuals changed their positions on the book in the ten years following its publication. Many swung from hating it to admiring it – Jung comes to mind, and the influential Parisian reviewer Louis Gillet, who went from describing it as "indigestible" and "meaningless" to congratulating Joyce on having written the great masterpiece of his time. But many others turned from adulation to suspicion. Samuel Beckett went from believing that Joyce had brought the English language back to life to wondering whether actually he wasn't simply pursuing the old error, as Beckett had come to see it, of imagining that language could ever evoke lived experience. Faced with something new, we may take a while to arrive at a settled response.

And this uncertainty of ours, as we tackle, say, our first Eggers, our first Pamuk, our first Jelinek, our first Ferrante, or as we switch from an early Roth to a late Roth, is actually part of the pleasure. And this pleasure in adjusting to the new – waiting to see if it will seduce us or bore us, understanding the nature of our readerly expectations precisely as they are challenged – can become addictive, or simply more interesting to us than the easier pleasure of finding yet another book pleasantly similar to others we have already enjoyed. Regardless of whether in the end we entirely enjoy a contemporary novel, we may nevertheless enjoy thinking about what is being asked of us. This was certainly my experience reading Murakami, Jelinek and Saramago. I don't greatly enjoy any of these writers. But I enjoyed grappling with them. Hence "it is even arguable", as Woolf says, "that we get actually more from the living, although they may be much inferior, than from the dead".

Objection: isn't there the same newness, or at least strangeness, when we tackle an older or foreign novel written in a tradition we're not familiar with? *The Tale of Genji*, for example, or *The Sorrows of Young Werther*, or even Nievo's *Confessions of an Italian*? There is, but with two important differences. A work like *The Tale of Genji* has already convinced millions of readers over centuries; I can go out on a limb and declare against it, but if I do so I'll also have to ask myself why so many other people have enjoyed it over so many generations. More pertinently, the fact that I know nothing of eleventh-century Japan rather hampers me when I come to wondering whether this story is an appropriate response to the world the author lived in. When *The Tale of Genji* is strange to me, it is likely because that world is strange to me, but not urgently so, since I don't have to live in it myself.

Even when I read Nievo, despite having lived in Italy for thirty years and having read a few other Italian novels of the nineteenth century (not that many are in print), I really don't know, in any depth, what it was like being alive in Venice and Bologna and Milan in the early nineteenth century. I won't react with the same engagement to Nievo's take on the 1848 revolutions as I will to, say, Martin Amis's account of life in 1980s London in *London Fields*. I could make all kinds of objections to Amis's book for the simple reason that I was there. And I can get very excited when he hits the nail on the head (as I see it). This won't happen reading Fielding's *Tom Jones*, where half the pleasure is: "Wow, how different the world once was."

The excitement of tackling the new novel that dares to recount the contemporary scene is always galvanized by these questions: how is it that someone sharing my world wrote this book that I perhaps find strange and difficult? What are they trying to tell me about it, about the way I perceive it? Is it a useful difficulty? Could I too, perhaps, react to our times in this way, and would it make sense if I did so? This was certainly the question readers faced when tackling *Ulysses*, but also *Mrs Dalloway*, or *A*

Farewell to Arms, or Beckett's Trilogy, or *The Lost Honour of Katharina Blum*, or *Gravity's Rainbow*, or DeLillo's *Underworld*. And these are the books that eventually convinced sufficient numbers of readers to find a place for them in the public mind. Many others, equally fascinating to read at the time perhaps, have fallen away. B.S. Johnson comes to mind. Yet the pleasure of thinking about the work's relation to the contemporary world was the same with Johnson as it was, say, with Beckett. And many were convinced for a while.

To read the *Iliad*, claims Roberto Calasso in *The Marriage of Cadmus and Harmony*, is to appreciate that there is no progress in art. It's hard not to agree. But that does not mean that everything has been done. The world changes and people change, and it is the way the author is sensitive to things as they are now that excites us in contemporary fiction. When I wrote my novel *Cleaver* in 2005, one of my European editors complained about my including text messages between the characters in the book. Old and unaccustomed to the mobile phone, he felt this was a gimmick. Eight years later, it is hard to imagine anyone objecting to the presence of text messages in a novel. To recount modern life one has to have characters with iPads and smartphones who take trains and planes, and to be aware how this alters consciousness, identity and the kind of experiences people have. They are constantly exposed to contact from everyone they know and many they don't.

In fact, what becomes suspicious in a new novel is when it merely pastiches the effects of past novels, when it takes us back to a past the author doesn't know except through books, so as to be able to repeat the pleasures of the books of the time. Which are never quite repeated. The pleasure of reading Nievo has to do with the fact that he really was in the fray of the Risorgimento and seeking to establish a position that made sense in the changed world he lived in. That gives the book its immediacy. To read Tomasi di Lampedusa's *The Leopard*, written in the 1950s, is to read a charming and effective pastiche. It seems to spring mainly from the author's determination to write a stylish and sophisticated novel, imagining the upheavals of the Risorgimento safe in the knowledge of hindsight, safe in the knowledge of how good traditional novels are written.

"Into thirty centuries born," Edwin Muir began his most celebrated poem, "At home in them all but the very last." Much is said about escapism in narrative and fiction. But perhaps the greatest escapism of all is to take refuge in the domesticity of the past, the home that history and literature become, avoiding the one moment of time in which we are not at home, yet have to live: the present.

> This is the place of hope and fear,
> And faith that comes when hope is lost;
> Defeat and victory both are here.
> In this place where all's to be...

The Pleasures of Pessimism

Why do we read writers who are profoundly pessimistic? And what sense are we to make of their work in our ordinary, hopefully not uncheerful lives?

I am not speaking about the sort of pessimism concerned with the consequences of our electing this or that president, or failing to respond to world famine or global warming, but what in Italy came to be called *il pessimismo cosmico*. The term was coined in response to the work of the nineteenth-century poet and thinker Giacomo Leopardi, who at the ripe old age of twenty-one decided that "all is nothing, solid nothing", and he, in the midst of nothing, "nothing myself". The only reasoned and lucid response to the human condition, Leopardi decided, was despair: hence all positive action and happiness must always have the quality of illusion.

This is existential pessimism of the most uncompromising kind. Who needs it? What could possibly be the attractions?

Towards the end of my graduate course in literary translation I introduce the students to Samuel Beckett, in particular Arsene's speech in the novel *Watt*. Watt has just arrived at Mr Knott's house and, since when one servant arrives another must depart, Arsene is leaving. Before he does so, he gives Watt the benefit of a lifetime's disillusionment in a twenty-page monologue. This is the passage I offer my students:

> Personally of course I regret everything. Not a word, not a deed, not a thought, not a need, not a grief, not a joy, not a

girl, not a boy, not a doubt, not a trust, not a scorn, not a lust, not a hope, not a fear, not a smile, not a tear, not a name, not a face, no time, no place, that I do not regret, exceedingly. An ordure from beginning to end. And yet, when I sat for Fellowship, but for the boil on my bottom… The rest, an ordure. The Tuesday scowls, the Wednesday growls, the Thursday curses, the Friday howls, the Saturday snores, the Sunday yawns, the Monday morns, the Monday morns. The whacks, the moans, the cracks, the groans, the welts, the squeaks, the belts, the shrieks, the pricks, the prayers, the kicks, the tears, the skelps, and the yelps. And the poor old lousy old earth, my earth and my father's and my mother's and my father's father's and my mother's mother's and my father's mother's and my mother's father's, and my father's mother's father's and my mother's father's mother's and my father's mother's mother's and my mother's father's father's and my father's father's mother's and my mother's mother's father's and my father's father's father's and my mother's mother's mother's and other people's fathers' and mothers' and fathers' fathers' and mothers' mothers' and fathers' mothers' and mothers' fathers' and fathers' mothers' fathers' and mothers' fathers' mothers' and fathers' mothers' mothers' and mothers' fathers' fathers' and fathers' fathers' mothers' and mothers' mothers' father's and fathers' fathers' fathers' and mothers' mothers' mothers'. An excrement.

The students' collective response is always the same, at first perplexity, faint smiles, frowns, widening eyes as the long list of "mother's" and "father's" begins, and finally a blend of giggles and incredulity: is "prof" really going to read that list to the end? So the passage becomes an exercise in showing how the most negative of visions can be smuggled into our minds without our hardly noticing, we are so distracted by the form. On my computer the autocorrect function of Word has underlined much of the passage in blue: "Avoid repetition," it suggests.

Not all pessimists have the same fondness for bizarre comedy. To read Thomas Hardy's *Jude the Obscure*, Joseph Conrad's *Lord Jim*, J.M. Coetzee's *Disgrace*, or indeed many other fine novels, is to feel at times that any optimism we might unwisely entertain is being systematically ground into the dirt; anything that can go wrong will. All the same, these works differ from Beckett's in that unhappiness is the result of adverse circumstance, or the combination of a particular character and a particular situation. There is, that is, in these novelists, a denunciation of the customs of their times, customs that contribute to their characters' downfalls. Jude and Sue would not have ended up so badly if people had had a more lenient view of unmarried couples. Jim would never have wound up as he did without the race discrimination which underlies so much of what happens in the book. David Lurie's story could only happen in modern South Africa. So the reader is permitted to think that such disasters occur to certain people in certain situations, but not of absolute necessity. Precisely the feeling that the happy life is possible, yet has been missed out on, intensifies the distress, but prevents the story from becoming a general, existential condemnation. The reader can close the book with a grim smile and a "there but for the grace of God…"

Pessimistic essayists and philosophers may not cast the same narrative gloom as fiction writers, but the implications of their work tend towards the universal. Indeed, to believe that unhappiness was *merely* a question of immediate circumstance and particular character might be seen as a crass form of optimism. "Our chief grievance against knowledge is that it has not helped us to live," observes Emil Cioran, dismissing the whole Enlightenment enterprise in a few dry words. Or again: "No one saves anyone; for we save only ourselves, and do so all the better if we disguise as convictions the misery we want to share, to lavish on others." Or again: "Being busy means devoting oneself to the fake and the sham." And: "Trees are massacred, houses go up – faces, faces everywhere. Man is *spreading*. Man is the cancer of the earth."

Here there is no question of a certain person making certain mistakes in certain circumstances. Here we have an across-the-board dismissal of the very idea of progress or improvement, or engineered happiness. So why do we, or some of us, read such material, and read it *with appetite*? Is it perhaps a perverse form of indulgence? Self-pity even? Leopardi noted,

the pleasure the mind takes in dwelling on its downfall, its adversities, then picturing them for itself, not just intensely, but minutely, intimately, completely; in exaggerating them even, if it can (and if it can, it certainly will), in recognizing, or imagining, but definitely in persuading itself and making absolutely sure it persuades itself, beyond any doubt, that these adversities are extreme, endless, boundless, irremediable, unstoppable, beyond any redress, or any possible consolation, bereft of any circumstance that might lighten them; in short in seeing and intensely feeling that its own personal tragedy is truly immense and perfect and as complete as it could be in all its parts, and that every door toward hope and consolation of any kind has been shut off and locked tight...

This certainly rings a bell, and the very accuracy of the description brings with it a certain pleasure and relief. How absurd that we do this! "Our pleasures like our pains," Cioran comments, pushing the disillusionment a step further, "come from the undue importance we attribute to our experiences."

Perhaps the best way to understand our engagement with pessimism is to observe those occasions when it does *not* attract us, when we put it aside with distaste or boredom. In novels this occurs when we feel the author is *merely* piling on the pain, without our feeling there was anything necessarily fatal about the combination of character and circumstance. A car accident occurs at the point when someone is happiest. Or our hero contracts a fatal disease. So what? We know that there are people who have interminable bad luck. Why torture us with it? We can all forgive, or at least condone, an unconvincing happy ending – *David Copperfield*, for example – for the ambiguous relief it brings, but not an unconvincing unhappy ending, or an ending that seeks to generalize distress from the merest individual accident. We have been made to suffer for nothing.

Recently I went to see Edward Bond's 1971 play *Lear*, a reworking of Shakespeare's story that presents a king obsessed with building a wall to protect his kingdom and (in this version) his two daughters, who are intent on marrying the rulers on the other side of the wall. The play amounts to a long denunciation of political violence and subterfuge, and offers no character with whom the spectator might remotely sympathize. People change position constantly, but always repeat old mistakes that bear obvious resemblances to the horrors of twentieth-century Europe. Most spectators will be in wholehearted agreement with the playwright's thesis from the beginning; but there is no pleasure either in the quality of expression (it is unwise to encourage comparison with Shakespeare), or in watching scenes of rape, torture and execution. The literary symbolism and interminable allusions are heavy-handed. One leaves the theatre exhausted and disgruntled. Mulling over this response, I realized that what is positive about *Jude*, or *Lord Jim*, or *Disgrace*, or indeed Shakespeare's *King Lear*, is that the lives and feelings of the individual characters do seem important, and the trajectories of the stories told, however unhappy, are clear and convincing.

For essayists and philosophers, what we cannot forgive is, first, the suspicion that our writer has a personal axe to grind, and second, perhaps even worse, *dullness*, a lack of panache. The slightest feeling that facts are being manipulated in order to support a position in which, for some spoilsport reason, the author has a personal investment, is fatal. The reader, that is, must recognize that a genuine truth is being acknowledged. Beckett can get away with his long list of "father's" and "mother's" because it tells an undeniable truth: mine really is the same earth that all my ancestors walked, the same life all my forebears lived. And it is true, unavoidably, that as one goes backward in time so one's forebears multiply – two parents, four grandparents, eight great-grandparents, sixteen great-great grandparents – so that one's own life becomes steadily less significant and could be construed as mere repetition.

But why is dullness a problem, if what we care about is the truth? Why does it matter that a pessimist deliver his or her message with brio? Here I think we are approaching the key to an aesthetic of pessimism, particularly in essay form.

Modern society, as a whole, tends towards a sort of institutional optimism, espousing Hegelian notions of history as progress and encouraging us to believe happiness is at least potentially available for all, if only we would pull together in a reasonable manner. Hence the kind of truth pessimists tell us will always be a *subversive* truth. All the quotations I chose from Cioran, almost at random, could be understood as rebuttals of the pieties we were brought up on: that knowledge is a vital acquisition, that we must work to help and save each other, that it is positive to be industrious and healthy, that freedom is supremely important and so on.

Such a radical deconstruction may be alarming, yet, when carried out with panache, zest and sparkle, it nevertheless creates a moment's exhilaration, and with it, crucially, a feeling of liberty.

Reading Leopardi or Cioran or Beckett, one is being freed from the social obligation to be happy. Here is Schopenhauer:

> There is not much to be got anywhere in the world. It is filled with misery and pain; and if a man escapes these, boredom lies in wait for him at every corner. Nay more: it is evil that generally has the upper hand, and folly that makes the most noise. Fate is cruel and mankind pitiable.

Espousing this kind of vision might seem like madness, but elsewhere Schopenhauer explains its usefulness:

> If you accustom yourself to this view of life, you will regulate your expectations accordingly, and cease to look upon all its disagreeable incidents, great and small, its sufferings, its worries, its misery, as anything unusual or irregular; nay, you will find that everything is as it should be, in a world where each of us pays the penalty of existence in his own peculiar way.

Cioran pushes the notion to extremes, and makes it more exciting:

> The only way of enduring one disaster after the next is to love the very idea of disaster: if we succeed, there are no further surprises, we are superior to whatever occurs, we are invincible victims.

Invincible victims! Here is a curious optimism lurking at the very heart of pessimism. And notice again how important form is. Life is chaos, a long sequence of uncontrollable disasters, but this idea is expressed with great control and elegance, suggesting heroic adaptation, appropriation even, rather than capitulation; in the midst of disasters we can formulate witty sentences. "No, future here," observes Beckett's narrator in *Worstward Ho*. And proceeds: "Alas, yes." With even greater virtuosity, Robert Lowell, in 'Her Dead Brother', creates a punch line by omission when he gives us: "All's well that ends." With these flashes of creativity it's as if a turbulent seascape were fleetingly illuminated by lightning; we are shown our shipwreck *brilliantly*.

The pleasure detonated by these clever devices does not last, of course, which is why one is never enough. Aphorisms of the negative kind are addictive. To read Cioran's *Cahiers* is to see a man obsessed with transforming his negative intuitions into these splendid little firecrackers, repeating and honing and refining one after another until they achieve the maximum effect in the most concise formulation, the brilliance becoming a kind of anaesthetic that actually makes it a pleasure to feel the knife turn in an old wound. The form is a triumph over pain.

"Do you believe in the life to come?" Clov asks Hamm in Beckett's *Endgame*. And Hamm replies, "Mine was always that."

Stories We Can't See

"What do we see when we read (other than the words on the page)?" asks Peter Mendelsund in a welcome and fascinating new book. Or more precisely: "What do we picture in our minds?"

Do we see Anna Karenina with her shining grey eyes under thick lashes, her faint smile and red lips; or Uriah Heep with his red eyes, red hair, dinted nostrils and lank forefinger? Or Captain Ahab, who "looked like a man cut away from the stake, when the fire has overrunningly wasted all the limbs without consuming them"? Certainly this sounds vivid enough. But do we *see* him?

Mendelsund is convinced that readers already know, or think they know, the answer to this question. "When we remember the experience of reading a book," he tells us – and throughout *What We See When We Read* he assumes that this experience is more or less the same for everyone – "we imagine a continuous unfolding of images." And again, "When we read it is important that we believe we are seeing everything."

Apparently we have a vested interest in supposing that we are capable of projecting a kind of continuous movie of the events in a novel, or indeed the events of our own past experience, to the point that we find it "terrifying and disorienting that we can't recapitulate the world in perfect facsimile". We must possess the world, visually, in our minds.

Art Director at Knopf and a highly respected book-cover designer, Mendelsund himself has an investment in all things visual, and sometimes seems to think of visualizing as a necessary part of reading, a sort of proof of our readerly abilities: "I wonder," he says, speaking of the reader's passage from illustrated children's books to adult novels, "if we... need, over time, to learn how to picture narratives unassisted." Ironically, the least successful aspect of his book is its own obtrusive use of visual "support". When Mendelsund talks about the timing involved in literary description, the fact that a novelist might withhold one feature of a character's appearance for many pages – something a film can't easily do and that readers will instantly recognize – he gives us a photo of a digital wristwatch. It is more a distraction, exhibitionism even, than an "illustration".

The problem is that upon close examination the reading experience is far more complex and far less visual than is commonly supposed, or than Mendelsund supposes is commonly supposed. One of the pleasures of his book is his honesty and perplexity at the discovery that every account he offers of the process of visualization very quickly falls apart under pressure. We do not really "see" characters such as Anna Karenina or Captain Ahab, he concludes, or indeed the places described in novels, and in so far as we do perhaps see or glimpse them, what we are seeing is something *we* have imagined, not what the author saw. Even when there are illustrations, as in many nineteenth-century novels, they only impose their view of the characters very briefly. A couple of pages later they have become as fluid and vague as so much of visual memory. At one point Mendelsund posits the idea that perhaps we read in order *not* to be oppressed by the visual, in order not to see.

So what do we see when we read? First the page, of course, and the words printed on it. No "image" we have of the characters or settings will ever be as concrete, as indisputably and continuously present, as the solid book, or e-reader, itself. Meantime, characters and places are given to us in discontinuous fragments – this kind of nose, that kind of hair, a scar, a limp, a grimace – and in a process that Mendelsund recognizes as having a lot to do with memory we come to have the impression that we know this sort of person, this sort of place. "A man of about forty-five," says Orwell of Big Brother, "with a heavy black moustache and ruggedly handsome features," and we are satisfied we could pick out the man in a police lineup. Just find the guy who looks like Stalin.

So the faculty of recognition is important. The novelist says "wry smile", and we are satisfied we know what a wry smile is because we have attached those words to someone's smile in the past. But do we visualize or picture this smile? Mendelsund never really puts any pressure on these words – *visualize, picture* – which curiously do not have parallels for the other senses. There is no word for our deliberately recreating sounds or smells or touch or taste in our heads, as if it was generally accepted that memories of these other sensory experiences are more passive, while visually we can actively reconstruct an experience.

But can we? If I think of people I know, even those closest to me, the shadowy impression I have of their faces, bodies, gaits, has nothing of the intensity, immediacy and solidity of their real presence. They may "flash upon that inward eye", as daffodils did for Wordsworth, at the most unexpected moments, in a kind of echo of their presence, but this is not something I can control, and it doesn't last, it can't be sustained. Often our visual memory is a sort of liminal waiting for the known person to appear: we stand at the airport arrivals gate thinking of the son or daughter who is returning home. They are vaguely there, in our minds, waiting to be recognized, to become real. But we don't see them yet.

More banally we may stand at the luggage collection carousel watching endless bags tumble onto the belt. We hold in our minds a shadowy idea of our own bag. Then suddenly it is there and the effort of "visualizing" ceases. Perhaps we realize that the bag is not quite as we remembered it. There are three zips, not two. Or at least this is my experience. And when I read, I do not so much see the characters and the places as feel satisfied that if they were to appear to me I would recognize them. Hence our discomfort when we see the film of the book and the actors look nothing like the people we supposed we knew.

In general, as Mendelsund points out, the act of visualizing, struggling to see something that isn't there, depends largely on semantics, on words. It is verbal as much as visual. If I'm sitting in a park by a river, close my eyes and try to visualize the scene, I say to myself, "river", "trees", "benches", and I seek to place them in relation to each other, though no idea I build up in my mind will compare with the intense presence of the scene when I open my eyes again. Quite simply, we do not possess the world, visually, in our minds. And if there is no word corresponding to *visualize* for the other senses – it may be because the other sensory experiences are verbally more difficult to reconstruct: of a smell we could say it was sweet, it was sour, or we could say the name we have given it – "musk", "lavender" – but we cannot piece it together bit by bit, as we might a tree, thinking "trunk", "bark", "branches", "leaves", etc. An old half-forgotten smell may flash upon us with great intensity, but it is difficult to evoke at will, difficult even to trick ourselves into believing we can evoke it.

"The practice of reading," Mendelsund says, "feels like and is like consciousness itself: imperfect; partial; hazy; co-creative." This seems astonishing to me. My consciousness of the environment about me has nothing hazy or partial about it at all. As I type now, screen, fingers, keyboard and the room around are all very present and wonderfully real, at least so long as I keep my eyes open. Perhaps Mendelsund means that our experience while reading, or on remembering what we have read, feels like our normal apprehension of all that is not immediately present to us, the places and people we try to imagine when we are far away from them. The reading process reactivates patterns of past experience to create new stories, pseudo-memories, in our minds.

But if we are not actually visualizing the people and places we read about in novels, what is the function of literary description? Quoting Nabokov on Dickens and his "intensely sensuous imagery", Mendelsund gives these lines from *Bleak House*: "When the sun shone through the clouds, making silvery pools in the dark sea..." and Nabokov's enthusiastic response: "These silvery pools in the dark sea offer something that Dickens noted for the very first time with the innocent and sensuous eye of the true artist, saw and immediately put into words."

Mendelsund is unconvinced. The specificity of an image sparks our recognition and convinces us the author is attentive to a world we know and share. But it doesn't really make us *see*. What neither man mentions is that Dickens always gives us lead characters – David Copperfield, Pip in *Great Expectations* – whose moods oscillate between gloomy depression and bright cheerfulness – and that these states are frequently evoked with references to weather and landscape. The description is part of an emotional pattern, what Mendelsund calls a "play of elements". Its meaning is other than its visual content.

More generally, descriptions are exercises in voice and part of the overall verbal enchantment – literally, "entering into chant" – that Mendelsund never really discusses in his book, and which remains, for me at least, the central experience when we read good fiction. Here is a passage he quotes from *Huckleberry Finn*. The phrases in square brackets show a few words that Mendelsund omits:

The first thing to see, looking away over the water, was a kind of dull line – that was the woods on t'other side; you couldn't make nothing else out; then a pale place in the sky; then more paleness spreading around; then the river softened up away off, and warn't black any more, but grey; [you could see little dark spots drifting along ever so far away – trading scows, and such things; and long black streaks – rafts]; sometimes you could hear a sweep screaking; or jumbled-up voices, it was so still, and sounds come so far; and by and by you could see a streak on the water which you know by the look of the streak that there's a snag there in a swift current which breaks on it and makes that streak look that way; and you see the mist curl up off of the water, and the east reddens up, and the river, and you make out a log-cabin in the edge of the woods, away on the bank on t'other side of the river.

Mendelsund remarks that the accumulation of detail in the passage doesn't help one "see it all": "I saw the dull line, and then the spreading paleness, and then I heard a screaking, and then voices, and then I saw the current…" The passage has a rhetorical power, he says, not a combinatory visual power. He is right about the rhetoric, but it is strange that he presents this as somehow a disappointment. To me it seems a triumph. What we have is a description of drifting down a river where things do come at you one after another, not all at once (the section he omits clinches that). As we read it we enter into Huck's distinctive voice, his earnest wakefulness, his constant concern that the river will throw up some unhappy surprise. A powerful suspense is generated (the passage continues for a couple of pages) in a manner that reminds us that fiction began in the oral tradition of the spellbinding voice, the voice that allows us to entertain the illusion that we have seen things we have not seen and heard things we have not heard, and in general participated in the experience of someone we never met except through this dazzle of words on the page, which are the only things we ever truly see when we read.

The Books We Don't Understand

What is going on when a book simply makes no sense to you? Perhaps a classic that everyone praises. Or something new you're being asked to review, something a publisher has warmly recommended.

I don't mean that you find the style tiresome, or the going slow; simply that the characters, their reflections, their priorities, the way they interact, do not really add up. You feel you're missing them in the dark. And your inevitable reaction, especially if you are an experienced reader, is that this must be the author's fault. He or she is not a good observer of life.

The most dramatic example of this in my reading career is, or was, *Ulysses*. Leopold Bloom knows that his wife is planning to betray him with the vulgar braggart Blazes Boylan. It's something he deeply cares about. It is distressing and humiliating. Yet he spends page after page reflecting on all kinds of other things, thinking of puzzles and puns, marvelling over shop-window displays, sounds and smells.

I first read the book in my teens, then again at university in my twenties. I could appreciate that Bloom might not feel able to confront his wife, but I could not imagine that the distressing situation, with all its implications for his future life, would not be hammering in his head through the day. Surely a betrayal like this would occupy his entire mind in the most urgent and obsessive fashion. Hence it seemed to me that the book's plot had been set up in the most casual manner merely as a vehicle for Joyce's "stream of consciousness", an opportunity to write page after lyrical page about the ordinary world. Had the book only just been published and had I been asked to write one of the first appraisals, my review would have been, to say the least, mixed. But then if we look at early reviews of many novels now considered masterpieces, we find, perhaps among the many positive responses, frequent examples of experienced readers who, in the best of faith, simply missed the point.

Here is the great critic John Middleton Murry writing about D.H. Lawrence:

> *Women in Love* is five hundred pages of passionate vehe-
> mence, wave after wave of turgid, exasperated writing im-
> pelled towards some distant and invisible end; the persistent
> underground beating of some dark and inaccessible sea in
> an underworld whose inhabitants are known by this alone,
> that they writhe continually, like the damned, in a frenzy of
> sexual awareness of one another. Their creator believes that
> he can distinguish the writhing of one from the writhing of
> another... To him they are utterly and profoundly different;
> to us they are all the same.

Murry cannot see what differentiates Lawrence's characters; as a result the melodrama makes no sense to him, and the plot becomes tedious. His failure is all the more curious in that he and Lawrence were actually friends; one would have supposed that Murry was all too aware of Lawrence's obsessions. After teaching *Women in Love* for many years, I find the characters to be almost over-defined, close to schematic. As a couple, Gudrun and Gerald cannot escape from a logic of conflict; one must dominate the other. They live in fear of being overcome by the other. That is what a relationship is for them: war. In contrast, Birkin and Ursula are aware of the dangers of conflict. They live in fear that they will fall into the trap the other couple has fallen into. It's all painfully clear. Fear is everywhere and always related to conflict, in one way or another. But Murry, though he was a fine critic and in many ways describes the book well, can't see it. It hasn't occurred to him that there are people who live in this way.

The same is true of this anonymous contemporary of Thomas Hardy's, reviewing his great novel *The Return of the Native* in *The Spectator* in 1879:

> Mr Hardy's tragedy seems carefully limited to gloom. It gives us the measure of human miserableness, rather than of human grief – of the incapacity of man to be great in suffering, or anything else, rather than of his greatness in suffering... The hero's agony is pure, unalloyed misery, not grief of the deepest and noblest type, which can see a hope in the future and repent the errors of the past.

In particular, the reviewer has problems with the character who in many ways is the soul of the book:

> [The] coldly passionate heroine, Eustacia Vye, never reproaches herself for a moment with the inconstancy and poverty of her own affections. On the contrary, she has no feeling that anything which happens within her has relation to right and wrong at all, or that such a thing as responsibility exists.

"Coldly passionate" is an excellent summing-up of Eustacia's character. The critic has read carefully and receptively. But he can't accept that such people exist, or that if they do they should be put forward to us in novels as deserving of our attention and sympathy. Various hints – "repent", "responsibility" – suggest that he thinks of life in moral terms, good and evil, and expects to see it represented in this way. He can't get over the fact that Hardy appears to move in a different world of feeling, a world in which Eustacia's desire for intense living at all costs is natural and even endearing, entirely overriding moral concerns. Unable to respond positively to this, the reviewer becomes prescriptive, appealing to traditional notions of what "tragedy" should be and complaining that Hardy has got his formula wrong.

Can anything useful or enlightening be said about such misunderstandings or blind spots? Certainly, in the case of Thomas Hardy, one can say it was fairly common to misunderstand him *in this way*, demanding a morality that wasn't there. "Has the common feeling of humanity against seduction, adultery and murder no basis in the heart of things?" protested the reviewer Mowbray Morris against *Tess of the D'Urbervilles*. "*Jude the Obscene*," thundered another reviewer. Could it be, then, that we have an indication here that a writer is out of line with the Zeitgeist? Or in other cases, where everyone else gets a book – *Ulysses* – and you don't, that you're out of line. You live in a different world.

Some years ago, reading a book of systemic psychology, I came across the idea of "the enigmatic episode". The idea is simple enough. Two people from quite different backgrounds meet and become involved in a relationship. Attracted erotically perhaps, each fascinated by the other, they become good friends. Then something occurs – meeting the other's parents perhaps, participating in a political movement, contemplating some particular sexual activity – that reveals to them that they have quite different outlooks on life. Not just that they don't agree, but that they don't, as we say, understand where the other is coming from; the other person's position is inexplicable, perhaps threatening.

In her book *Semantic Polarities and Psychopathologies in the Family*, the Italian psychologist Valeria Ugazio draws on two characters in Milan Kundera's novel *The Unbearable Lightness of Being* to explain the idea:

> [Franz and Sabina's] relationship is marked from the very beginning by enigmatic episodes: Kundera calls them "words misunderstood" and develops a short glossary of them...
>
> Sabina asked Franz at a certain point: "Why don't you sometimes use your strength on me?" Franz replied: "Because love means relinquishing strength." And Sabina realized two things: firstly, that Franz's words were noble and just; second, that with these words Franz disqualified himself in her eyes as a sexual partner.
>
> Franz often told Sabina about his mother, perhaps with a sort of unconscious calculation. He imagined that Sabina would be attracted by his capacity for faithfulness and thus would have been won over by him. Franz did not know that Sabina was attracted by betrayal, and not by faithfulness.
>
> When Sabina told him once about her walks in cemeteries, Franz shuddered with disgust. For him, cemeteries were "bone and stone dumps", but for her they provided the only nostalgic memory of her country of birth, Bohemia.
>
> Franz admired Sabina's homeland. When she told him about herself and her Czech friends, Franz heard the words prison, persecution, tanks in the streets, emigration, posters and banned literature, and Sabina appeared even more beautiful because behind her he could glimpse the painful drama of her country... Sabina felt no love for that drama. Prison, persecution, banned books, occupation and tanks were ugly words to her, devoid of the slightest romantic intrigue.

For Franz and Sabina to go on being a couple beyond the first phase of intense erotic attraction, each will have to open up and change, learn to see the world differently. But since, as Ugazio points out, not everyone is eager to step outside the positions they have grown up with, many relationships will founder on the hazards of "words misunderstood". So Franz and Sabina eventually break up. Yet that is not quite the end of the matter. After they have parted, Sabina begins to miss Franz. In the Montparnasse Cemetery she suddenly finds herself able to see, perhaps even to feel, cemeteries the way Franz did. To understand where he was coming from. Then she wishes she hadn't been so impatient with him. The enigmatic episode has prompted a moment of growth.

Is there an analogy with the way we read? Could the book that initially seems plain wrong to us be precisely the one that allows us to understand something new about other people? Let's suppose that when we begin a novel, the invitation to share a story, to get close to a group of characters, works as an erotic charge. We are drawn in. The opening pages of novels can be wonderfully seductive. "All happy families are alike; each unhappy family is unhappy in its own way," Tolstoy writes at the beginning of *Anna Karenina*. I'm not sure I really agree with either side of this aphorism, but who could resist such a promising proposition? "It was a bright cold day in April and the clocks were striking thirteen," Orwell announces, introducing us to the world of *1984*. How can we not read on? "All children, except one, grow up," opens *Peter Pan*. We want to know who that one is. Giovanni Verga's great story 'Black Bread' has one of the most immediately engaging first sentences I know: "No sooner did neighbour Nanni close his eyes, and the priest still there in his stole, than war broke out between the children over who should pay the costs of the funeral, so that the priest was sent off with his aspersorium under his arm."

Once we have been hooked, then so long as the narrative moves along and intrigues us we won't have too much trouble dealing with things that don't make sense to us. On the contrary, any early perplexities will come across as exotic, part of the fascination. But eventually, with some novels at least, we will baulk. After a hundred or two hundred pages, we will start to feel that this just doesn't add up. Early reviews of, but also many more recent responses to, Lawrence's *Sons and Lovers* offer an excellent example. As long as the novel dwelled on Paul Morel's fearful infancy, his growing up in the shadow of his parents' violent conflict, readers were sympathetic. But as the timid boy moved into adulthood many bailed out, as indeed I remember my mother bailed out when I encouraged her to read the book.

"To our grief and our amazement," wrote a reviewer in *The Nation*, "the book suffers a sea-change, and not into something rich and strange, but into something – the terms must, paradoxically, be used for all this stretch of startling verbal frankness – thin and commonplace. As we feel this more and more decidedly, as we revolt in weariness from the incessant scenes of sexual passion…"

One wonders if sometime later this reader grasped that Paul has identified the fear that characterized his childhood, a fear that inhibits him in every way, above all sexually, as his primary enemy. He is determined to overcome fear, determined to open up to life's impulses rather than shrinking from them. So the second half of *Sons and Lovers* is in a very obvious, even optimistic relation to the first.

So much is said about the "uses of literature", which almost always have to do with our becoming more liberal and compassionate in response to reading about injustice. I very much doubt whether our behaviour changes for the good in this way. All the same, by drawing us into visions that are quite different from and alien to our own, novels may, even if we initially throw them down in disgust, open our eyes to different worlds of feeling from our own. Many years later, on a third or fourth reading of *Ulysses*, since studying and then teaching English literature kept forcing me back to it, I did eventually begin to sympathize with Leopold Bloom. Where Stephen Dedalus simply "will not serve" and is eternally resentful of anyone who has claims on him, always determined to come out on top, Bloom is more than happy to serve his wife, to cook her breakfast and to pick up the books she drops on the floor, perhaps because he has an inner intellectual life to retreat to where he feels comfortable and at home. His is the pathos of the *generous loser*, the man determined not to be resentful, and in this regard he is Stephen's opposite. In the end it is precisely this generosity of Bloom's that keeps Molly saying yes to him even when attracted to others. And although this would never be my mode of operation, long mulling on the book got me to feel his was an authentic position – that there really are people like this, and the character is not just an excuse for endless pages of poetic cerebration.

I remember similarly changing position on Nicholson Baker's *The Fermata* (1994). When I initially reviewed this story of a man who uses his magical ability to stop everyone else's lives while he remains active merely to undress pretty women and masturbate at the sight, it had seemed to me a rather embarrassing exercise in literary erotica. But after being unkind to Baker in print, I gradually realized that what his novel was about was the conflicting desires of wanting to live life to the full, to be utterly transgressive, yet at the same time never to damage anyone, never to leave the slightest trace of oneself on others – to remain, that is, if not quite pure, at least utterly innocuous. And this suddenly seemed interesting to me as a way of seeing fiction in general, a vicarious, sometimes transgressive experience that does no damage.

Not that every novel we dislike will eventually prove instructive. Far from it. But where we find ourselves confronted with complete enigma – Peter Stamm's *Seven Years* (2010) was another novel whose characters initially seemed to be behaving in ways that made no sense to me – it is perhaps worth giving the author the benefit of the doubt, or coming back to the book after putting it down for a while. Certainly it was worth going back to Stamm. For unlike the people we make our lives with, novels need not be threatening. They will not bitch about our slowness to appreciate that they have quite other values than ours. And though we may never be able to accept those values, it is fascinating, and useful, to appreciate that there are people who move in quite different worlds of feeling from our own.

Bob Dylan: The Music Travels, the Poetry Stays Home

No one has been a fiercer critic of the Nobel Prize in Literature than I. It's not the choices that are made, though some (Elfriede Jelinek, Dario Fo) have been truly bewildering; it's just the silliness of the idea that a group of Swedish judges, always the same, could ever get their minds round literature coming from scores of different cultures and languages, or that anyone could ever sensibly pronounce on the best writers of our time. The best for whom? Where? Does every work cater to everybody? The Nobel for literature is an accident of history, dependent on the vast endowment that fuels its million-dollar award. What it reveals more than anything else is the collective desire, at least here in the West, that there be winners and losers, at the global level, that a story be constructed about who are the greats of our era, regardless of the impossibility of doing this in any convincing way.

At times I have even thought the prize has had a perverse influence. The mere thought that there are writers who actually write towards it, fashioning their work, and their networking, in the hope of one day wearing the laurels, is genuinely disturbing. And everyone is aware of course of that sad figure, the literary great who in older age eats his or her heart out because, on top of all the other accolades, the Swedish Academy has never called. They would be better off if the prize did not exist. As for the journalists, one might say that the more they are interested in the prize, the less they are interested in literature.

All that said, this year I have to admit that the judges have done something remarkable. And you have to say, *chapeau*! For they have thrown the cat among the pigeons in a most delightful manner. First they have given the prize to someone who wasn't courting it in any way, and that in itself is cheering. Second, in provoking the backlash of the purists who demand that the Nobel go to a novelist or poet, and the diehard fans who feel their literary hero has been short-changed, they have revealed the pettiness and boundary-drawing that infests literary discourse. Why can't these people understand? Art is simply not about a solemn attachment to this or that form. The judge's decision to celebrate a greatness that *also* involves writing is a welcome invitation to move away from wearisome rivalries and simply take pleasure in contemplating one man's awesome achievement.

But the most striking thing about the choice of Dylan has little to do with his primary status as a musician rather than novelist or poet. Far more interesting, at least from my point of view as a long-term resident in Italy, translator and teacher of translation, is that this prize divides the world, geographically and linguistically, in a way no other Nobel has done. Which is quite something when you think that the Nobel was invented precisely to establish an international consensus on literary greatness.

Why? Because while Dylan's greatness seems evident in English-speaking countries, even to those scandalized that he has been given the Nobel, this is simply not the case in all those places where Dylan's music is regularly heard, but his language only partially understood. Which is to say, in most of the world.

When the prize is given to a foreign poet – Tomas Tranströmer, Wisława Szymborska, Octavio Paz – whose work one perhaps has not read, or is not even available in English, one takes it on trust that the judges know a thing or two. For however arbitrary and absurd the prize might be, the judges themselves no doubt take it seriously and do their best. Even in those cases where there are translations, those few people who read and think about poetry are usually sophisticated enough to realize that a poem in translation is not, or only rarely, the real thing. More a shadow, a pointer, a savouring of impossibility.

But everyone has heard Dylan – everyone who has a radio or watches television – worldwide. In this sense the jury has exposed itself as never before. And they have heard him in the pop culture mix alongside other musicians and bands whose lyrics are perhaps banal and irrelevant. Outside the English-speaking world people are entirely used to hearing popular songs in English and having only the vaguest notions of what they might be about. They do not even ask themselves whether these are fine lyrics or clichés, just as we wouldn't if we heard a song in Polish or Chinese. Even those who do speak English to a certain level and have heard 'Mr Tambourine Man' a thousand times will very likely not react to it in the same way that a native English speaker would.

> Though you might hear laughing, spinning, swinging
> madly across the sun
> It's not aimed at anyone
> It's just escaping on the run
> And but for the sky there are no fences facing
> And if you hear vague traces of skipping reels of rhyme
> To your tambourine in time
> It's just a ragged clown behind
> I wouldn't pay it any mind
> It's just a shadow you're seeing that he's chasing.

Dylan sings the words clearly enough. But for the foreign listener this is hard work. He doesn't see them written down. He can't linger over them. He doesn't know if they exhibit great facility or are merely nonsense. In particular, when he gets three verbs in a row ending in "ing" – "laughing", "spinning", "swinging" – it isn't clear to him whether they are gerunds or participles. How to parse this phrase? And how to understand the charm of "But for the sky there are no fences facing" if you don't immediately grasp that in English we can say that fences "face" each other?

Let's not even begin to imagine the difficulties with 'Subterranean Homesick Blues'.

When we read poetry on the page we take time over it. We puzzle over it. We relish it. When we hear poetry sung, and sung intensely as Dylan sings, drivingly, with a snarl and a drawl, which is also a sophisticated form of irony, how can we, if we are not native speakers, be expected to appreciate it?

So we have this fantastic paradox. Of all Nobel winners, Dylan is surely and by far the best known worldwide. Hurrah. But only known in the sense that people have heard the songs, not understood, not relished the words. So, barely an hour after the Swedish Academy made its announcement, I was receiving messages and mails from Italian friends, of the variety, "I've always loved Dylan, but what on earth has he got to do with literature?" And these are people who know English fairly well. Until finally someone wrote, "I've always suspected Dylan's words were something special." And in this message there was an element of pride, in knowing English well enough to recognize this.

Needless to say, there are some translated versions of Dylan in Italy. In 2015 the excellent singer-songwriter Francesco De Gregori came out with an album *Amore e furto* (*Love and Theft*), which has some fine renderings of Dylan, or "stolen" from Dylan, in Italian. He calls 'Subterranean Homesick Blues' 'Acido seminterrato' and does his best to keep up with Dylan's mad rhymes:

ragazzino cosa fai
guarda che è sicuro che lo rifarai
scappa nel vicolo,
scansa il pericolo
nel parco uno con un cappello ridicolo
ti dà la mano
vuole qualcosa di strano

But this kind of virtuosity is the exception that proves the rule, and even then, one is mainly marvelling at De Gregori's getting so near, while remaining so far away. For the most part cover translations are just a trite dumbing-down of the original, entirely at the whim of the music's rhythm and the need for rhyme. I would argue that they actually undermine rather than enhance the singer's reputation.

We should hardly be surprised then if outside the English-speaking world the controversy over this Nobel is even fiercer than within it. For the award has laid bare a fact that international literary prizes usually ignore, or were perhaps designed to overcome: that a work of art is intimately bound up to the cultural setting in which it was created. And language is a crucial part of that. Quite simply Dylan's work *means* more, and more intensely, in the world that produced Dylan. To differing degrees, and in the teeth of internationalism and globalization, this will be true of every literary work.

Italy: Writing to Belong

Is there a continuity of behaviour between the stories we tell and the way we live? And if there is, does it hold at the level of the community, as well as at the level of the individual? Might we hazard the hypothesis that fiction and real behaviour are mutually supporting and reinforcing?

Take the case of Italy. It's generally agreed that one of the most distinctive features of Italian public life is factionalism, in all its various manifestations: regionalism, familism, corporativism, campanilism, or simply groups of friends who remain in close contact from infancy through to old age, often marrying, separating and remarrying among each other. Essentially, we could say that for many Italians the most important personal value is belonging, being a respected member of a group they themselves respect; just that, unfortunately, this group rarely corresponds to the overall community and is often in fierce conflict with it, or with other similar groups. So allegiance to a city, or a trade union, or to a political party, or a faction within the party, trumps solidarity with the nation, often underwriting dubious moral behaviour and patently self-defeating policies. Only when fifteenth-century Florence had a powerful external enemy, Machiavelli tells us in his *Florentine Histories*, did its people unite, and as soon as the enemy was beaten they divided again; then any issue that arose, however marginal, would feed the violent battle between the dominant factions. This would not be an unfair description of Italian society today.

But if these observations seem commonplace, one question rarely asked is how this phenomenon is reflected in the country's literature. Famous titles like Enrico Brizzi's *Jack Frusciante Has Left the Band* or Paolo Giordano's *The Solitude of Prime Numbers* might seem eloquent in themselves; or again the fact that in Elena Ferrante's *My Brilliant Friend* the two main characters are obsessed with using their writing skills to escape the Neapolitan community they grew up in and gain admission to a more worthy society. Vincenzo Latronico's recent novel *La mentalità dell'alveare* (*The Honeycomb Mentality*) imagines an Italy where an organization like Beppe Grillo's Movimento 5 Stelle has taken power, an organization that originally drew inspiration from its opposition to the excesses of factionalism only to become itself a dominant faction. One of the most disturbing characteristics of the Movement, which Latronico well describes, is the way its members are frequently invited to vote online for the expulsion of others who have shown themselves in some way unworthy of the group.

But perhaps such examples are merely anecdotal. Maybe a more sensible way to start is to ask: what are the emotions and narratives typical of familism and factionalism, and how have Italian authors described them? Do they simply condemn this kind of social organization, or do they rather celebrate and foster it? Or both? Perhaps it's not the worst way of arranging life, in the end.

As soon as we start to think along these lines, the first thing that strikes us is how many Italian writers over the centuries have been exiles of one kind or another. In a society where the value of belonging is paramount, people are manically vigilant as to who is worthy of inclusion in a family, group or community, while forced exclusion becomes a punishment that threatens to undermine the whole purpose of existence. Dante was exiled from Florence in 1302 and spent the remaining twenty years of his life seeking to get back there. Again and again the *Inferno* expresses the contrasting emotions of the desolation of exclusion and the joy of inclusion, the shame of being despised by one's peers, but also the indignation in finding that one's peers are not worthy of one's own respect. Almost all the dead are obsessed with how friends and family back in Florence think of them, to the point that they seem more exiled than dead, more concerned with not being within a stone's throw of the Arno than with being damned.

In general the *Inferno* condemns factionalism, but scholars have long since shown how the choice of those Dante criticizes and praises changes through the *Commedia* depending on his sense at any given time of which powerful people in Florence might be able to help him return. Towards the end of *Paradiso*, when it was clear that none of his politicking was going to get him home, Dante expresses the hope that it will be the "sacred poem" itself that will "overcome the cruelty that locks me out". As with Ferrante seven hundred years later, writing is seen as a means to gain access to the desired group.

One reason why so many Italian writers experienced exile and still experience exclusion of milder kinds (one thinks of the Nobel winner Dario Fo's frequent lament that he has been excluded from Italian public television) is because they were and are themselves intensely involved in public affairs. The logic of this Italian spirit of belonging is that dominant groups always seek to enrol talented artists to their cause, while the artists themselves rarely hold back, since group participation is always the path to prestige, in Italy. From the city states of the Renaissance to today's world of political parties, newspapers and Facebook, there have been few major Italian authors who have not been active in public life in some way, or who did not seek to be so.

And often it is precisely the fact that writers are at the centre of public life that leads to their being exiled. This was true of Dante and arguably of Torquato Tasso and Ugo Foscolo. Removed from his government position after the return of the previously exiled Medici family in 1512, Machiavelli went into forced retirement on his farm outside the city and wrote a book – *The Prince* – that he hoped would get him back into the political role he loved. The notion that took hold in England and France in the later nineteenth century that a writer should be absolutely outside public life, his art pure and at no one's service, never really caught on in Italy.

The downside to this is that no sooner does a young Italian writer have any kind of success – one thinks of Claudio Magris in the 1980s, Enrico Brizzi in the 1990s and more recently Roberto Saviano and Paolo Giordano – than they are signed up to write endless opinion pieces for one of the major newspapers, which of course will be deeply offended if the writer then writes for a different newspaper, since that would be a betrayal of their group. It is astonishing how many utterly ordinary articles a great poet like Eugenio Montale continued to write for *Corriere della Sera* long after he had any financial need.

Unsurprisingly, the very nature of literary language is influenced by this pattern of behaviour, since style becomes a way of expressing a writer's position in relation to various embattled factions. Dante insisted on writing *The Divine Comedy* in vernacular Tuscan, thus taking primacy away from the narrow circle of those who read and wrote in Latin, a privileged elite he was not himself born into, and always worried about being excluded from. Later, in exile, he would be astonished to discover the range of different and mutually incomprehensible dialects that existed in Italy. The vernacular was not the unifying factor he had imagined.

Nor would it be for five hundred years. In the 1840s, Alessandro Manzoni complained about how irritating it was, when enjoying a conversation with Milanese friends, if some outsider turned up from Naples or Venice or Florence and they all had to start speaking Italian rather than the local dialect. All immediacy of expression was lost. Yet it was Manzoni who would twice rewrite his great book *The Betrothed* so that it could become the model of the national language, available to everybody and indeed, after unification in 1861, *imposed* on everybody by an education system desperate to achieve cultural unity throughout the peninsula. And, of course, being imposed, it was also resented. Poetry in local dialects continues to flourish in Italy, together with novels that, like those of the Sicilian detective-story writer Andrea Camilleri, are dense with local usage. One way or another, prose style in Italy always involves a gesture of allegiance and belonging, whether to an elite, a youth culture, an ideology or a class. The only absolutely neutral and hypercorrect Italian is to be found in the country's endless translations, mostly of American novels, that make up about fifty per cent of the fiction Italians read. One is less likely to be irritated by something brought in from abroad and alien to the conflicts that galvanize Italian life. So readers can unite around a Jonathan Franzen or a Toni Morrison in a way they might not around Eco or Saviano.

The continuity of this dynamic in Italian life is extraordinary. In the Fascist period, many writers with suspect loyalties were sent into internal exile, split off from the groups that gave their lives meaning. Others supported the regime and reaped the benefits of being included in the Party. Some, like Curzio Malaparte, oscillated between the two positions, one moment in with the establishment, the next out, then in again. When you look at what novelists of the period wrote, even where it is apparently private and determinedly apolitical, the issue of belonging is almost always central. In Natalia Ginzburg's writing the moments of greatest pathos always come with the lonely death of someone excluded from the group, while the comedy is generated by people who find ways of forcing the group to assist them by appearing helpless and inept. Elsa Morante's wonderful hero Arturo, in *Arturo's Island*, dreams of his inclusion at a round table of noble heroes only to discover that the father he imagined as supremely worthy in fact moves in a world that is irretrievably squalid. Almost all Cesare Pavese's novels have a protagonist drawn into involvement with a group and then suddenly withdrawing from it in disgust.

More recent novels update rather than change this preoccupation. Some Italian authors prefer to write and publish in groups, Wu Ming being the most famous, but Kai Zen, Mama Sabot and Babette Factory have all joined the trend, while the Lyceum school in Milan even offers courses in collective creative writing, something hard to imagine in the Anglo-Saxon world. Interestingly, the solidarity within the group is also presented as opposition to groups outside, particularly in the media: Wu Ming, whose four – but once five – members travel together and present their work together, refuse to be photographed by the media or to appear on television. As so often, forming a group becomes a way of distinguishing oneself from other groups in the constant Italian obsession with inclusion and exclusion. Even Elena Ferrante's anonymity can be seen as a provocative "staying outside" in a society where being inside – known and prominent – is a priority.

In short, if Italian writers have always condemned factionalism, their work inevitably expresses the emotions, values and stories of a world where belonging is more important than any other value, freedom, goodness and success included. So Italy is a country where "regional insults" are now (rather absurdly) banned in football stadiums, but admired in Dante:

> …Ah, Genovese, people strange to all good custom and full of all corruption, why are you not driven from the world?

Clearing Up Ambiguity

"I like middles," said John Updike. "It is in middles that extremes clash, where ambiguity restlessly rules."

"A marvellously ambiguous ending," says Barry Norman of *One Flew Over the Cuckoo's Nest*.

"*Blood Meridian* is wonderfully ambiguous on these questions," says Scott Esposito of Cormac McCarthy's novel.

"The greater the ambiguity, the greater the pleasure," declares Milan Kundera.

"Françoise Sagan's *Bonjour Tristesse* is a beautifully composed, wonderfully ambiguous celebration of sexual liberation," says a publisher's blurb on Amazon.

So what is it about ambiguity that it has to be praised to high heaven by all and sundry? Above all, how did it come to take on, at least for some, a cloak of liberal righteousness, to shift from being an aesthetic to a moral virtue, as if the text that wasn't clear, that didn't state its preferences clearly, were ethically superior to the text that does.

In every other sphere of expression ambiguity is a flaw. Clarity is prized. Politicians are condemned for their ambiguity. There is nothing worse than bureaucratic forms or technical instructions that are not clear. It is famously said that the disastrous charge of the Light Brigade during the Crimean War was the result of an ambiguously worded order. Hundreds died. But in literature ambiguity is positive. "Authors and readers alike have a stake in textual ambiguity," writes critic Janet Solberg, because "literature both illustrates and depends on the ability of language to create and to obscure 'meaning'."

At the same time, of course, in order to evoke experience for the reader, literature has to be precise. The more we recognize what is being described the more likely we are to engage with the narrative. Here is Thomas Hardy describing Tess in *Tess of the D'Urbervilles*: "She had stretched one arm so high above her coiled-up cable of hair that he could see its satin delicacy above the sunburn; her face was flushed with sleep, and her eyelids hung heavy over their pupils."

Nothing ambiguous here. Hardy wants us to see Tess. But isn't this kind of precision at loggerheads with the idea of the ambiguous text? Or are we to take it that ambiguity only has to do with point of view, character and narrative outcome, not with the details? To set my mind straight on this, I recently went back to the fountainhead, the first man to acclaim ambiguity as somehow essential to literature, William Empson.

And what struck me as I opened the pages of *Seven Types of Ambiguity* (1930) was the precision with which different manifestations of ambiguity are described. In examples ranging from Greek tragedy to the present day, but concentrating above all on Shakespeare and the Elizabethans, Empson always distinguishes between the merely (but perhaps excitingly) vague and the semantically complex, between the suggestive nebulousness of Thomas Nashe's "Brightness falls from the air" and the complexity of possible meanings in a later line in the same stanza, "Dust hath closed Helen's eye", where, as Empson points out, the poet hints at a statue with dust falling on it, rather than an eye turning into dust. In any event, towards the end of his exposition of "the first kind of ambiguity" (when a detail is effective in several ways at once), he remarks:

People, often, cannot have done both of two things, but they must have been in some way prepared to have done either; whichever they did, they will have still lingering in their minds the way they would have preserved their self-respect if they had acted differently; they are only to be understood by bearing both possibilities in mind.

Setting aside the question of an exact definition of ambiguity, it's soon clear that what Empson is really trying to do is pin down all the ways literature can be dense, can create complexity, with always the implication that in doing so it in fact achieves a kind of realism, since experience itself is complex and dense and not easily deciphered. He speaks persuasively of "a general sense of compacted intellectual wealth, of an elaborate balance of variously associated feeling". After a wonderful analysis of the ambiguous placing of "alas" in these lines by Ben Jonson,

> Pan is our All, by him we breathe, we live,
> We move, we are;...
> But when he frowns, the sheep, alas,
> The shepherds wither, and the grass.

he goes on to claim that,

> Both in prose and poetry, it is the impression that implications... have been handled with more judgement than you yourself realize, that with this language as text innumerable further meanings, which you do not know, could be deduced, that forces you to feel respect for a style.

That is, contrary to the drift of Janet Solberg's remarks, language in general actually tends to the simplistic, offering a reductive account of what it seeks to represent – it could hardly be otherwise. Hence we prize someone who has managed to put into language, with its relentless and crude semantic segmentation of experience, some of the density and indeed perplexity we feel as we try to get a grip on what is going on around us.

At this point you might say that, if our experience of reality is that it is far from clear, any literature with a mimetic vocation will have to be on the one hand precise in the presentation of the physical detail and on the other ambiguous in its vision of the whole, of what the details add up to. But there are those who see a value for ambiguity and multiplicity beyond mimesis.

In a previous piece I discussed the anthropologist Gregory Bateson's comments on art and painting in Bali. Alarmed by the modern world's tendency to privilege the conscious, purposeful, "problem-solving" mind at the expense of less conscious practices and traditions, Bateson suggested that one of the purposes of ambiguity in art might be its capacity to confound and undermine this hubristic, hands-on impulse to be forever sorting the world out. So a painting of a cremation procession, which, curiously, can also be read as a phallic symbol (the tall cremation tower in the centre has a roundish elephant on each side at the base) is not, Bateson feels, "really" about any of the elements we see, but an invitation to reflect on their possible relatedness. As such it encourages a contemplative rather than a purposeful state of mind, a dazzled respect for the world's mysterious complexity, undermining the thirst for active engagement. Unsurprisingly, one of Bateson's favourite works of literature was *Through the Looking Glass*; his *Steps to an Ecology of Mind* has a charming discussion of the scene where croquet is played with flamingos for mallets and hedgehogs for balls, in which he suggests that Carroll is inviting us to contemplate the madness of seeking to bend the natural world to our purposes.

Arguably, D.H. Lawrence was thinking on the same lines as Bateson and anticipating Empson's enthusiasm for ambiguity when in 1925 he asserted that the greatness of the novel was that within fictional narrative "everything in the world is relative to everything else", hence novels are incapable of assuming an absolute position on anything. An author like Tolstoy might have a Christian purpose "up his sleeve", but for a fine novelist the sheer process of paying attention to life's complexity would, in the end, subsume this purpose and make it merely, or intriguingly, only one of the work's elements to be put in relation to the others.

So the novel "won't let you tell didactic lies", Lawrence concludes. Like Bateson, he is praising art for a resistant, or negative quality. At which point we realize that, going back even further, this idea was already there in Keats's notion of negative capability, "that is when man is capable of being in uncertainties, mysteries, doubts, without any irritable reaching after fact and reason".

Case closed then? Ambiguity, uncertainty, multiplicity are positive in literature in so far as they act as a corrective against a dominant and potentially harmful manipulative hubris. This seems well and good. But in order for art to achieve this quality, Bateson observes, the artist has to be genuinely open to the unconscious, to all that lies outside rational, control-oriented behaviour. Lawrence agrees: for the novel to avoid didacticism, the novelist has to be truly open to the world he describes; it is the multiplicity he then inevitably lets into the text that overwhelms the petty habit of knowing better.

But what are the consequences of recognizing "ambiguity" as a quality of literature, something to be encouraged in creative-writing courses and invariably praised with blandly intensifying adverbs – "wonderfully ambiguous", "marvellously ambiguous" – with no discussion of how and why the text is indeed complex? Nothing is less attractive, in a poem or novel, than the feeling that "ambiguity" has simply been constructed or contrived.

Anyone looking for an example of this might turn to Haruki Murakami's recent novel *Colorless Tsukuru Tazaki and His Years of Pilgrimage*, where structural ambiguity – mysterious trigger points on the anatomy alerting us that a relationship is important, strange stories of amputated sixth fingers preserved in a bag by an artist doomed to die, etc. – has become little more than a mannerism, or signature, at the service of the very rational and purposeful goal of producing another Murakami best-seller.

Worse still is the hijacking of literary ambiguity for use as a political tool against fundamentalism. Reviewing Salman Rushdie's *Haroun and the Sea of Stories*, in which an evil "Cultmaster" seeks to destroy a fertile ocean of fiction where stories of many different kinds flow together, Hilary Mantel remarked: "This tyrant hates stories because he aims to rule the world, and fiction creates an alternative world, a multiplicity of worlds he can never command." Here the structural ambiguities of fiction are purposefully deployed in the battle against obscurantism. Nothing could be further from Bateson's vision of art as an invitation to a contemplative state of mind, or Lawrence's sense that the novelist's enterprise was simply greater than the didactic purposes he might have.

And we arrive at the core issue. To have learnt how a piece of literature affects and stimulates us – and nobody gets closer to explaining such effects than Empson in *Seven Types of Ambiguity* – is not to have learnt how to create a similar piece of literature. For this reason, it would be as well when we talk about ambiguity in this or that novel to be as precise as possible about its nature and implications, and above all to avoid the sort of perfunctory, reflexive praise that simply aligns this quality with a special kind of cleverness. As if we could just all decide to be "wonderfully ambiguous".

The Writer's Shadow

How is it possible that even when I know nothing about a novelist's life I find, on reading his or her book, that I am developing an awareness of the writer that is quite distinct from my response to the work? I might enjoy a book while feeling a certain dislike or even hostility for the person I take to be its writer, or I might be attracted to both work and author, but in different ways. Philip Roth's novels are provocative to the point of bludgeoning; the confrontation is invigorating. At the same time I find myself endeared to the writer who needs to do this, who is determined to get away with it. To me he seems attractively vulnerable.

Of course my intuitions regarding the author may be quite wrong, but all the same I have them. It seems impossible, at least for me, to read almost anything without being aware of the person behind it and without putting that person in relation to what he or she has written and indeed to readers of the book, to the point that I sometimes wonder, in the teeth of a literary critical tradition that has always told us the writer's personality is irrelevant to any appraisal of the work, whether one of the pleasures of literature isn't precisely this contemplation of the enigma of the person creating it. We know so little about Shakespeare's life, and yet, as we read his sonnets or watch his plays, we develop an idea of Shakespeare, and we are aware of a continuity of "personality" behind the writing. We have the impression that if someone ever did find the full story of his life, we would immediately recognize the person we had in mind.

It is difficult to pin down where and how this awareness of the writer starts. Like so much of what happens when we read, it has an elusive, shadowy existence. However, over the last year or two, I have found it clarifying to play this game: I try to identify a kind of conversation, encounter or transaction in a novel that seems to be characteristic of its author, something that recurs frequently; when I've established that, I try to think of the reader's relationship with the writer in the same terms.

First the recurrent encounter or exchange. An easy example might be the question of loans in *Ulysses*. An awful lot of the book is about characters asking each other for loans or favours, errands and chores, and every request is a little power game. People make demands – Stephen on Buck Mulligan, Buck on Stephen, the Englishman Hine on both and both on him – and others define themselves in the way they respond.

In Dickens, we frequently have powerful figures befriending weaker ones, or appearing to befriend them, offering them help, inviting them to be part of a group that may or may not be welcoming or beneficent. Likewise the person befriended may or may not be worthy and loyal. He may, like Uriah Heep, accept another's patronage in order to manipulate him and steal from him.

Rereading Antonio Tabucchi's work recently, I noticed that a great deal of it is made up of conversational sparring between strangers, in which one character is seeking information and the other is teasing, both giving and refusing to give what is asked. Often both characters are teasing each other, and always looking for paradox rather than clarity:

"Photographing wretchedness," Christine replied...
"It's my job... Have you ever been to Calcutta?"
"Well, let's suppose I'm writing a book, for example."
"A book."

"Something like that."

"Oh no," I said, "it's just an experiment, my job is something else, I look for dead mice."

In *romans durs*, there is always a long struggle between two central characters, in which one holds on triumphantly (as Maigret always does), soaking up every kind of insult, provocation and equivocation to come through on top, or, in the grimmer books, to die in some kind of glorious defeat.

Now for the second part of the game. Can I think of my reaction to the book, the emotions brought into play by its story and style, as in some way analogous to that recurrent transaction? Is the author beginning to form with me this kind of relationship that recurs so frequently in his novels?

In this regard, Joyce, usually considered such a difficult writer, is easy. If anyone is making demands, it is Joyce asking us to give inordinate amounts of time to decoding the complexities of his work. All those enigmas and puzzles would "keep the professors busy for centuries", he famously said, as if this was what writing was about: reducing the reader to a busy acolyte. With Joyce, the act of literary seduction is also a serious imposition on the reader and establishes at once, thanks to the relentless brilliance and erudition of the style, who is important in this relationship, who is smart. Some people fall to their knees, others resist. Jung complained that Joyce made him feel stupid. H.G. Wells thought it a scandal to demand so much of our time. So a gap can open up between our acknowledgement of the work's genius and our irritation at the way the genius is forced upon us. After the first few pages of *Finnegan's Wake* most readers will bail out.

On the other hand, Dickens befriends us. That's evident at once. He reaches out his paternal hand. He writes inviting prefaces. He talks about both characters and readers as his family. His seductive prose is brilliant but never really difficult, witty but never abstruse, always warm. We feel an attraction to the man that reinforces or perhaps even exceeds our appreciation of the writing. We would like to be part of his world, his club. Dickens loved clubs and of course his first novel is about a club. The Pickwick Club. Even today there are Dickens clubs in countries round the globe. Readers love to aggregate around the man. And we notice that happiness in Dickens is almost always a happiness with a group of people, a small community, not with passionate couples.

All the same, Dickens's plots encourage us to be alert to friendships that seem attractive and easy. David Copperfield is mistaken when he allows the older and more charismatic Steerforth to take him over. Anyone who befriends the Micawbers will be let down. Perhaps this anxiety that one can get it wrong when befriending others explains those sudden odd lapses in Dickens when rather than lavishing attention on his readers he suddenly seems determined to be rid of us as quickly as possible, to wrap up his story and be away. The last part of *Dombey and Son* is emblematic. But even *David Copperfield* ends in a hurried, unconvincing fashion, as if Dickens felt it might have been a mistake to befriend us, and we too feel disappointed; the relationship we hurried into is not quite as rewarding as we hoped. Or is it that relationships in general can never sustain that Dickensian festivity for long?

Perhaps this is whimsical, but what I am trying to suggest is that literary creativity, far from being the impersonal thing Eliot and Joyce spoke of, may largely involve finding the form, the stories, the style that will allow readers to enter into the aura that the writer habitually moves in and to experience the kind of relationships he or she tends to form. Muriel Spark writes about con artists, phoneys and impostors and at the same time her own style has a glittering surface dazzle, a playfulness and far-fetchedness that forces readers to ask whether they are not themselves the victims of a kind of literary charlatanism. Is all this believable? Am I being taken for a ride?

Natalia Ginzburg uses such a simple, apparently ingenuous style that we almost feel we must come to her aid. She needs our help, the way so many of her protagonists are inept and need help. Meantime, someone we have barely paid attention to, someone independent who refuses help, is in trouble; quite suddenly we hear that he is dead and died alone, unassisted, mugged in some squalid side street or overcome by illness in a seedy apartment. Our sense of the author when reading Ginzburg is of someone offering a relationship, through her novels, that can be a comfort to both of us, but quite inadequate to help others who adventure outside this intimacy. We become friends to mourn their loss.

J.M. Coetzee, in his trilogy – *Boyhood, Youth, Summertime* – writes about John Coetzee, and above all his misdemeanours, his towering ambitions, his pretensions to goodness. The style is spare and the facts clearly, even austerely laid out. The reader would appear to be invited to pass judgement on the man. At the same time we are told the books are fiction – novels, not autobiography – and that anyway John Coetzee rejects the opinions that others have of him. It's a conundrum and conundrums are seductive. But it's not a conundrum to which Coetzee is going to offer any solutions. Enjoying the book, we nevertheless have a strong sense of the author as prickly, torn between an impulse for self-revelation and a preference for decorous or defensive reticence. Or perhaps this sense of the author is precisely part of our enjoying the book.

I remember meeting Coetzee, after having read his books for many years, and being astonished by a feeling of recognition; the atmosphere induced in the conversation, the odd awareness of both austerity and warmth on his part, withdrawal and openness, was exactly the feeling one has reading the novels. Indeed it was after that meeting that it first occurred to me that literary genius is the ability to draw readers into one's own world of feeling, with all its nuance and complexity, and to force them to position themselves in relation to you.

Too Many Books?

Is there a relationship between the quantity of books available to us, the ease with which they can be written and published and our reading experience?

At present, for example, it's hard not to feel that we are in an era of massive overproduction. Just when we were already overwhelmed with paper books, often setting them aside after only a few pages in anxious search of something more satisfying, along came the Internet and the e-book, so that, wonderfully, we now have access to hundreds of thousands of contemporary novels and poems from this very space into which I am writing.

Inevitably, this tends to diminish the seriousness with which I approach any particular book. Certainly the notion that these works could ever be arranged in any satisfactory order, or that any credible canon will ever emerge, is gone for ever. I'm disoriented and don't expect things to be otherwise any time soon.

So would it be provocatively reductive to say that in the end our experience of literature might be crucially influenced by the mere supply and availability of the materials necessary for its production? If there hadn't been all that paper, if printing costs had been higher, if the computer and Internet hadn't opened up endless oceans of space on which to write, would we take our books more seriously? Would we find our way around more easily?

The idea is hardly new. In the *Dunciad* (1742), responding to what he already saw as a deafening chorus of incompetent poets, Alexander Pope spoke of "snows of paper" providing space for the ever more widespread publication of the "uncreating word". A century later, with paper mills and printing presses ever more mechanized and publishers rapidly expanding the number of titles, Thomas Carlyle has this passage in his satire *Sartor Resartus* (1835) – remember that at this point paper was still being made from recycled rags:

> If such supply of printed Paper should rise so far as to choke up the highways and public thoroughfares, new means must of necessity be had recourse to... In the mean while, is it not beautiful to see five million quintals of Rags picked annually from the Laystall; and annually, after being macerated, hot-pressed, printed on, and sold, – returned thither; filling so many hungry mouths by the way?

To sort out the serious from the superficial in the mounting snowdrifts of paper, critics were needed. Johnson had been an early example. But critics rarely agree, and they themselves are under pressure from the market, from employers, from literary friends and perhaps from the publishers with whom they themselves publish novels. In his excellent book *White Magic*, an account of the history of paper, Lothar Müller has a lengthy section on Balzac's trilogy *Illusions perdues*, where the crucial illusion lost is that a writing career could genuinely remain serious in a philistine world. And one of the reasons for this was the conditions under which critics worked, the high fees paid for apparently authoritative criticism that would make or break books and hence have a direct influence on sales. The critic feels impelled to create a new celebrity or destroy an old one, something all too evident today in the writing of even the most respected critics we have. The resulting rhetoric often borders on the grotesque: Knausgaard's *My Struggle*, a *Guardian* reviewer writes, "has strong claim to be the great literary event of the twenty-first century". As a reluctant afterthought, he adds " – so far".

Needless to say, it wasn't always like this. Anyone who has studied English literature in college will remember observing that in courses on early medieval literature or Old English there are really very few texts to choose from. In the pre-modern era social conditions were vastly different, but, crucially, paper itself was scarce and text reproduction was difficult. With little writing around there was little reason for most people to be literate. For those who could read and write, each text was more likely to be precious and important. It was easy to get your bearings.

True, in the early 1300s, with the establishment of the first partially mechanized paper mills in Italy, a more generous supply of paper began to circulate and the number of people able to write rapidly increased. All the same, the only way to have more than one copy of what you'd written was to write it out again on another piece of paper, or pay someone else to do that for you. These limitations naturally encouraged people to keep things short and to invest the act of writing with a certain solemnity.

For centuries, if what you had written was going to be shown to others, it would have to be placed in a library, usually a church library. And since the one of the only ways anyone would know that a new piece of literature had been written was if the writer personally put the word around, there would usually be some kind of social connection between writer and readers. At best, then, you could appeal to a literate elite, sharing the same written language – Latin – that was inaccessible to the masses. Perhaps the offspring of these elite would also read you. In fact it was easier to imagine a reputation in centuries to come than widespread diffusion in one's own time. The perception was that the essential quality of writing was its separation of mental material from mortal grey matter. Word and idea were disembodied and stabilized in order to travel through time, not to be infinitely multiplied in the present.

In general, then, the conditions for supporting the independent professional writer who makes a living from his work just weren't there. At most, one could hope to come under the patronage of a king, or a city state, or the Church. You could be commissioned to write a treatise or a history. These were not circumstances where it would be easy to write things your patrons didn't agree with. Or you might attach yourself to a theatre company, where actors would repeat things you had written, though not necessarily word for word. Now your writing might travel a little if the theatre company travelled. But most likely it wouldn't. Travelling companies would not be performing elaborately scripted plays until the sixteenth century.

With the arrival of print in the late fifteenth century, it was suddenly possible to start thinking of a mass audience; twenty million books had been printed in Europe by 1500. Yet it was the printing shops – often more than one if a book was popular – rather than the authors, who made the money. You might write out of a passion to get your ideas around, or out of megalomania – never a condition to be underestimated where writers are concerned – but there was still no steady money to be had producing writing of whatever kind. In economic terms, it was hardly worth insisting you were the author of a text, hence the anonymous book was rather more common than it is today.

Meantime, with this new possibility of printing so many books it made sense to start thinking of all those people who didn't know Latin. The switch to writing in the vernacular had begun; this meant that, though more copies were being sold, most books were now trapped inside their language community. There were scholars capable of translating of course, and a book that made a big impression in one country would eventually be translated into another. But it took time, and it wouldn't happen if a book didn't impress in its original language. Nor for the most part were these translators under contract with publishers. Initially, they were simply scholars who translated what they were interested in and what they believed was worth disseminating. Think of that.

In 1710, Britain's Queen Anne introduced the first of a series of laws recognizing an author's right to control the copying of his or her work. Suddenly it made economic sense to address yourself to everybody who could afford to pay for a book, rather than to your peer group; much better to write one book that sold in huge quantities than many books that were of interest only to a chosen few. And if the work could be sold in another country it was now worth paying a translator to translate, even if he or she – but usually at this point he – was not especially interested in the work, or perhaps actively disliked it. Writing, translating and publishing were all becoming jobs.

It was really at this point – when one could imagine pursuing literature as a source of income and, thanks to copyright, dream of making a lifetime's fortune from a single book (I have frequently dreamt this dream) – that we became preoccupied with the decline of serious writing. In 1750, Samuel Johnson was already remarking of the novels of the previous generation that the typical author "had no further care than to retire to his closet, let loose his invention, and heat his mind with incredibilities; a book was thus produced without fear of criticism, without the toil of study, without knowledge of nature, or acquaintance with life".

Two and a half centuries later, the abundance and daunting multiplication of possible reading material, combined with a feeling that some of it at least ought to be tremendously serious and even spiritually enlightening, has created an exasperated, delusive determination to establish prominent landmarks. The literary prize, needless to say, is part of the phenomenon, each sponsor eager to lay claim to having crowned the new king or queen of the now global empire of literature and spared the reader the disorientation of the teeming marketplace. But anyone who has sat on the jury for a literary prize knows how arbitrary the final verdict often is, dependent on the meshing and conflict of the people who happen to be on the jury. And even if prizes were a reliable way of establishing that one book is better than others, there are now so many literary prizes that it is simply impossible to read all the winners, never mind those shortlisted.

How to respond, then, to this now permanent condition of overproduction? With cheerful scepticism. With gratitude for those rare occasions when we come across a book that speaks to us personally. With forgiveness for those critics and publishers who induce us to waste our time with some literary flavour of the day. Absolutely without indignation, since none of this is anyone's particular "fault". Above all with a sense of wonder and curiosity at the general and implacable human determination (mine included) to fill endless space with dubious mental material when life is short and there are so many other things to be done.

Reality Fiction

It has long been a commonplace that fiction provides a way to break taboos and talk about potentially embarrassing or even criminal personal experiences without bringing society's censure on oneself. Put the other way round, you could say that taboos and censorship encourage creativity, of a kind. But what happens if the main obstacles to free and direct expression fall away?

Eager to find a form of expression for ideas or feelings that would upset a status quo we are all heavily invested in, writers have often invented stories quite different from their own biographies or from the political situation in which they find themselves, but that nevertheless reconstitute the play of forces, the dilemmas and conundrums behind their own preoccupations. "Shall I be incapable, to the end, of lying on any other subject?" Beckett has his ageing narrator, Malone, ask himself of himself, as he tries and fails to tell a story that will be the merest escapism.

Consider Dickens's late novels, *Little Dorrit* and *Our Mutual Friend*, where so many of the characters labour under the psychological strain of keeping a deep secret that can never be revealed. Is Dickens aware that he is reconstituting his own anxieties as he tries to combine the experience of being a very public figure with keeping a young mistress year after year? Probably yes. He had complained to friends that rules of propriety prevented him from talking about large areas of experience. At the end of *Our Mutual Friend* he puts together an extraordinary series of events to allow a lawyer to marry a boatman's daughter and then to have this unlikely development discussed around a well-to-do dinner table where all but one person present describes the union as grotesque and disgraceful. Close friends of Dickens would have seen he was reflecting on what would happen if he tried to bring his beloved mistress Ellen out into the open.

But Dickens lived 150 years ago. Society has changed. Taboo after taboo has fallen away. People can now boast about coming from humble origins. Homosexuality is no longer something to be hidden; there may even be social and commercial advantages to a writer's "coming out". Marriages are no longer conceived of as fortresses of propriety, such that every difficulty or infidelity must be strenuously denied. And in any event it's becoming harder and harder to deny things. Everyone's posting photographs on Facebook, everybody's leaving traces of what they do or say on email and Twitter. Those who suffer abuse of any kind are more willing to speak up. With or without the NSA, the kind of collective reticence and sense of privacy that allowed Dickens to keep his young woman hidden from the public eye for so many years is a thing of the past.

What does all this mean for creativity? Readers have become so canny about the way fiction works, so much has been written about it, that any intense work about sexuality, say, or race relations, will be understood willy-nilly as the writer's reconstituting his or her personal involvement with the matter. Not that people are so crass as to imagine you are writing straight autobiography. But they have studied enough literature to figure out the processes that are at work. In fact, reflecting on the disguising effects of a story, on the way a certain set of preoccupations has been shifted from reality to fiction, has become, partly thanks to literary criticism and popular psychology, one of the main pleasures of reading certain authors. What kind of person exactly is Philip Roth, Martin Amis, Margaret Atwood, and how do the differences between their latest and previous books suggest that their personal concerns have changed? In short, the protection of fiction isn't really there any more, even for those who seek it.

Naturally, one response to this is the confessional novel, or simply autobiography. Knausgaard's *My Struggle* is the most recent example: six long volumes of intimate and sometimes scabrous personal minutiae. Arguably Thomas Bernhard's *Gathering Evidence*, five brief but almost unbearably intense autobiographical volumes, and Coetzee's three-volume third-person novelized autobiography, *Scenes from Provincial Life* (*Boyhood*, *Youth* and *Summertime*), are further, though more austerely structured examples. Coetzee insists that his books are "novels" not memoirs, and in fact they have competed for novel prizes; yet the main character is John Coetzee, his early life follows the same trajectory as the author's and he is presented in the most unflattering light: in bed with another man's wife, brushing off a girl who has aborted his child and so on.

Such "confessions" would have been dangerous a hundred years ago. By calling these books novels you might say that Coetzee is holding onto a fig leaf. More interestingly, I suspect he is telling us that the word "fiction" was always a fig leaf, that literature can always be deconstructed to arrive at a play of forces that is essentially autobiographical, so that in a sense these more candidly autobiographical works are no more revealing than the fiction that came before them. Certainly, rereading Coetzee's great novel, *Disgrace*, after *Scenes from Provincial Life*, the continuity between the two projects is obvious.

But another response to the collapse of taboo, censorship, privacy, is for authors to step back from narrative altogether and reflect instead on the whole impulse to tell, or to tell things in a certain way. That is: a young writer may set out by imitating past novelists he loves, but then begin to wonder why on earth they are telling stories in this elaborate roundabout way, fighting so hard to cover things up, when now there is just no need to do so, to the point that borrowing a working method from say, Thomas Hardy, or even Muriel Spark, simply makes no sense today.

Geoff Dyer's *Out of Sheer Rage* is a fine example of this. Torn between writing a novel of his own or a biography of D.H. Lawrence, Dyer at one point admits that he hasn't read all of Lawrence's fiction and probably never will; he has reached a point where Lawrence's life and letters are more interesting to him than his fiction. This shift of focus, which seems to surprise Dyer even as he acknowledges it, is in line with his dwindling enthusiasm for writing a novel of his own, such that every time he tries to start a novel he finds himself preferring to think of D.H. Lawrence and, in particular, D.H. Lawrence in so far as he does or does not resemble Geoff Dyer.

However, since Dyer is not a professional biographer, and has no patience for compiling a traditional work of non-fiction, what exactly is he going to write? The answer is that strange intertwining of fraught memoir, biography manqué and to an extent fiction that is *Out of Sheer Rage*, a book that suggests that D.H. Lawrence's direct non-fictional statements about himself were more immediately engaging than the fictional works where he found ways of putting his most intimate concerns before the public. Who needs the novels, Dyer asks, if we can get a lively expression of Lawrence's concerns and character in the letters? And why should I create unnecessary fictions if a changed world now allows me to express my own concerns without any reticence at all?

Dyer is determinedly avant-garde, so it's not surprising to find him at the forefront of developments in the literary world. The more traditional novelist David Lodge is a different case altogether. In his recent *Lives in Writing*, Lodge tells us that as he gets older he finds himself more interested in "fact-based writing" than in fiction and goes on to offer an account of the lives of eleven writers, most of them novelists. Lodge had already written novelized accounts of the lives of Henry James and H.G. Wells and mentions his embarrassment that in the same year he published his novel on James, Colm Tóibín also published a novel on James and in the year he published a novel about Wells, A.S. Byatt published a novel largely based on the life of Wells. We have a trend.

Lodge explains his new interest in fact rather than fiction in his typically low-key manner, as merely "a common tendency in readers as they age, but it also seems to be a trend in contemporary literary culture in general". Very casually, without any further elucidation, that is, Lodge has suggested that both as individuals and as a culture we can expect to *grow out of fiction*. It was a phase. All the same, the facts that Lodge turns out to be interested in, when we turn to his recent novels or to *Lives in Writing*, are the lives of people who wrote fiction – Kingsley Amis, Graham Greene, Muriel Spark, Anthony Trollope – and what interests him is how these people transformed their personal concerns into novels. That is, he is interested in the phase that he himself seems to be emerging from, or in the process of change that is occurring. Again, as with Dyer, we have the sense that a situation that once made the novel extremely important, as a space where difficult questions could be fielded with impunity, has now altered, such that the author brought up on this model is now bound to reflect on what to do with his ambition and creativity.

So has fiction now outlived one of its sustaining purposes? That is the question Lodge, Dyer, Coetzee, Knausgaard and many other writers are posing (one thinks in particular of David Shields's madly provocative *Reality Hunger*). It could be we are moving towards a period where, as the writer "gets older" – as Lodge has it, carefully avoiding the positive connotation of "matures" or the negative of "ages" – he or she finds it increasingly irrelevant to embark on another long work of fiction that elaborately reformulates conflicts and concerns that the reader anyway assumes are autobiographical. Far more interesting and exciting to confront the whole conundrum of living and telling head on, in the very different world we find ourselves in now, where more or less anything can be told without shame. Whether this makes for better books or simply different books is a question writers and readers will decide for themselves.

Six Chairs in Search of an Audience

Last night I walked out of a play. It was too painful. Too boring. At the same time I understood why so much that is experimental in literature has come to us via the theatre.

This is Milan. The play was advertised as Pirandello's *Six Characters in Search of an Author*. A friend had encouraged me to go, and it was years since I had seen the piece. Only on arrival at the theatre did we realize that this was not quite what was on offer. The cast would not be using Pirandello's script, or indeed any script. In an attempt to recover the revolutionary spirit of the original and unmask the bourgeois and authoritarian mechanisms of the theatre, each player would play his part as he chose. Actors they were not. Or not professional actors. They were youngsters, apparently politically motivated, or with strong opinions about themselves and about the theatre. After about five minutes it became clear the evening would be dire.

But it is not this performance or these particular pretensions that I want to talk about, but the absolute difference between bailing out of a book, a movie and a theatrical performance. When you head for the exit in the cinema before the end, something I do fairly often, you possibly bother the person next to you for a few seconds, but you can't upset what's happening on the screen or change the mood of the evening. However bad or good, the film is done and dusted. As for a book, when you're not impressed by what you're reading, your only resistance to putting it aside is the money spent and the time already invested.

No one will be disturbed or offended when you send it off with the old newspapers for recycling.

The theatre is quite different, especially the small, intimate stages where experimental material first gets an airing. In this particular case, for example, our only exit from torment was via a door to the left of the stage. Leaving thus meant not only upsetting the people sitting either side of us, who might well themselves be struggling to get into the spirit of the piece, but likewise alerting the actors to our negative verdict, perhaps with disastrous consequences. Maybe the cast would lose what confidence they had. Perhaps others seeing us leave would get up and follow. So no sooner had my friend and I whispered to each other our desire to escape than I began to feel guilty. Give them a chance, I thought. Another ten minutes. No, another twenty.

Unfortunately, there were no scenes or acts in this play, at least not so far, and no interval when one might disappear discreetly. Even *Godot* has two acts, I thought. And it was at this point that it occurred to me why Beckett was so much better known for his plays than for his novels, even though for the Beckett fan the novels are infinitely more interesting than the plays. Anyone new to Beckett, opening the *Trilogy* and seeing those long pages – no paragraph breaks, no dialogues, or none punctuated, no immediately obvious plot, strange ideas, strange emotions, strange non sequiturs – might well be daunted, might even imagine the writer was merely incompetent or self-indulgent. Likewise with the baroque prose of *Murphy*, or the mad computations of *Watt*, or the repetitive bleakness of *How It Is*, or the knotty, gnomic compression of *Texts for Nothing*. You have to be a determined, patient, ultra-receptive reader the first time you approach Beckett in prose.

In the theatre, on the other hand, the flesh-and-blood presence of the actors, good or bad as they may be, creates a sense of reality and immediacy, a heightened state of attention. Having paid for your seat, having promised yourself a special evening and finding yourself sitting in the middle of a long row beside others who have also paid and promised themselves a special evening, others whom you imagine have similar interests to your own, people willing to spend time and money supporting avant-garde culture, a community almost – in these circumstances you are probably always going to hang on at least thirty minutes, however bewildered and sceptical you may be. And thirty minutes should be enough for Beckett's enchantments to begin to work. Simply the emotional experience of *being in the theatre*, the sense of occasion, the positive atmosphere of people engaging in an intellectual pursuit together provide the necessary momentum for tackling the great enigma of Beckett's work.

And not only Beckett. I remember in particular an experience with Ionesco's play *The Bald Soprano*, which imagines the tedious dialogue of two mindless and spectacularly insignificant English couples. Again I was watching it in Milan, so this was an Italian translation of Ionesco's French, which in turn was his own translation of his original version in Romanian. I had never seen a Ionesco play before. For the first twenty minutes or so the performance seemed wooden to a degree, and, being English myself, the satire of Englishness, as it initially came across in the play, something the Italian cast were perhaps over-stressing for reasons all their own, seemed way off the mark.

Had this been a movie, I would definitely have headed for the nearest pub. But I was trapped in the very front row of a small experimental theatre with people sitting cross-legged on the floor around me. There was a definite feeling of *shared* watching, nothing like the separateness one has in the cinema. It would have been unkind of me to go. And suddenly the play began to work. The sheer mechanical inanity of the dialogues and the weird dislocation of the non sequiturs began to excite me, to the point that at the end of the performance, when, after the final mad scene, it appears that the whole play is simply start-ing over in a kind of loop, I was actually rather disappointed when it didn't continue.

One appreciates then why certain avant-garde departures might only take off in the theatre, and particularly in the kind of theatre where the public attaches some self-regard to their willingness to tackle difficult material. Alas this also means that a lot of long-suffering folks will end up sitting through hours of tedious nonsense, and then try to cheer themselves up by imagining the work was not so bad after all.

This I am not willing to do. It may be a question of age. After about forty minutes of the Pirandello that wasn't Pirandello, there came a moment when, quite suddenly, all the actors re-treated into the deep shadow at the back of the stage. Whether they had actually gone and this was a scene change, or whether they had faded in order to rematerialize in some revolution-ary statement of the way theatre ought to be, I do not know. I grabbed my friend's hand and said, "Now!"

It was a matter of seconds. How much we disturbed the others and whether the actors were aware I just don't know. But the fact is that no sooner were we out on the street than we both experienced a sort of mad euphoria. We had done it! Overcome inhibition, reclaimed our lives and our time, refused to succumb to high-minded conventions governing proper behaviour in the theatre. Stepping into the nearest bar and ordering a beer, we even began to feel we had had an experience worth paying for. Perhaps the actors had succeeded in their revolutionary intent.

Looking for Primo Levi

Can one ever know "too much" about a writer?

Take the delicate case of Primo Levi, the Holocaust survivor who combined the careers of writer and professional chemist. Until recently I had only read Levi's three most renowned works, his two great war memoirs, *If This Is a Man* and *The Truce*, and then *The Periodic Table*, a series of autobiographical pieces exploring the author's relationships in the light of his work as a chemist. My response – many years ago – was in line with that of most of the articles I had read on the author, which tend to hagiography. The story of Auschwitz in *If This Is a Man* is so overwhelming, Levi's humanity and healthy bewilderment in the face of the surreal collective cruelty of the Nazi camps so resolute and right that one cannot help but admire the book. *The Truce*, in contrast, is full of positive energy and optimism, describing Levi's experiences in Russian refugee camps after Auschwitz and up to the moment of his repatriation and return to his home town of Turin, while *The Periodic Table* is clearly the work of an older, more determinedly sophisticated writer. Neal Ascherson's 1985 review in *The New York Review* sets out the typical reader reaction: "a wonderful store of irony, of humour and observation", Ascherson calls it, coming out of Levi's work not as "a supervisor... in some enormous multinational concern, but a struggling freelance chemist... a sort of packman-chemist, an alchemist on the road".

How different things begin to look when one tackles the almost three thousand pages of *The Collected Works* and browses the long chronology of Levi's life offered in the first of these three hefty volumes, as I have just done for a review essay.

The first surprise is the dates: *If This Is a Man* (1947), *The Truce* (1963), *The Periodic Table* (1975). What was Levi doing in the years in between? On the road with his chemistry? No, from 1948 to 1975 he worked for the same locally based paint and chemical company, first as a chemist, then as technical director and later (when he was writing *The Periodic Table*) as general manager. So Ascherson had got an entirely skewed and romanticized view of Levi's working life. But this was hardly his fault. It's the view *The Periodic Table* suggests. So was Levi unhappy, one wonders, with his long managerial career?

The next curiosity is that while there are no publications in the eighteen years between the first two books, between *The Truce* and *The Periodic Table* there are two collections of short stories that no one ever mentions: *Natural Histories* (1966) and *Flaw of Form* (1975). Reading through them, I'm astonished at the fall-off in performance. It's not that they are badly written, but there is a frivolity, a childishness almost, that strives for but never quite achieves comedy. Essentially, these are science-fiction pieces in which the twin fears of sexual experience and invasive impersonal power structures play out in a wide variety of paranoid fantasies, but without the urgency or commitment that might really involve us. They are, as it were, at once frightened and complacent. "Little transgressions," Levi called them. Why was he writing this stuff?

The question pushed me to look at a proper biography. Obscurely, I felt that if I could understand the inspiration behind the short stories, I might learn something new about the memoirs. Here again there were surprises. Ian Thomson's *Primo Levi: A Life* (2003) offers a wealth of facts, some of the most important of which are not in the chronology provided by the new *Collected Works*. For example, a number of the details in the three autobiographical works are distorted or invented. Thomson lists these details, and I pondered them. It seemed that Levi tended to make his close companions less cultured and educated, but more vital and enterprising than they actually were, such that they become foils for the cautious and highly educated Levi; they are not as smart as he is, but admirably courageous and above all free. However, doing this involved inventing details that the people in question found insulting, or just plain false.

What is most surprising in the biography, though, and barely hinted at in *The Collected Works*, is the intense monotony and eventually chronic unhappiness of Levi's domestic life, his deep depressions and profound pessimism. Aside from the two-year parenthesis that was Auschwitz and the Russian refugee camps, he spent his whole life in the same Turin apartment in the company of his mother, to whom he was intensely attached. After the war, the still-virgin Levi married in very short order the virgin Lucia Morpurgo, but rather than set her up in a new home, Levi brought her, against her wishes, into the apartment with his mother and sister, bringing up two children in an atmosphere fraught with frustration and resentment. Meantime, Levi, who desperately wished to leave his office job for a literary career but feared he wouldn't make it, spent much of his free time corresponding with Auschwitz survivors and establishing intimate but non-sexual relations with other women, and in general stayed out of his home as much as possible.

But is this information "important" or even useful when we read a great book like *If This Is a Man*? Though his mother was absolutely central to Levi's life, she barely gets a mention in his autobiographical work, nor is there any projection of her that one can see in the fiction. Surely the book is the book is the book, and that's that. The rest, gossip.

None of us can read a story without relating it to the knowledge and experience we bring to it. When we read Levi's memoir, our reaction is conditioned by what we already know about the Holocaust, about fascism, about Judaism. The story stands in relation to the things we know. That, after all, is the main reason for including a life chronology at the beginning of *The Collected Works*: the facts of the life condition or inform our response. Returning to the celebrated works equipped with the rich context of the extended biography, I began to notice things I hadn't really seen before. "If, from inside the Lager," Levi writes at one point of *If This Is a Man*, "a message could have seeped out to free men, it would have been this: be sure not to tolerate in your own homes what is inflicted on us here."

What can Levi mean? Surely not that there may be beatings and gas chambers and forced labour in our homes. The comment comes immediately after a reflection that the deprivations of Auschwitz have forced him to acknowledge how little he really lived when he was a free man. Is Levi suggesting that one's manhood can be challenged as profoundly in the domestic environment as in the camps? Towards the end of *The Truce*, with Levi now in sight of home after his long travels, he offers a reflection that at once explains the book's curious title and throws the whole narrative into a new perspective:

> We knew that on the thresholds of our homes, for good or for ill, a trial awaited us, and we anticipated it with fear... Soon, even tomorrow, we would have to join battle, against still unknown enemies, within and outside us... Although the months just passed, of wandering at the edge of civilization, were harsh, they now seemed to us a truce, an interlude of unlimited openness, a providential gift of destiny, never to be repeated.

Never to be repeated! Writing almost twenty years after that truce, Levi appears to be telling us that this had been his one experience of real freedom. A page later the book ends with the author safely home, but dreaming that he is again back "in the Lager, and nothing outside the Lager was true". Home and the camps are bizarrely superimposed.

Realizing only now how frequently notions of freedom and imprisonment occur throughout Levi's work, I began to suspect that the small changes to the facts that Levi makes in his memoirs are driven by a desire for freedom. His commitment to bearing witness to the truth of Auschwitz was becoming a kind of straitjacket, something people expected of him, imposed almost. He was also expected to behave in a proper fashion, receiving warnings from the Turin synagogue when it became known he was flirting with a female journalist. Was writing about the imprisonment of Auschwitz becoming itself a kind of prison? The short stories are largely frivolous perhaps because Levi yearned for the freedom of frivolity; many of those who knew him report his occasionally infantile behaviour ("My impression was of a child trapped in a man's body," said one close associate). But the short stories did not bring him the respect that the memoirs did, and Levi wanted both the freedom and the respect.

In the later works it's easy to see Levi searching in every way for a freedom of expression that will nevertheless carry the weight of the memoir; the books, that is, become part of his search for a modus vivendi, one that will allow him both to stay home with mother *and* feel courageous and free *and* be respected and admired. This is particularly the case with *If Not Now, When?*, Levi's only novel, where an alter ego in the guise of a Russian Jew becomes an anti-Nazi partisan, successfully fighting and killing, and seducing women, being simultaneously, as it were, free and good, committed to the right cause but not trapped in it. This is wishful thinking, and in fact the story is unconvincing from start to finish.

The picture of this man deeply conflicted between the imperatives of freedom and the fear of disappointing his nearest and dearest inevitably influences the way I come to his last book, written in the early Eighties. Levi's mother was now an invalid. His wife's mother was blind. Whenever he left home for a day or two he was extremely anxious about them. He was on antidepressants. Philip Roth, the writer Fulvio Tomizza and the great German publisher Michael Kruger all found Levi "pathetic", even "excruciatingly pathetic".

It was in this miserable atmosphere, in his sixties now, that Levi turned away from the freedoms he had been looking for in fiction and went back to Auschwitz, this time in a moral essay of ferocious reflection, without any suspect details. The book is called *The Drowned and the Saved* and is remarkable for its sense of exasperation, its masochism almost. As I note in my review, Levi sometimes seems more determined to insist that Auschwitz survivors were degraded and contaminated, and that all "the best" inevitably died, than to explore the psyche of the Nazi torturers. He seeks, that is, in every way to break down the consoling image of the sanctified survivor, the image he himself had become trapped in.

It is hard not to feel how this stands in relation to Levi's domestic situation and general feeling of entrapment. He goes back to Auschwitz, as so many of his readers wanted, but claims the freedom to tell them things they don't want to hear. Meanwhile, he was frequently referring to his mother and mother-in-law as "the drowned" and "like Auschwitz victims", a comparison that made any "betrayal" (putting his mother in a home, for example) unthinkable, while simultaneously confirming that Levi himself felt he was somehow still in prison.

Nothing of what I said here diminishes Levi or his writing. Great works come out of great psychological intensity, in his case great suffering, great frustration. Why insist, then, in offering a sanitized, optimistic version of an author's life, as if his work might be the less if we acknowledged his difficulties? Isn't this, in the end, precisely the kind of denial that Levi fought against? Even the way the chronology of *The Collected Works* acknowledges Levi's suicide is anodyne and vague, as if hoping the fact might go away: "April 11 [1987] Levi dies, a suicide, in his apartment building in Turin."

In fact, Levi threw himself down the stairwell of the building he had lived in all his life. "Suicide is an act of will, a free decision," he had written years before to his German translator. "Either you die or your mother dies," the editor Agnese Incisa, a Jewish female friend of Levi's, put it to him a few days before his death. In any work of fiction the symbolism of Levi's suicide would be clear enough and amply commented. The household becomes the instrument of death; using it to kill himself he simultaneously frees himself from its imprisoning grip. It was the drama he had never quite put in his books.

Reading and Writing

How I Read

How can we read better? Recently I suggested the value of reading with a pen in the hand, ready to mark the pages at any moment. In return I received a score of emails from readers lamenting that even thus armed they felt the text was passing them by. "Tell us how you read and mark a novel," more than one correspondent challenged me.

Well, I would not want to be prescriptive. We all read from different places, different backgrounds, and my meeting with Proust or Woolf, or Lydia Davis or J.M. Coetzee, will not be yours, nor should it be. On the other hand I do believe reading is an active skill, an art even, certainly not a question of passive absorption. Borges would often remark that he was first and foremost a professional reader, not a writer, and he meant the claim as a boast, not a confession; certainly his wonderful essays on other writers, the fruits of that reading, are at least as fine an achievement as his stories. So if reading is a skill, there must be techniques and tools that everyone can use or try, even if we use them differently.

Experience is important. No one is born a fine reader. If you write a lot yourself obviously you become more curious about how certain effects can be achieved or avoided, and with application over the years your sensibility is enhanced. In my case translation has been important. I came to Italy when I was twenty-five. Living in a second language, I became more aware of how language drives and shapes thought. Translating and teaching translation forced me constantly to take texts to pieces in order to put them back together in my own tongue. I became very conscious of elements of style, if only because I felt the tension between the author's habits and my own. Translating texts together with students, I have also had the benefit of discovering all the things they saw that I didn't.

This will not be much help for those who do not write, translate or teach. So, to honour the promise made to those who wrote to me, let me try to say a few words about how I go about reading a novel.

As I dive into the opening pages, the first question I'm asking is, what are the qualities or values that matter most to this author, or at least in this novel? I start Murakami's *Colorless Tsukuru Tazaki and His Years of Pilgrimage*, and at once it is about a man who has been excluded from a group of friends without knowing why; the mishap has plunged him into a depression that seems disproportionate to the damage suffered. So I begin to look for everything relating to community and belonging, to the individual's relationship to the community, to loneliness and companionship. I underline any words that fall into this lexical field. Is the community positive or negative or both? Are there advantages to being excluded, even when it is painful? Do loneliness and depression produce strength, creativity? Is the book aligning itself with the position of the person excluded?

Or I start a novel by Hemingway and at once I find people taking risks, forcing themselves toward acts of courage, acts of independence, in a world described as dangerous and indifferent to human destiny. I wonder if being courageous is considered more important than being just or good, more important than coming out a winner, more important than comradeship. Is it the dominant value? I'm on the lookout for how each character positions himself in relation to courage. Sometimes, if you're reading an e-book it's fun to run a search on a key word: *fear, strength,* in this case maybe; *alone, loneliness, company* in Murakami's. You can see all the ways the word is used and who it is applied to. E-books certainly offer a reader new tools for getting a grip on a novel.

What is the emotional atmosphere behind this narrative? That's the question I suppose I'm asking – and what is the consequent debate arising from that atmosphere? When I start reading Coetzee or Marilynne Robinson, it soon seems that what matters most is good and evil, finding a way to be good while acknowledging the thrust towards transgression. Yet the tone of these two authors could hardly be more different. Why? Again I'm looking at all words and expressions that have to do with these qualities and putting them in relation to each other. When I read Muriel Spark I am immediately up against people who seek to dominate and dupe each other. Life is a struggle, a competition. Every Spark novel is a battle to see who will come out on top. And I want to know which side in the struggle I'm being drawn towards and why. Very soon it's clear that the only person who will really come out on top is Muriel Spark.

Getting a sense of the values around which the story is organizing itself isn't always easy; I might change my mind two or three times. But let's say that the mere attempt to do that gives me something to look for. After that the next step is to wonder what is the connection between these force fields – fear/courage, belonging/exclusion, domination/submission – and the style of the book, the way the plot unfolds. How is the writer trying to draw me into the mental world of his characters through his writing, through his conversation with me?

Per Petterson opens *Out Stealing Horses* with a description of titmice banging into the window of the narrator's remote cabin home and falling dizzily into the evening snow. Warm inside, the ageing Trond Sander remarks, "I don't know what they want that I have." The natural world is an enigma, possibly a threat. Collisions, deaths and bitter cold are the norm. The reader knows at once that something will go terribly wrong, and that the catastrophe will present itself as a mystery. We are anxious for Trond, and even for ourselves. Soon we will be reading about unhappiness. All the same, reading about another man's troubles in the safe space of book can be a pleasure, as watching foul weather can be a pleasure when warm and safe inside a cabin. We savour our safety in comparison to Trond's predicament. Petterson's focus on the material world, presenting characters who know how to cut wood, build a cabin and light a fire, suggests that perhaps the book too, with its short terse sentences, its carefully constructed paragraphs, is a kind of resource, a shelter against a dangerous world.

Asking these questions is at best a tricky business, but precisely because of that exciting and intriguing. It gives direction to the pen in our hands, the active attitude of our reading. Let me use a book everyone knows as an example.

Imagine we are approaching *Ulysses* for the first time. What is it about? In the opening pages Stephen Dedalus jokes and vies with Buck Mulligan. It is a battle of wits. Each tries to get the better of the other intellectually. Stephen is anxious that he will seem Buck's servant when he returns him the shaving equipment he forgot outside. Stephen does not want to serve, to be subordinate, as he does not want to lose the battle of wits. Both he and Buck feel superior to the Englishman Haines and resent the fact that the circumstances of history allow an Englishman to feel superior to an Irishman. Stephen is irritated that the woman who brings the milk affords more respect to Buck because he studies medicine not literature. Teaching in school, Stephen is in a position of easy superiority to his pupils, but has to kowtow to a headmaster he feels is inferior to him. People are measured by their cleverness, their sensitivity. Often they accrue pathos by being more intelligent and sensitive than those who dominate them socially, economically.

So much for the first section. Already the extravagantly ambitious style, at its most poetic when inside Stephen's head, aligns the narration – and possibly Joyce himself – with Stephen and his cleverness, his hurt. We are to be on his side. However, the style is really so clever, so full of eloquence, imagery, musicality, that there is no doubt that if we put ourselves in relation to Joyce the way he puts his characters in relation to each other then certainly we are inferior to him. Joyce is better with words than we are, and he wants that to be felt, as Stephen wants Buck to feel he is the better. On the other hand, Joyce needs us to buy his book, as Stephen and Buck will look for money from Haines by selling him cleverly resentful formulations of how Irish art has been reduced to "the cracked looking glass of a servant".

I'm not suggesting that we have got to the heart of *Ulysses*, but we now have something to think about and a way into the text. The book seems to be very much about establishing a hierarchy between people where the value that matters is not the value that society recognizes. And in fact the second chapter opens with Bloom religiously serving his wife, where Stephen refused to serve – except when Molly comes across the word "metempsychosis", she has to ask her husband what it means. Like Stephen, Bloom has a superior mind, but he is not resentful about service, since it's his wife he's serving, even though he knows she is planning to betray him.

While this process of putting the characters in some relation to each other and the author in relation to the reader is going on, another crucial question is hammering away in my head. Is this a convincing vision of the world? Is it really such a disaster, Murakami, if four friends exclude you from their circle? Would they really have done that and would anyone have reacted as Tsukuru Tazaki did? Is it really true, Hemingway, that courage is so crucial and the world so indifferent? Does it make sense, Joyce, to be constantly using wit and aesthetic sensibility as a way of measuring people against each other? In short, are these real concerns, or have they just been brought together to "do literature"?

If there is one thing I dislike, and this perhaps tells you more about me than the books I read, it is the suspicion that the whole construct was put together merely out of opportunism, to write a literary book, to win a literary prize. But how one might hazard some assessment of a novel's authenticity is a question I shall leave to another time.

In Search of Authenticity

"Are these real concerns? Is this work convincing?"

Behind all the other questions one asks oneself about a novel, these are perhaps the most determining – and the most slippery. Probably we should accept that in many cases a straight yes-or-no answer just won't be possible. There will be shades of grey. Still, the matter of whether a work of fiction – its setting and characters, its interactions and preoccupations, etc. – feels "authentic" may have much to do with how we ultimately judge it, whether we like it, whether we take it seriously. But what do we mean by authenticity? Since we can hardly ask for documentary accuracy from fiction, what is it exactly we're looking for?

Let's take some easy cases. All Dickens is packed with orphans or people in uncertain relation to family groups or clubs. It's impossible to read anything he wrote without feeling that the question of belonging was a major issue for him. He had to write about these matters. If we read Lovecraft's science-fiction horror stories, weird and unpleasant as they may be, they are all obsessively about fear of otherness – women's, people of other races', aliens'. All the overheated horror of the books arises from this gut fear. He can't leave it alone. Whether or not we like the books and quite regardless of any verisimilitude, it's clear that the author is writing directly from his personal concerns. The stuff wasn't just constructed for a literary prize. A certain form of repetition, particularly the endless reformulation, in dozens of different guises, of the same core conflict is probably the hallmark of authenticity.

Now consider a contemporary American. Dave Eggers's *A Heartbreaking Work of Staggering Genius* posits a tension between the need to tell an unhappy personal story and the desire to exploit and manipulate that story to accrue fame and celebrity. He wishes to use his suffering to become special, but fears he has betrayed fellow sufferers and to an extent himself in the process. This anxiety that the project is flawed becomes itself another form of suffering that again can be exploited in witty description for the purposes of self-affirmation. The autobiographical nature of the work, which gives a version of Eggers's adolescence and early adulthood, the constantly and comically reiterated clash between the desire to respond charitably to suffering (in short, to be good) and the yearning to be recognized as a genius and achieve celebrity status, pretty soon convinces us that whether or not we "like" the book, it is coming out of something genuine.

Even when Eggers is not talking about himself, the same problem turns up: at one point a certain Adam Rich agrees to have Dave's magazine report him as murdered as part of a rather pious project to ridicule the public obsession with celebrity. However, Dave is soon wondering,

> Could he really be doing all this for attention? Could he really be milking his own past to solicit sympathy from a too-long indifferent public?
>
> No, no. He is not calculating enough, cynical enough. It would take some kind of monster, malformed and needy. Really, what sort of person would do that kind of thing?

Dave, that is, is projecting his own concerns about motivation on Adam. Authenticity doesn't preclude monomania, quite the contrary. Novelists do this all the time. All Shakespeare's tragic heroes have the same concerns about appearance and reality, performance and inner life.

In his later work *Zeitoun*, however, Eggers writes a novelized but declaredly non-fiction account of an Arab man wrongly accused and mistreated by police and judiciary after he chose to stay in his New Orleans home in the wake of Hurricane Katrina. The book is a *J'accuse*. It seems then that the drive for visibility of the earlier work has been tamed and put at the service of altruism. But has it? *Zeitoun* is very "written", very stylish; it draws attention to its own melodramatic telling. And the insistence on the protagonist's goodness frequently seems forced, exaggerated, manipulative. Non-fiction the story may be, but we're not convinced. Rather than confronting these conflicting impulses – the desire to be good tangling with the determination to be famous – the book pretends that the second has been put to rest. But we suspect that this is not the case.

On the other hand the crazy plot of his novel *You Shall Know Our Velocity*, where two Americans try to go around the world in a week giving away $32,000 in cash to anyone whose poverty might make them worthy recipients, once again sets up the clash between monomania and altruism in grand comic style. Here are Eggers's heroes in Senegal:

We found a group of boys working in a field... They were perfect. But I couldn't get my nerve up...
"This is predatory," I said.
"Yeah but it's okay."
"Let's go. We'll find someone better."
We drove, though I wasn't sure it would ever feel right. I would have given them $400, $500, but now we were gone. It was so wrong to stalk them, and even more wrong not to give them the money, a life-changing amount of money here, where the average yearly earnings were, we'd read, about $1,600. It

was all so wrong and now we were a mile away and heading down the coast.

Finally someone – and it sounds like Eggers himself speaking – points out to these would-be benefactors that, far from doing good and relinquishing the control that money gives, they are actually exercising their control in the very arbitrariness of their choice of recipient. Precisely because we now have a completely different plot, but nevertheless the same issues, you can't help feeling that the story arises from a real personal concern.

Authors who switch between genre writing and "serious" fiction introduce a further dimension to this question. Is the literary work "authentic" and the genre work not? Georges Simenon wrote seventy-five detective novels featuring Inspector Maigret and, starting somewhat later, forty-four serious novels that many believed should have won him the Nobel Prize. Frequently autobiographical (and we remember here Simenon's boast to have made love to ten thousand women), the serious fiction endlessly reworks the same territory – like it or not, this does seem to be a hallmark of literary authenticity. Life, in Simenon's literary novels, is ruthless self-affirmation: "Some [people] seem powerful," remarks one character typically, "and maybe for the moment they are. But they're never – and don't forget it – as powerful as they pretend, because no matter how powerful they are, there are always others who are more powerful still."

The resulting struggle may occasionally be quieted and contained in mutual understanding, but more often leads to open conflict and catastrophe. In one of the strongest of these novels, *Dirty Snow*, a young man seeks to assert himself by theft, murder and deceit. But paradoxically he contrives to do so in such a way that he will be observed by a "good" neighbour whose adolescent daughter he seduces and betrays in the most ugly fashion. Monstrously provocative, the young hero seems simultaneously to seek recognition and condemnation, victory and defeat. Flashing around money that is the reward for theft and murder, he knows he is attracting attention, but reflects, "Why say he was worried when he was perfectly calm, when it was he, of his own free will and in full awareness, who was doing everything to bring about his own destruction?" It's hard to imagine more conflicted books than Simenon's *romans durs*.

What has all this to do with Inspector Maigret, whom the author had invented years earlier as part of a lifelong project to become extremely wealthy, and then trotted out four or five times a year for much of his adult life? Inevitably the plots tend towards the formulaic and are often wearily mechanical. Clearly, the temptation to read all of them amounts to a form of addiction, rather than the kind of fertile engagement one associates with literary fiction. Yet Maigret himself is absolutely *sui generis* and, for all the far-fetched action that surrounds him, convincing. In the rapidly sketched world of suburban Paris or seedy, small-town France, ambition, passion and consequent conflict has led to murder. This is the territory of the serious novels, but reduced now to caricature.

After the crime has taken place, the murderer enters into a different kind of conflict, this time with Maigret. It is a battle of wits and wills. Bovine, dogged and brilliant, Maigret always wins. But he wins not through violence, a mere assertion of power, but by understanding his quarries on a human level, to the point that, having arrested them, he often personally "forgives" the assassins. It is as if both sides of the conflict in *Dirty Snow* had been resolved in one fantasy figure; Maigret was the kind of man who would have understood and forgiven Simenon himself for his endless philandering (some of it bordering on rape), and the ruthless ambition that produced all those books, often provoking outrage among family and friends who felt they had been grossly misrepresented.

This is how I construe authenticity: however many ways the author reworks his material, it is recognizably his. We might say he or she is obedient to a need, or an inspiration, even when setting out to work in a different genre. Tackling an author who is new to us, it can be hard to tell whether the work is authentic or not. In which case, best to enjoy the perplexity of not quite knowing how serious our author is, weighing the arguments on both sides, reading another novel to see how it fits. This is part of the fun of reading too, the attempt to get one's mind round the work, accepting a long game played out over three, four, five books. I have had this pleasure reading Annie Proulx. Or again Damon Galgut, the latter's work being intensely focused around questions of fear and courage.

In general, when a novel manipulates its material to conform to the pieties of the day, or alternatively to attack those pieties for no other reason than the visibility such an attack will generate, when its literary tropes are all too familiar, its clever prose reminiscent of other clever prose, then the compass needle is slipping away from true north. William Giraldi's *Busy Monsters*, Andrés Neuman's *Traveller of the Century*, Eleanor Catton's *The Luminaries* are all recent examples. (James Walton, writing in *The New York Review*, speaks of the "feeling that *The Luminaries* is more a careful simulacrum of a great novel than the real thing".) When, on the other hand, the author renounces some easy twist, some expected payoff, to take us into territory we didn't expect but that nevertheless fits with the drift of the story, then the novel gains force and conviction. And when he or she does it again, telling quite a different story that is nevertheless driven by the same urgent tensions, then we are likely moving into the zone of authenticity.

This approach to novels, which is only one of many, inevitably has implications for how we see the relationship between an author's work and life. Explore a biography of Dickens or Simenon and one's intuitions on reading the novels are quickly confirmed. The conflicts in their fiction emerge very clearly in their lives. "The artist," Simenon remarked, "is above all else a sick person, in any case an unstable one."

This is not an easy concept to teach in a creative-writing course.

Do Flashbacks Work in Literature?

Every few days, working on my new novel, my thoughts flash back to something Colm Tóibín said at the Hay-on-Wye literary festival nine months ago: that flashbacks are infuriating. Speaking at an event to celebrate the two hundredth anniversary of Jane Austen's death, Tóibín said Austen was marvellous because she was able to convey character and plot in the most satisfying way without the "clumsiness" of the flashback. Today, on the other hand, we have to hear how a character's parents and even grandparents met and married. Writers skip back and forth in time filling in the gaps in their shaky stories. It is dull and incompetent.

Is Tóibín right? I worry, as I prepare to put together a flashback myself. Is there no merit or sense in the device? Didn't Joyce use it? And Faulkner? Or David Lodge, for that matter? Or John Updike? Or going back before Austen, Laurence Sterne? In which case, can there really be, as Tóibín appears to suggest, an association between the flashback and "our unhappy age"?

Certainly, use of the flashback is widespread and mainstream. Jonathan Franzen's *Purity* opens with his eponymous heroine being invited to work at the WikiLeaks-style organization of the charismatic Andreas Woolf, based in a remote valley in Bolivia. Among many other narrative developments, there is then an extensive flashback to Woolf's tormented youth in East Germany. This is told over a hundred and more pages and will eventually allow us to understand that the woman who shares Purity's apartment is, in fact, an ex-lover of Woolf's on a mission to find ingenuous recruits for his shady project – while Purity's father, whose identity Purity has never learnt, is both Woolf's associate in a crime and his bitter rival. It is melodramatic, paranoid stuff, suggesting that the whole world spread over space and time is conniving to draw Purity into a fatal trap. A certain use of the flashback, that is, implies a certain vision of the world. You could never give your fiction a Jane Austen feel with this kind of technique, nor a Franzen feel without it.

One advantage of this sort of flashback is that it allows the writer, first, to declare where our central narrative interest is – with Purity right now, as she decides whether or not to work with Woolf – and, second, to build up the past that gives importance to that decision. The problem in Franzen's novel is that the flashbacks are so very long and elaborate that we lose sight of the initial focus. The book is called *Purity* and the character Purity would appear to be its author's declared centre of interest, but the energy of the extensive backstory is all elsewhere. It's confusing.

Peter Stamm's elegant short novel *On a Day Like This* uses the device more efficiently. Andreas, a diligent high-school teacher, heavy smoker and desultory Don Juan, is invited to the hospital to discuss the results of a lung X-ray, but bails out on the appointment at the last minute. His behaviour, particularly with his various girlfriends, becomes erratic. Gradually, a series of short flashbacks suggest that fear of cancer and death has activated a profound regret from late adolescence, his failure to declare himself to the one woman he was ever really in love with. Based in northern France, Andreas buys an old Citroën Dyane and sets out with a new girlfriend on a trip to his childhood home in Switzerland to visit the other woman whose memory, at this time of crisis, calls to him. Since everything here, past and present, is focused on Andreas, there is none of Franzen's dispersiveness, and when our hero actually meets his old flame, now a married mother, and makes his much delayed declaration, the juxtaposition of flashback and present action reaches its incongruous but brilliant climax, something you feel just couldn't have been achieved any other way. In his praise of Austen, Tóibín insists that she can tell us all we need to know about the Mr and Mrs Bennet of *Pride and Prejudice* from their conversation, manner and behaviour, without filling us in on their pasts. But that is perhaps because there is nothing remarkable there to know.

Flashbacks come in all shapes and sizes, from the fragments of reverie in Joyce's short story 'Evelyn' to the huge chunks of backstory in thrillers by Stieg Larsson or Stephen King, or the near delirium of the tormented narrators of William Faulkner and Thomas Bernhard. However, the crucial distinction is whether the content of the flashback is to be understood as present in the mind of one of our characters, or as narrated separately. In Franzen's *Purity*, extended flashbacks are narrated to establish the circumstances of Purity's birth, which she knows nothing about, so that the reader understands her as the product of a conflicted relationship she is entirely unaware of.

In Faulkner's *The Sound and the Fury*, on the other hand, Benjy compulsively relives traumatic moments in the past, precisely because he is unable to digest or come to terms with them. This is now a commonly used technique in both literary and popular fiction. The flashback merges with the interior monologue, and we have the idea of a person whose psychological present is a constant reverberation of the past, a person for whom, as Faulkner observed, "The past is never dead. It is not even past." Needless to say, this is a vision of human experience that owes much to Freud and the concept of trauma – two ideas that simply weren't around when Jane Austen was writing.

In one of the most ingenious uses of flashback, Beckett's Krapp plays himself old audio tapes he recorded on various birthdays in the distant past to create a log of his life. Rarely celebrated for his realism, Beckett wonderfully captures the way so much past experience is lost and meaningless, Krapp not even recognizing events he spoke eagerly about years ago. This is comedy. But other remembered moments, in particular the end of a relationship on a summer-afternoon boat trip, have Krapp pouring drinks with shaking hand and reaching for the comfort of his beloved bananas. This is pathos, if not quite tragedy.

But beyond comedy and pathos, what *Krapp's Last Tape* gives us is the overwhelming clutter of the past in the present, the spools in their dusty boxes unravelling, poorly catalogued, mostly irrelevant, occasionally devastating. And this is the absurd. Perhaps one reason Tóibín is so viscerally negative about the flashback is the chaos it threatens to introduce into an otherwise composed artistic form; present and past all mixed up. His own novels, as I recall, while usually sad, are always reassuringly crafted. But wasn't the whole achievement of modern art to allow a little chaos into forms that had become restrictive?

The idea that an individual is in some special way burdened by the past inevitably leads to the more general reflection: what is a character if not the incarnated accumulation of past behaviour and circumstances? The very idea of personhood demands a narrative and a meshing of present and past. When Sabina and Franz constantly misunderstand each other in Milan Kundera's *The Unbearable Lightness of Being*, it is because they come from such dramatically different circumstances that they have no idea what certain concepts – faithfulness, heroism – mean to the other. Their relationship breaks down over this. They have no access to flashbacks. And again, one can see here a connection between our "unhappy age", as Tóibín has it, and flashbacks. Jane Austen's characters are usually aware of each other's backgrounds; they come from the same milieu. But that is rarely the case in our metropolitan lives today.

Stuck with my novel, I sit idly reflecting on all this, wondering how my character's past, the presence of his past, the drama of his past's impact upon the present, can be introduced into the story without falling into the kind of clumsiness that Tóibín is no doubt right to complain about.

Perhaps the solution is to question the very linearity of language itself. The sentence sets off, word by word, instant by instant, from A to B, capital to full stop, but its meaning emerges across time, the end often altering or clarifying the sense of the beginning, with some sentences seeming to challenge just how far the reader's mind can spread itself in time and space. Here is a classic example of flashback working with extended syntax as Virginia Woolf's Clarissa Dalloway ventures forth from her Chelsea home to buy flowers for her dinner party:

What a lark! What a plunge! For so it had always seemed to her when, with a little squeak of the hinges, which she could hear now, she had burst open the French windows and plunged at Bourton into the open air. How fresh, how calm, stiller than this of course, the air was in the early morning; like the flap of a wave; the kiss of a wave; chill and sharp and yet (for a girl of eighteen as she then was) solemn, feeling as she did, standing there at the open window, that something awful was about to happen; looking at the flowers, at the trees with the smoke winding off them and the rooks rising, falling; standing and looking until Peter Walsh said, "Musing among the vegetables?" – was that it? – "I prefer men to cauliflowers" – was that it? He must have said it at breakfast one morning when she had gone out on to the terrace – Peter Walsh. He would be back from India one of these days, June or July, she forgot which, for his letters were awfully dull; it was his sayings one remembered; his eyes, his pocket-knife, his smile, his grumpiness and, when millions of things had utterly vanished – how strange it was! – a few sayings like this about cabbages.

Again and again, in *Mrs Dalloway*, the mind is returned to the past by something in the present, then expands and explores across time and space, the syntax stretching out and out, until we are returned to the present by some new incident impinging on the reverie. Here's another little gem, as Clarissa stands on the curb waiting to cross the road:

> For having lived in Westminster – how many years now? over twenty – one feels even in the midst of the traffic, or waking at night, Clarissa was positive, a particular hush, or solemnity; an indescribable pause; a suspense (but that might be her heart, affected, they said, by influenza) before Big Ben strikes. There! Out it boomed.

This is all very well, but I'm not Virginia Woolf and not interested in my hero's indulging in reveries. I want the reader to understand that, despite all his effort to engage with the present, an incident in the past constantly forces itself on his mind. In fact, it is this pressure from the past that makes him so frenetically determined to engage in the present. And so unpredictable.

Perhaps one useful reflection is that all language comes to us from the past. We learnt the words we use years ago, and though we put them together in different ways each time, their past activities cast an aura in the present. This gives us the power of association, of words that simply demand a flashback, forcing us back to some previous use.

Could I perhaps just drop a single name into the flow of a paragraph, completely out of place, causing a gross interruption of the sense and rhythm of the prose, interrupting its linearity with a word from that past? Would that make the reader feel the drama of my character's being mentally elsewhere? Or maybe drop in a whole but brief sentence – "I should never have said such a thing to a child" – in the middle of a paragraph that talks in measured fashion about something quite different. "I should never have forced that truth on her." That might do it. Or might there be some object in the room, or in my character's pocket, that is attached to the past? Henry Green, who uses no flashbacks at all in his masterpiece *Party Going*, has a character named Julia who carries around with her three small charms – an egg, a wooden pistol and a spinning top – and is so morbidly attached to them that we cannot help thinking they are related to some decisive moment in the past.

I don't know. I can't decide. But until I do, it's quite clear that Colm Tóibín's attack on flashbacks is just going to keep coming back to me.

Reading: The Struggle

The conditions in which we read today are not those of fifty or even thirty years ago, and the big question is how contemporary fiction will adapt to these changes, because in the end adapt it will. No art form exists independently of the conditions in which it is enjoyed.

What I'm talking about is the state of constant distraction we live in and how that affects the very special energies required for tackling a substantial work of fiction – for immersing oneself in it and then coming back and back to it on numerous occasions over what could be days, weeks or months, each time picking up the threads of the story or stories, the patterning of internal reference, the positioning of the work within the context of other novels and indeed the larger world.

Every reader will have his or her own sense of how reading conditions have changed, but here is my own experience. Arriving in the small village of Quinzano, just outside Verona, Italy, thirty-three years ago, aged twenty-six, leaving friends and family behind in the UK, unpublished and unemployed, always anxious to know how the next London publisher would respond to the work I was writing, I was constantly eager for news of one kind or another. International phone calls were prohibitively expensive. Likewise the fax, which no one we knew had. Which left only snail mail, as we called it then. Each morning the *postino* would, or might, drop something into the mailbox at the end of the garden. I listened for the sound of his scooter coming up the hairpins from the village. Sometimes when the box was empty I would hope I'd heard wrong, and that it hadn't been the *postino*'s scooter, and go out and check again an hour later, just in case. And then again. For an hour or so I would find it hard to concentrate or work well. "You are obsessed," I would tell myself, heading off to check the empty mailbox for a fourth time.

Imagine a mind like this exposed to the seductions of email and messaging and Skype and news websites constantly up-dating on the very instrument you use for work. In the past, having satisfied myself that the postman really had come and gone, the day then presented itself as an undisturbed ocean of potential – for writing (by hand), reading (on paper) and, to pay the bills, translating (on a manual typewriter). It was even possible in those days to see reading as a resource to fill time that hung heavy when rain or asphyxiating heat forced one to stay indoors.

Now, on the contrary, every moment of serious reading has to be fought for, planned for. Already by the late 1990s, translat-ing on computer with frequent connections (back then through a dial-up modem) to check email, I realized that I was doing most of my reading on my two or three weekly train commutes to Milan, two hours there, two hours back. Later, with better laptop batteries and the advent of mobile Internet connections, that space too was threatened. The mind, or at least my mind, is overwhelmingly inclined towards communication or, if that is too grand a word, to the back and forth of contact with others.

We all know this. Some have greater resistance, some less. Only yesterday a smart young Ph.D. student told me his supreme goal was to keep himself from checking his email more than once an hour, though he doubted he would achieve such iron discipline in the near future. At present it was more like every five to ten minutes. So when we read there are more breaks, ever more frequent stops and restarts, more input from elsewhere, fewer refuges where the mind can settle. It is not simply that one is interrupted; it is that one is actually *inclined* to interruption. Hence more and more energy is required to stay in contact with a book, particularly something long and complex.

Of course long books are still being written. No end of them. We have Knausgaard after all. People still sit on the Tube with the interminable *Lord of the Rings* and all the fantasy box sets that now fill our adolescent children's bookshelves. Certainly *Fifty Shades of Grey* and its variously hued sequels were far longer than they needed to be. Likewise Stieg Larsson's *Millennium Trilogy*. Never has the reader been *more* willing than today to commit to an alternative world over a long period of time. But with no disrespect to Knausgaard, the texture of these books seems radically different from the serious fiction of the nineteenth and early-twentieth centuries. There is a battering-ram quality to the contemporary novel, an insistence and repetition that perhaps permits the reader to hang in despite the frequent interruptions to which most ordinary readers leave themselves open. Intriguingly, an author like Philip Roth, who has spoken out about people no longer having the "concentration, focus, solitude or silence" required "for serious reading", has himself, at least in his longer novels, been accused of adopting a coercive, almost bludgeoning style.

Let's remember just what hard work it can be to read the literary novel pre-1980. Consider this sentence from Faulkner's *The Hamlet*:

He would lie amid the waking instant of earth's teeming minute life, the motionless fronds of water-heavy grasses stooping into the mist before his face in black, fixed curves, along each parabola of which the marching drops held in minute magnification the dawn's rosy miniatures, smelling and even tasting the rich, slow, warm barn-reek milk-reek, the flowing immemorial female, hearing the slow planting and the plopping suck of each deliberate cloven mud-spreading hoof, invisible still in the mist loud with its hymeneal choristers.

This is the kind of complexity one needs to work up to. Coming cold to it, on an early-morning Tube, for example, might not be ideal and would certainly lead to a different reading than if I arrive at it on the roll of what comes before. On the other hand, if I read mainly on public transport because these are the only moments when I'm not at a keyboard, I cannot really decide where to break off. I might be right at the flowing immemorial female when a voice announces Piccadilly Circus, or Times Square. Then when I restart I'll have to figure out how much of a run-up I need, how far back I have to go, to tackle this waking instant again.

Going back further, here is Dickens in a single sentence in *Our Mutual Friend*:

Having found out the clue to that great mystery how people can contrive to live beyond their means, and having over-jobbed his jobberies as legislator deputed to the Universe by the pure electors of Pocket-Breaches, it shall come to pass next week that Veneering will accept the Chiltern Hundreds, that the legal gentleman in Britannia's confidence will again accept the Pocket-Breaches Thousands, and that the Veneerings will retire to Calais, there to live on Mrs Veneering's diamonds (in which Mr Veneering, as a good husband, has from time to time invested considerable sums), and to relate to Neptune and others, how that, before Veneering retired from Parliament, the House of Commons was composed of himself and the six hundred and fifty-seven dearest and oldest friends he had in the world.

The passage comes towards the end of this eight-hundred-page novel. All kinds of previous references have to be kept in mind and some knowledge of the English parliamentary system and the jargon of the time is essential. Dickens is a world to immerse yourself in for periods of not less than half an hour, otherwise the mind will struggle to accustom itself to the aura of it all and the constant shift between different voices and rhetorical ploys. It is so endlessly playful.

Returning to the twentieth century, here, for connoisseurs of suicidally elaborate prose, is Henry Green describing a graveyard in his novel *Back*:

For, climbing around and up these trees of mourning, was rose after rose after rose, while, here and there, the spray overburdened by the mass of flower, a live wreath lay fallen on a wreath of stone, or on a box in marble colder than this day, or onto frosted paper blooms which, under glass, marked each bed of earth wherein the dear departed encouraged life above in the green grass, the cypresses and in those roses gay and bright which, as still as this dark afternoon, stared at whosoever looked, or having their heads to droop, to grow stained, to die when their turn came.

Coming as it does on the opening page, this sentence amounts to a stern warning not to imagine that this book can be picked up and put down lightly. There are sentences in Green's work that seem to mesmerize the mind and invite three or four readings before moving on. Set aside some quiet time for me, Green is protesting. Let's move into an entirely different frame of mind.

"In a good novel – it hardly needs to be said – every word matters." Thus Jay Caspian Kang giving us the lit-crit, text-is-sacred orthodoxy in a recent *New Yorker* blog post. Honestly, I wonder whether this was ever really true: authors have often published then republished their work with all kinds of alterations but arguably without greatly changing a reader's experience (one thinks of Thomas Hardy, Lawrence, Faulkner), while many readers (myself included), in the long process of reading a substantial novel, will simply not register this or that word, or again will reread certain sections when they've lost their thread after a forced break, altering the balance of one part to another, so that we all come away from a book with rather different ideas of what *exactly* it was we experienced during perhaps a hundred hours of reading.

But today Kang's claim seems less and less likely to be true. I will go out on a limb with a prediction: the novel of elegant, highly distinct prose, of conceptual delicacy and syntactical complexity, will tend to divide itself up into shorter and shorter sections, offering more frequent pauses where we can take time out. The larger popular novel, or the novel of extensive narrative architecture, will be ever more laden with repetitive formulas, and coercive, declamatory rhetoric to make it easier and easier, after breaks, to pick up, not a thread, but a sturdy cable. No doubt there will be precious exceptions. Look out for them.

Reading Upward

"Frankly, I don't mind what they're reading, *Twilight*, *Harry Potter*, whatever. So long as they are reading something there's at least a chance that one day they'll move on to something better."

How many times have we heard this opinion expressed? On this occasion the speaker was a literary critic on Canadian radio with whom I was discussing my recent blog post 'Reading: The Struggle'. Needless to say, the sentiment comes along with the regret that people are reading less and less these days and the notion of a hierarchy of writing with the likes of Joyce and Nabokov at the top and *Fifty Shades of Grey* at the bottom. Between the two it is assumed that there is a kind of Neoplatonic stairway, such that from the bottom one can pass by stages to the top, a sort of optimistic inversion of the lament that soft porn will lead you to hard and anyone smoking marijuana is irredeemably destined to descend through coke and crack to heroin. The user, that is, is always drawn to a more intense form of the same species of experience.

Of course, while the fear that one will descend from soft to hard drugs tends to be treated as a near certainty, the hope that one might ascend from Hermione Granger to Clarissa Dalloway is usually expressed as a tentative wish. Nevertheless, it serves to justify the intellectual's saying "Frankly, I don't mind what they're reading, etc." (as if this were some kind of concession), and underwrites our cautious optimism when we see an adolescent son or daughter immersed in George R.R. Martin. It's not Dostoevsky, but one day it might be, and in any event it's better than a computer game or TV, since these are not part of the reading stairway.

Is any of this borne out by reality? Do people really pass from *Fifty Shades of Grey* to Alice Munro? (Through how many intermediate steps? Never to return?) And if it is not true, why does a certain kind of intellectual continue to say this kind of thing? To what end?

In 1948, W.H. Auden published an essay, 'The Guilty Vicarage', on what he calls his "addiction" to detective novels. The point he makes is that these schematic narratives serve the escapist needs of readers who share his particular psychological make-up. These people will not, as a rule, Auden claims, with some elaborate argument, be the same readers as readers of light romances or thrillers, or fantasy fiction. Each genre has its pull on different types of minds. In any event, if he, Auden, is to get any serious work done, he has to make sure that there are no detective novels around, since if there are he can't resist opening them, and if he opens them he won't close them till he's reached the end. Or rather, no new detective novels; for Auden notes this difference between the stuff of his addiction and literature: that the detective novel is no sooner read than forgotten and never invites a second reading, as literature often does.

The implications are clear enough. Auden denies any continuity between literary novels and genre novels, or indeed between the different genres. One does not pass from lower to higher. On the contrary, one might perfectly well fall from the higher to the lower, or simply read both, as many people eat both good food and junk food, the only problem being that the latter can be addictive; by constantly repeating the same gratifying formula (the litmus test of genre fiction), it stimulates and satisfies a craving for endless sameness, to the point that the reader can well end up spending all the time he has available for reading with exactly the same fare. (My one powerful experience of this was a spell reading Simenon's Maigret novels: after five or six it gets harder and harder to distinguish one from another, and yet one goes on.)

Auden, it should be noted, does not propose to stop reading detective novels – he continues to enjoy them – and expresses no regret that people read detective novels rather than, say, Faulkner or Charlotte Brontë, nor any wish that they use detective novels as a stepping stone to "higher things". He simply notes that he has to struggle to control his addiction, presumably because he doesn't want to remain trapped in a repetitive pattern of experience that allows no growth and takes him nowhere. His essay, in fact, reads like the reasoning of someone determined to explain to himself why he must not waste too much time with detective novels, and at the same time to forgive himself for the time he does spend with them. If anything, genre fiction prevents engagement with literary fiction, rather than vice versa, partly because of the time it occupies, but more subtly because while the latter is of its nature exploratory and potentially unsettling, the former encourages the reader to stay in a comfort zone.

I'm forced to pause here to admit the objection that much supposedly literary fiction also repeats weary formulas, while some novels marketed as genre fiction move towards the exploratory by denying readers the sameness the format led them to expect. And of course many literary writers have made hay "subverting" genre forms. However, if the "I-don't-mind-people-reading-*Twilight*-because-it could-lead-to-higher-things" platitude continues to be trotted out, it is because, despite all the blurring that has occurred over recent years, we still have no trouble recognizing the difference between the repetitive formula offering easy pleasure and the more strenuous attempt to engage with the world in new ways.

So do people pass from the genre to the literary up our Neoplatonic ladder? Do they discover Stieg Larsson and move on to Pamuk? With no studies or statistics available to settle the question – at least I have not come across any – I can only resort to anecdotal evidence, as a father of three and a university teacher for many years. And the first thing to say is that no one has ever spoken to me of having made this progression. My children all enjoyed listening to the classic canon of children's stories in their infancy, but this did not automatically lead to "serious reading" later on, despite, or quite possibly because of, their parents' highly developed reading habit. My son spent his adolescence switching back and forth between computer games and compulsive rereadings of *The Lord of the Rings*, equally happy with both forms of entertainment. Later, he gathered together complete collections of Jo Nesbø and Henning Mankell. When I have suggested trying the work of certain novelists I like – Coetzee, Moravia – his complaint is invariably that they are too disturbing and too close to home. My eldest daughter oscillates between pulp fiction and literary fiction with the greatest of ease, perfectly aware of the entirely different pleasures they offer. My youngest daughter pursues vast fantasy chronicles and seems entirely happy with them; they have never prompted her to consider opening any of the more literary works our bookshelves are stacked with. In fact she reads fantasy chronicles because they are not to be found on the family bookshelves and offer a distinctly different experience from literary fiction. She does not want, she says, to be troubled with the kind of realities she sees quite enough of. She likes the costumed world of bold exploits and special powers.

When I speak to my students, what is most striking is that the majority of them, who are content on a diet made up exclusively of genre fiction, simply do not perceive any difference in kind between these and literary works; they do not see the essentially conservative nature of the one and the exploratory nature of the other. They register no need to widen their reading experiences. Often they propose theses on genre works of no distinction whatsoever, unable to understand why their teachers might put these in a different category from, say, Doris Lessing or D.H. Lawrence.

If we assume, then, for the sake of argument and in the absence of persuasive information to the contrary, that narratives do not form a continuum such that one is naturally led from the simpler to the more complex, but offer quite different experiences that mesh with readers' psyches and requirements in quite different ways, why do the right-thinking intellectuals continue to insist on this idea, even encouraging their children to read anything rather than nothing, as if the very act of reading was itself a virtue?

It's evident that publishers have a commercial interest in the comforting notion that any reading is better than none. They can feel virtuous selling a hundred million copies of *Fifty Shades*, strong in the hope that at least some of those folks might move on to Pulitzer and Nobel winners, and perhaps eventually to some of the more obscure and adventurous writers in their stables – just as, in *Fifty Shades* itself, the heroine Anastasia can indulge in a little S&M as part of a project to lead Christian Grey out of his perversion and on to the joys of the missionary position in conventional wedlock. It's always a relief to have reasons for supposing that what one is doing might have a bit more to it than the merest self-interest.

At a deeper level, there is a desire to believe in an educational process that puts the intellectual in a pastoral relationship to an ingenuous public who must be coaxed in a positive direction; that is, the notion of this pathway upward from pulp to Proust allows for the figure of the benign educator who takes the hands of blinkered readers and leads them from the stable to the stars, as the Italians say. It's good to posit a scheme of things in which possibly obsolete skills like close reading and critical analysis in fact have an important social role.

What no one wants to accept – and no doubt there is an element of class prejudice at work here too – is that there are many ways to live a full, responsible and even wise life that do not pass through reading literary fiction. And that consequently those of us who do pursue this habit, who feel that it enriches and illuminates us, are not in possession of an essential tool for self-realization or the key to protecting civilization from decadence and collapse. We are just a bunch of folks who for reasons of history and social conditioning have been blessed with a wonderful pursuit. Others may or may not be enticed towards it, but I seriously doubt if E.L. James is the first step towards Shakespeare. Better to start with *Romeo and Juliet*.

How Italy Improved My English

It has become commonplace, in this age of globalization, to speak of novelists and poets who change language, whether to find a wider audience or to adapt to life in a new country. But what about those writers who move to another country and do not change language, who continue to write in their mother tongue many years after it has ceased to be the language of daily conversation? Do the words they use grow arid and stiff? Or is there an advantage in being away from what is perhaps only the flavour of the day at home, the expressions invented today and gone tomorrow? Then, beyond specifically linguistic concerns, what audience do you write towards if you are no longer regularly speaking to people who use your language?

The most famous candidate for a reflection on this situation would be James Joyce, who left Ireland in 1904 aged twenty-two and lived abroad, mainly in Trieste and Paris, until his death in 1941. Other writers one could speak of would be W.G. Sebald, writing in German while living in England, Dubravka Ugrešić writing in Croatian while living in the Netherlands, or Aleksandr Solzhenitsyn and Joseph Brodsky, who went on writing in Russian after being forced into exile in the United States. One could go back and look at Robert Browning's fifteen years in Italy, or Italo Calvino's thirteen years in Paris. There are many others. Yet the easiest example, the only one I can write about with some authority, and, frankly, one of the most extreme, for length of time away and level of engagement with the foreign language and foreign country, is myself. What has happened to *my* English over thirty-five years in Italy? How has this long expatriation – I would never call it exile – changed my writing?

One's age at the time of leaving home and reasons for doing so are important. I left London in 1981 at twenty-five, in part because my wife, who was Italian and whom I had met in the States, wasn't happy with England, and again because, having failed to secure a publisher for any of my first four novels, I needed to get away from friends and family who were pressing me to settle on a decent career before it was too late. I knew no Italian. I had no desire to leave England. Indeed, I was extremely anxious about losing touch with English. Two years previously, I had abandoned a Ph.D. at Harvard because I wanted to be in England to write about the English, not the Americans. So this new move felt a little like a failure. My hope was that I'd be back in a couple of years bringing a publishable novel with me. What changed my mind was learning Italian.

It was a huge effort. I had never been good at languages, at least orally. At school I regularly failed the oral side of German and French exams, and at Cambridge chose Latin for my language requirement precisely to avoid the oral. Also, I love to talk; not knowing the language is a big privation for me. Added to which, my wife spoke four languages fluently, she couldn't see my problem, so there was quite a shift in the relationship as I found myself obliged to rely on her. I was floundering.

We had chosen to live in Verona because my wife's brother was studying there. There was not a large English community in the city at the time, and anyway we did our best to avoid it so that I could learn Italian. For four or five years, aside from the language lessons I taught to make ends meet, I spoke little English and read even less, concentrating entirely on Italian fiction, Italian newspapers, Italian history books, checking every word I didn't know in the dictionary. It was exhausting. There was no radio in English, no satellite TV, no Internet. I was immersed in Italian in a way that I think has become difficult today.

I say I was learning Italian, but in fact I was learning English too. Relearning it. Nothing makes you more aware of your own language, its structure and strategies, than the differences of a new one. And very soon I had my first major pay-off from all this effort. I had been reading the work of Natalia Ginzburg – *È stato così*; *La strada che va in città*; *Caro Michele*. I had chosen Ginzburg merely because friends advised that she was the easiest Italian writer for foreigners. But something in the laconic, colloquial voice meshed with my own writing. Trying to imagine how that voice and downbeat storytelling style might work in English, I wrote two short novels, *Tongues of Flame* and *Loving Roger*, in rapid succession. Oddly, though I had taken both voice and, to an extent, structure from Ginzburg, these would be the most English of all my novels, acts of pure memory of places and people: my family in the first book, an office where I had once worked in the second. Though both books were rejected dozens of times, I felt confident that I had got it right. Five years later both were published and won prizes.

In a previous piece I mentioned that early on in Italy I wrote a novel in Italian. This came immediately after *Tongues of Flame* and *Loving Roger* and this too was influenced by Ginzburg. The curious thing was how differently influence plays out when you are writing in the same language and when you are transferring to another. In the same language, influence can look dangerously like imitation. My Italian book was hopelessly derivative. This had been true too of my earlier love affairs in English with Henry Green and with Beckett. The writing was too obviously hankering after its model. But transferring Ginzburg, whom I doubt I understood perfectly at the time, into my English world, linguistic and cultural, made something new happen, something that was neither Ginzburg nor the old me.

I began to understand that I could use my immersion in Italian to become a different writer in English.

Translation helped. I had started to translate at a commercial level after a couple of years in Italy, and shortly after my thirtieth birthday, the very same week that *Tongues of Flame* was finally accepted for publication, I was given my first "literary" translation, Alberto Moravia's *La cosa*, or *Erotic Tales* as it was to become. Over the next ten years I translated more Moravia, as well as Antonio Tabucchi, Italo Calvino, Roberto Calasso and others. In each case, the closeness to fine writers, the awareness of how differently they wrote, from each other and from myself, a difference I always strove to preserve, was the best possible school for writing. Again and again, one had to ask, how can this voice, this peculiar tone, this way of moving into a story be made to work in English? And once one had found a solution it became natural, on starting a story of my own, to wonder: how would Tabucchi do this? What would this story sound like if Calasso were writing it? My novel *Shear*, in particular, couldn't have been written without the rather bizarre combined influence of my regular translation of a trade magazine for the stone-quarrying business and the 450 pages of Calasso's *The Marriage of Cadmus and Harmony*. Writers whose work I felt wouldn't be helpful in this way – Oriana Fallaci, Aldo Busi, Pier Paolo Pasolini, in his last novel *Petroleum* – I simply refused to translate. The commercial work provided enough money to live on. And where I was open to an author's influence, there was always the abyss between his or her Italian and my English to prevent me from falling into imitation. I remember seven or eight intensely fertile years.

But how long would my English hold up against the daily attrition of Italian?

I worried about this. Going home for holidays I noticed that buzzwords had come and perhaps already gone – "nerd", "dink" – without my ever using them. Editors were forever picking up

Italianisms in my writing. Setting a new story in England I began to feel vulnerable. Often Italian expressions came to mind when what I needed was English. Even Italian situations. Often English expressions came to mind that quite likely no one was using any more. Nothing is more normal than for the expat's vision of his home country to remain anchored in the past. *Ulysses* we remember, published in 1922, was set in 1904, immediately before Joyce left Dublin.

I began to write non-fiction, about Italy, to draw this experience into my writing. Where fiction was concerned, I looked for a different kind of storytelling that didn't involve an intense contemporaneity, or was set outside the UK. A novel like *Europa*, where foreign-language teachers working in an Italian university travel together to the European Parliament to present a petition, was a deliberate attempt to turn this displacement from England into drama. Now I consciously played with Italianisms in English, to see what effects might be achieved that way. In *Destiny*, the disturbed son of an Italian mother and English father constantly provokes his father by introducing Italian idioms in English sentences.

Just when it seemed I had pushed these strategies to the limit, if not beyond, changes in my circumstances and indeed in technology came to my aid. The fact is that no two writers abroad are ever in quite the same situation. Had I come to Italy as a Korean, or a Norwegian, languages people rarely use or need here, I wonder if it would have been possible or sensible to go on using my mother tongue in the same way. And had I arrived twenty years earlier I could not have had the career that eventually offered itself to me in the late Nineties. First the fax, then email, then the Internet, opened the way to working regularly for British and American papers. In 1995 I wrote my first piece for *The New York Review*. As a result, I found myself reading mostly in English again, as a reviewer now rather than a translator. With the Internet came radio and television in English. One was no longer "isolated in Italy". Gradually, I could feel part of an English-speaking community again, without ever leaving my Italian home. It's hard to express how uncanny this seemed at the time, and how radically it changed expat existence.

Also, this was a community one could write towards. That is, writing in English, in Italy, I wasn't really writing towards my old life, England and London, any more. I was writing to all the people out there who read English. So I needn't worry that my English was no longer an idiomatic British English. For me, with my Italian experience long consolidated, this could not have happened at a better time.

There is a formative period in a writer's life when influences are crucial, when to go and live in another country, read in another language, discover this or that author, will matter intensely. And there is a time when, while still open to novelty and experiment, it can no longer blow you away or revolutionize your approach. For a writer to go to a foreign country as a young man, like Sebald, who went to England in his twenties, is quite a different matter than to go when most of one's major work is accomplished, as was the case with Solzhenitsyn's move to the States. For Sebald there was mostly gain, for Solzhenitsyn, much later in life, mostly loss.

Looking back, I have no idea what kind of writer I might have become had I stayed in the UK. Perhaps I would never have got published at all. Or perhaps I would have found my way to the centre of London literary life, though that was never an ambition. All in all, I feel immensely lucky to have gone to Italy when I did and experienced for a decade or so the relative linguistic isolation that made me focus so intensely on language, writing and translation. But equally lucky to be able to send this piece to New York by email, and to be part of that now global community that shares its thoughts, on literature and other matters, online, regardless of where we live.

How Best to Read Auto-Fiction

I am accused of auto-fiction. A British reviewer feels my recent novel *In Extremis* is too obviously about my life for him to assess it as a novel. That is, if I am going to focus on my own life in a book – and it's interesting the reviewer feels he can be sure about the facts of my life – I should, like Karl Ove Knausgaard, openly declare that this is autobiography, or at least, that it should be thought about in relation to my life, and stop pretending it is fiction.

This debate is as old as the hills: there are critics who feel it's good for the novelist to focus on his own experience, and then there are those who feel that the core of a novel must be invented. Just as there are writers who claim their work is never autobiographical, even when it seems it must be, and writers who claim their work is always autobiographical, even when it seems it can't be. Champions of truth and authenticity; worshippers of the artist's untrammelled imagination.

Can we say anything new about this? Anything deeper than a difference in literary taste?

Philip Roth, who died this week at the age of eighty-five, always defended himself vigorously against frequent accusations of "auto-fiction". Evidently, the criticism troubled him. In a series of essays and interviews republished in *Why Write?*, Roth insists that, while his novels draw on his background and experience, they are sovereign artefacts, quite distinct from biography. "Readers may have trouble disentangling my life from Zuckerman's," he says of the character who appears in so many of his novels and is commonly thought of as his fictional alter ego. All the same, these novels are "the result of a writing process a long way from the methods, let alone the purposes, of autobiography".

So the hero is not the writer. Fair enough. But the question is more complex than that, and in a later interview Roth defended *The Counterlife*, which offers various conflicting versions of the life of novelist Nathan Zuckerman and his brother Henry, in these terms: "People constantly change their story... we are writing fictitious versions of our lives all the time, contradictory but mutually entangling stories that, however subtly or grossly falsified, constitute our hold on reality and are the closest thing we have to truth."

Actually, most people don't write fictitious versions of their lives at any time, though they may invent such versions in conversation or reflection. Roth seems to be conflating, or confusing, the novelist's activity with the individual's construction of a personal history. This would appear to be in line with the conclusion of *The Counterlife*, in which Nathan explains to his wife, Maria, who is objecting to the way she has been presented in a novel of his, that there is "no you" and "no me". People are simply the sum of their performances.

So, behind the debate about whether this or that character in a novel is identical to the writer – auto-fiction – lies the perplexing question of selfhood, of what it means to be someone and to have an identity at all. Rather than a stable state, Roth suggests, selfhood is a perpetual performance, a character in a book being only one representation, one possible manifestation of that performance. It cannot be identical with the author himself, since his extra-literary performance of selfhood is involved in constructing the other, fictional self. Hence "even in a fiction that may have decidedly autobiographical roots, one is always at a distance from one's sources anyway, and that distance is always in flux".

Roth's arguments are hardly consistent when we look at them closely. By talking about "fictitious versions" of our lives, he implies that there is a true version. By talking about "the closest thing we have to truth", he suggests that this true version remains disappointingly unavailable. But if a version is unavailable, in what way can it be said to exist at all? By going on to contrast the "subtly falsified" version and the "grossly falsified" version, he nonetheless assumes that we know how to get closer to the truth if we want to. But might not that be an illusion?

In more defensive interviews, Roth simply insists on a manifest gulf between himself and his supposed alter egos. The author Philip Roth, he says, has lived most of his life alone in the country, writing novels, something that gives him "an enormous sense of personal freedom", of being out of the fray, while his characters for the most part get on with their much busier, sometimes scandalous lives. What links the two, author and character – beyond the obvious Newark Jewish backgrounds – is the common concern with freedom. Roth's heroes invariably seek to overcome fear as they kick against the curbs of social convention, particularly in the sphere of relationships and sex. Out in the country, mainly alone, Roth feels free from social pressure, free to write about characters with backgrounds similar to his own struggling to be free. If character is not stable, the performance nevertheless follows recognizable patterns.

Let's offer this formulation: a certain kind of writer, for whom the day-to-day performance of self – the interaction of personality with the world – is complex and conflicted, invents multiple fictional selves who deal with the same predicament in different ways. Rather than establishing any ultimate truth about identity, such a writer explores possibilities that might be dangerous or incompatible in real life. In short, the writing becomes an extension of the living. "Making fake biography... out of the actual drama of my life," Roth acknowledges, "is my life." According to this scheme, the novelist's creativity lies in the richness of variation with which the same underlying conflict is reconstituted in every new story.

Let's try out this formulation on one of the greatest exponents of auto-fiction, Leo Tolstoy. Almost every character, every scene, every conversation, claims the critic and biographer Angus Wilson, every object even, in Tolstoy's novels, can be traced back to something in his life. He is the most biographical of authors. The fictional reconstructions of events close to those in his own experience, Wilson goes on, frequently present an alter ego behaving as Tolstoy would like to have behaved, but didn't, in similar circumstances. Behaving better, that is, more nobly and honestly. Thus Konstantin Levin, in *Anna Karenina*, is in all kinds of ways similar to Leo his author, except that he is nicer. Levin has a sick and wastrel brother, exactly like Tolstoy's brother Dmitry, but behaves patiently and kindly at his deathbed, which Leo did not, leaving Dmitry to die in the country because there were parties he didn't want to miss in St Petersburg. Levin proposes to his Kitty in exactly the way Tolstoy proposed to his wife, Sophia (or Sonya, as she was usually called), just that the saintly Levin does not have sex with any number of peasant girls while agonizing over that proposal, as the profligate Leo did. Throughout his life, Tolstoy experienced, and indeed spoke openly about, a fierce conflict between an insatiable sexual appetite and a deep yearning for sanctity. Again and again, this conflict is played out in his fiction.

After *Anna Karenina* (1877), Tolstoy largely gave up fiction-writing, which he had begun to see as itself a form of self-indulgence, in order to "be good" – or "play at being good", as Sonya would disparagingly put it. The two quarrelled constantly and constantly produced children (thirteen in all). She kept him anchored, Tolstoy worried, to the world of the flesh and the world of material belongings. To achieve sainthood, it wasn't enough to stop writing novels and to stop having peasant girls: he would also have to stop having sex altogether, renounce his wealth, leave his wife and family, live like a hermit, or at least like a monk. But he couldn't. Instead, in 1887, he went back to fiction and wrote *The Kreutzer Sonata*. In that novella, a man who holds exactly Tolstoy's extreme views on sex (that it is utterly disgusting), and whose courtship and marriage in every way described corresponds to the author's own biography, kills his wife in a fit of jealousy when he assumes (probably wrongly) that she is betraying him with her handsome violin teacher.

Was this wishful thinking on Tolstoy's part? Was it a warning to himself of what he might be capable of? Was it an exploration of the relation of his extreme views to real behaviour? Whatever the case, Leo allowed Sonya to read the book aloud to his family. Did they find it too obviously about the author's life, about their own lives, to be enjoyed as a novel? Not at all. Despite the glaring and unflattering parallels, Sonya loved the book and, concerned as always about the family's finances, immediately set about promoting it. Shocked when Moscow gossips began to take it as a straight account of their marital crisis, she insisted on letting everyone know that, after twenty-five years of marriage, the two still enjoyed sex; in fact, a last child had been born while the book was being written. But of course this was exactly the problem as described in the story: an inability to stop having sex.

Six years after the novel's publication, still determined to leave Sonya, Tolstoy became furiously jealous when she fell in love with her much younger piano teacher. But he did not kill her.

One can enjoy *The Kreutzer Sonata* without knowing anything about Tolstoy's private life, as one can enjoy *Portnoy's Complaint* and *Zuckerman Unbound* without knowing anything about Roth. And one can enjoy them in a different way knowing what there is to be known about the life behind the work, or rather, the life performing itself through the work. Certainly, to read a number of Tolstoy's novels, or Roth's, is to be aware of a mapping, if not of some fixed point from which they are all projected, at least of a precise area of disturbance that throws up seemingly endless variations on the underlying theme. Roth's writing about characters with similar backgrounds struggling to be free would seem to be part of his own struggle. Tolstoy's writing about characters eager to be pure seems very likely to have been part of his own eagerness for purity.

Roth's struggle ended in 2012, when he put down his pen and settled for the safe, elderly man's freedom of not having to engage with the world any more. Tolstoy made his bid for absolute purity when, in 1910, at dead of night, aged eighty-two, he slipped out on his sleeping wife with thoughts of seclusion and monasteries. Two weeks later, he was dead from pneumonia.

In the case of my novel *In Extremis*, many events do follow more or less the events surrounding my mother's death. Many do not. Some conversations seem to me to correspond, at points, to what was actually said. Most do not. To an extent, I share the narrator's view of events. To an extent, I don't. What is clear is that at the time of those events, nobody could have imagined the book that is *In Extremis*; no filming of the events would have produced, or even hinted at, the story that is *In Extremis*. A majority of the people who come to the book knowing nothing of my life will simply enjoy it, or not, as a novel.

Those who disparage authors for practising auto-fiction tend to believe character is a steady state that can be adequately represented on the page and thus see the autobiographical as an easy option, a cop-out. What they want instead is a determined effort of the unbridled imagination representing many different characters, all stable and well-defined, interacting with one another. Both the stability and the creativity are reassuring, even when the drama may be tragic. Those who recognize the problem of being anyone at all, the difficulty of keeping the performance on the road from one moment to the next, will have priorities of a different kind.

Perhaps the first group should avoid reading author biographies, or too many novels by the same person, since the more you read of any author, the more the same patterns will emerge, making an awareness of the biographical element inescapable. The second will be happy settling down with the complete works of Tolstoy and Roth, Joyce and Dickens, Dostoevsky and Chekhov, of George Eliot and Virginia Woolf, Faulkner and Hemingway, Proust and Beckett, Bernhard and Coetzee, and even Dante and Boccaccio... auto-fiction has a long pedigree.

Why Write in English?

Why not write in a foreign language? If people feel free to choose their profession, their religion and even, these days, their sex, why not just decide which language you want to write in and go for it? Ever since Jhumpa Lahiri published *In Other Words,* her small memoir in Italian, people have been asking me: why don't you write in Italian, Tim? You've been in the country thirty-five years, after all. What keeps you tied to English? Is it just a question of economic convenience? That the market for books in English is bigger? That the world in general gives more attention to books written in English?

Is that it? Certainly economics can be important. And politics too. Arguably, these were the factors that pushed Conrad and Nabokov to abandon their Polish and Russian mother tongues. If it is not possible to publish at home, or to publish there as one would wish to publish, then one is more or less obliged to go elsewhere if one wants to have a viable career as a writer. And if to publish elsewhere one has to change language, then some authors are willing to take that step.

Something of the same logic no doubt drives the many writers from Africa, Asia and the subcontinent who have turned to writing in French and English in recent years. The opportunities are larger. There is also the fact that people in Europe and the West are interested in the countries they grew up in. Just as in the nineteenth century novelists like Thomas Hardy or Giovanni Verga could "sell" their familiarity with peasant, provincial life to a middle-class metropolitan public, so post-colonial writers have fascinated us with stories that might seem unremarkable in their home countries, where the narrative tradition very likely deals with different content and requires a different relationship between writer and reader.

But beyond any understandable opportunism, there is often a genuine idealism and internationalism in the decision to change language. If you have "a message", and if English is the language that offers maximum diffusion, then it would seem appropriate to use it. In the 1950s, the rebellious and free-spirited Dutch novelist Gerard Kornelis van het Reve felt that the Dutch language and culture was simply not open enough and not big enough for an artist with important things to say. Van het Reve moved to England in 1953, dropped the exotic "van het" from his surname and set about writing in his adopted language. "Let us no longer express ourselves in a local argot," he boldly declared. The revolutionary, the preacher and the megalomaniac will always tend toward the medium that offers the widest possible readership.

For writers from countries that were once colonies, the switch to the language of the colonial power could also be seen as a kind of counterattack. The post-colonial writer appropriates the ex-overlord's language, subverts it and adapts it to his or her own purposes, all this to the supposed chagrin of members of the once dominant culture. This is the depressing, confrontational and, I suspect, flawed logic of Rushdie's 1982 article 'The Empire Writes Back with a Vengeance' (it is interesting that references to this famous article tend to omit the last three words).

More simply – more probably – you could say that if a global culture really is developing, and if the lingua franca of that culture is English, then its energy will naturally draw in those from the peripheries, just as the excitement over the formation of the nation state in a country like Italy in the nineteenth century prompted many writers to switch from writing in the local idioms of Naples and Venice and Milan to address the whole nation in the standard Tuscan Italian that finally became the language of the institutions and the schools.

All this makes sense, yet critics tend to pay attention only to those who have made a success of writing in a new language. In April 2014, a *New York Times* article about the phenomenon essentially compiled a list of young literary stars who had switched to writing in the main Western languages. The piece, titled 'Using the Foreign to Grasp the Familiar', is full of enthusiasm and positivity. "All interesting literature is born in that moment when you are not sure if you are in one place with one culture," Yoko Tawada, a Japanese author who writes in German, is quoted as saying.

At this point, the native English speaker almost begins to feel at a disadvantage for having been born into the dominant culture. Should we perhaps head for Paris, like Beckett or Jonathan Littell, just to be between two worlds? Or look for something more exotic and have ourselves translated back into English afterwards? Why not Korean, or Swahili? One reason is that changing languages doesn't always work. Van het Reve, notorious in Holland for his deeply pessimistic postwar novel *De Avonden* (*The Evenings*, 1947), was never able to secure a publisher in England, where his style and politics seemed incomprehensible. His talent wouldn't flower again until he returned to Holland and threw himself back into his country's national debate, in Dutch of course, with an incendiary mix of Catholicism, homosexuality and obscenity. His genius needed his mother tongue, his home milieu and an atmosphere of intense antagonism.

Kundera was already a huge international presence by the time he switched to writing in French in the 1990s, one of those authors who need never fear they might not find a publisher. Yet his work has lost power and intensity with the switch of language. In French, he just doesn't seem able to produce novels of the quality of *The Book of Laughter and Forgetting* and *The Unbearable Lightness of Being*.

Both Reve's and Kundera's moves suggest a certain hubris: they supposed their individual talents were entirely separate from the culture and language in which they had developed. It's a hubris inherent, perhaps, in the Western obsession with freedom, and the consequent refusal to accept that we are conditioned and limited by circumstances of birth, family and education.

In this light, Lahiri's quite unusual decision to move away from global English to write in Italian begins to make a little sense. Growing up in Rhode Island between Bengali and English, triumphing as an author in the latter while feeling that she had betrayed the former and her parents' culture with it, she had conflicted feelings towards both languages, something she talks about quite candidly in one of the later chapters of *In Other Words*: "I was ashamed," she writes, "of speaking Bengali and at the same time I was ashamed of feeling ashamed. It was impossible to speak English without feeling detached from my parents..."

Yet these difficult emotions, transmuted into other people's stories, were recognizably the driving force of Lahiri's excellent early stories. To imagine they could simply be set aside by moving into a language for which she had a certain affection but of which she had no deep knowledge, was perhaps ingenuous. In the event, what Lahiri writes in Italian is little else than an account of her attempt to escape English. At no point does it draw energy from Italian culture, or even transmit a feeling that her life is now firmly based in the world of Italian. There are no Italian characters in the book – indeed, no characters at all aside from Lahiri, as if actually she were writing in a language that was all her own, and that just happened to coincide with the language sixty million Italians use. The decision to publish the American edition of the book as a parallel text, Italian on the left and English on the right, gives the curious impression that, though written in Italian – indeed published first in Italian – the book is somehow not written *for* Italians; rather, the achievement of Italian becomes a trophy to show off to the American reader. We never believe that Lahiri will really spend her life in Italy or go on writing in Italian. Reviewers have generally agreed that the book just didn't work.

Writing in another language is successful when there is a genuine, long-term need to switch languages (often accompanied by serious trauma), and when the new linguistic and social context the author is moving in meshes positively with his or her ambitions and talents. At which point, let me make an admission. After only two years in Italy, long before I had published any fiction in English, I did write a novel in Italian: *I nani di domani* (literally *Tomorrow's Dwarves*). It was a comic "thriller" about a Veronese rock band, I nani di domani, who turn out to be a cover for a rather amateur terrorist organization. I had arrived in Verona in 1981, around the time of the Red Brigades' kidnapping (from an apartment block only a mile from where I was living) of General James Lee Dozier, Deputy Chief of Staff at NATO's Southern European land forces. The novel satirized pretty much everyone and everything I had come across in Verona, the main character being a female version of myself, teaching at a seedy private school run by the father of one of the terrorists.

Having written half the book, I sent it to Italy's only major literary agent at the time, the popular and immensely respected Erich Linder, an Austrian Jew whose family had brought him to Milan as a child in 1934 to escape persecution. To my amazement – since all my attempts to write in English were collecting regular rejections in London – he liked my Italian book and offered to take it on. But no sooner had I sent him the final pages than Linder died and my chances of becoming an Italian author with him. His successor at the agency, in the more usual Italian style, did not reply to my letters.

Years later, when I had published a number of novels in English, *I nani di domani* came up in conversation with an Italian publisher. I showed it to him and he offered to publish. But after rereading it, I decided against it. Any charm it had was to do with my naive fun with the language; it was superficial and playful in a rather facile way, and I decided I wouldn't feel comfortable promoting the book. My real subject matter still had to do with England and English, and it was to my home culture that my books were addressed, something that put me in a tradition, I suppose, with any number of other expats – Muriel Spark, James Joyce, D.H. Lawrence, Robert Browning, Lord Byron – who never dreamt of changing language. Not to mention W.G. Sebald, who always wrote in German despite thirty years in England, or the excellent Dubravka Ugrešić, who continues to write in Croatian despite having been forced to leave her homeland for the Netherlands in 1993.

The critic Karen Ryan, who has written a great deal on Russian émigré literature, remarks that "all transnational writers" have "a sense of play and inventiveness". I think this is true. An acquired language feels like a playground, at least at first. It is easy to have fun and break rules, because they are not internalized, they don't weigh so heavily in the psyche. In particular, it's easy to make puns, because the sound of the language still often dominates over the sense. Hence, changing language can benefit the author whose genius lies in that direction. But along with the playfulness comes a loss of pathos. The second language never seems to mean quite as much as the first. Or not for many years. In any event, after my early experiment, I never went back to writing in Italian. Rather I began to see how I could use a life speaking and reading mainly in Italian to develop an English that would be very much my own. Changing language is not the only way to bring energy to your writing.

Malpractice

A Novel Kind of Conformity

What happens when a multi-million-dollar author gets things wrong? Not much. Take the case of Haruki Murakami and his recent novel *Colorless Tsukuru Tazaki and His Years of Pilgrimage*. The idea behind the story is fascinating: what do you do when your closest friends eject you from the group without the slightest explanation? But the narrative is dull throughout and muddied by a half-hearted injection of Murakami-style weirdness – people with six fingers and psychic powers – that eventually contributes nothing to the very simple explanation of what actually happened. The book received mixed to poor reviews from embarrassed admirers and vindictive critics. Nevertheless, millions of copies were quickly sold worldwide, and Murakami's name remains on the list of likely Nobel winners.

How many times would Murakami have to get things wrong, badly wrong, before his fans and publishers stopped supporting him? Quite a few. Actually, no matter what Murakami writes, it's almost unimaginable that his sales would ever fall so low that he would be considered unprofitable. So the Japanese novelist finds himself in the envious position (for an artist) of being free to take risks without the danger of much loss of income, or even prestige.

This is not the case with less successful authors. Novelists seeking to make a living from their work will obviously be in trouble if a publisher is not confident enough in their success to offer a decent advance; and if, once published, a book does not earn out its advance, publishers will be more hesitant next time, whatever the quality of the work on offer. Authors in this situation will think twice before going out on some adventurous limb. They will tend to give publishers what they want. Or try to.

The difficulties of the writer who is not yet well established have been compounded in recent years by the decision on the part of most large publishers to allow their sales staff a say in which novels get published and which don't. At a recent conference in Oxford – entitled Literary Activism – editor Philip Langeskov described how on hearing his pitch of a new novel, sales teams would invariably ask, "But what other book is it like?" Only when a novel could be presented as having a reassuring resemblance to something already commercially successful was it likely to overcome the sales-staff veto.

But even beyond financial questions, I would argue that there is a growing resistance at every level to taking risks in novel-writing, a tendency that is in line with the more general and ever increasing anxious desire to receive positive feedback, or at least not negative feedback, about almost everything we do, constantly and instantly. It is a situation that leads to something I will describe, perhaps paradoxically, as an intensification of conformity, people falling over themselves to be approved of.

How can I flesh out this intuition? At some point it slipped into the conversation that high sales are synonymous with achievement in writing. Perhaps copyright was partly responsible. A novelist's work is to be paid for by a percentage of the sales achieved. This aligns the writer's and the publisher's interests and gets us used to thinking about books in terms of numbers sold. Add to that the now obligatory egalitarian view of society, which suggests that all reader responses are of equal worth, and you can easily fall into the habit of judging achievement in terms of the number of readers rather than their quality.

So, when praising a novel they like, critics will often give the impression, or perhaps seek to convince themselves, that the book is a huge commercial success, even when it isn't. Such has been the case with Karl Ove Knausgaard. Apparently it isn't imaginable that one can pronounce a work a masterpiece and accept that it doesn't sell. Conversely, writer Kirsty Gunn recently spoke (again at the Literary Activism conference) of a revelatory moment when she, her husband, the editor David Graham, and others were celebrating another milestone in the extraordinary success of Yann Martel's *Life of Pi*, which Graham was responsible for publishing in the UK. "Suddenly I had to leave the room," Gunn said, describing a moment of intense dismay. "I realized we had reached the point where we were judging books by their sales."

Copyright has been with us two hundred years and more, but the consequent attention to sales numbers has been recently and dramatically intensified by electronic media and the immediate feedback it offers. Announce an article (like this one) on Facebook, and you can count, as the hours go by, how many people have looked at it, clicked on it, liked it, etc. Publish a novel and you can see *at once* where it stands on the Amazon sales rankings (I remember a publisher mailing me the link when my own novel *Destiny* amazingly crept into Amazon UK's top twenty novels – for about an hour). Otherwise, you can track from day to day how many readers have reviewed it and how many stars they have given it. Everything conspires to have us obsessively attached to the world's response to whatever we do.

Franzen talks about this phenomenon in his recent novel *Purity,* suggesting that, simply by offering us the chance to check constantly whether people are talking about us, the Internet heightens a fear of losing whatever popularity we may have achieved: "the fear of unpopularity and uncoolness... the fear of being flamed or forgotten". Hence the successful novelist is constantly encouraged to produce more of the same. "It's incredible," remarks Murakami in an interview. "I write a novel every three or four years, and people are waiting for it. I once interviewed John Irving, and he told me that reading a good book is a main line. Once they are addicted, they're always waiting."

Well, is "addiction" what a literary writer should want in readers? And if a writer accepts such addiction, or even rejoices in it, as Murakami seems to, doesn't it put pressure on him, as pusher, to offer more of the same? In fact it would be far more plausible to ascribe the failure (aesthetic, but not commercial) of *Colorless Tsukuru Tazaki*, and indeed Franzen's *Purity*, not to the author's willingness to take exciting risks with new material (Ishiguro's bizarre *The Buried Giant*, for example), but rather to a tired, lacklustre attempt to produce yet another best-seller in the same vein. Both writers have in the past taken intriguing distractions from their core business – Franzen with his idiosyncratic *Kraus Project*, Murakami with his engaging book on running – but when it comes to the novel, it's back to the same old formula, though without perhaps the original inspiration or energy. Financial freedom is not psychological freedom.

Yet to create anything genuinely new, writers need to risk failure, indeed to court failure, aesthetically *and* commercially, and to do it again and again throughout their lives, something not easy to square with the growing tendency to look on fiction-writing as a regular career. "How have you survived as a writer twenty years and more?" a member of the public asked Kirsty Gunn after she had spoken of her absolute refusal to adapt her work to a publisher's sense of what was marketable. "Day job," she briskly replied.

Is it really possible, then, to be free as a writer? Free from an immediate need for money, free from the need to be praised, free from the concern of how those close to you will respond to what you write, free from the political implications, free from your publisher's eagerness for a book that looks like the last or, worse still, like whatever the latest fashion might be?

I doubt it, to be honest. Perhaps the best one can ever achieve is a measure of freedom in line with your personal circumstances. Anyway, here, for what it's worth, are two reflections drawn from my own experience:

1. So long as it's compatible with regular writing, the day job is never to be disdained. A steady income allows you to take risks. Certainly I would never have written books like *Europa* or *Teach Us to Sit Still* without the stability of a university job. I knew the style of *Europa*, obsessive and unrelenting, and the content of *Teach Us to Sit Still,* detailed accounts of urinary nightmares, would turn many off. And they did: one prominent editor refused even to consider *Teach Us*, because "the word prostate makes me queasy". Yet both books found enthusiastic audiences who were excited to read something different.

2. When you're trying to write something seriously new, *don't show it to anybody until it's finished*; don't talk about it; seek no feedback at all. Cultivate a quiet separateness. "Anything great and bold," observed Robert Walser "must be brought about in secrecy and silence, or it perishes and falls away, and the fire that was awakened dies."

Oddly enough these are conditions that are most likely to hold at the beginning of your writing career, when you're hardly expecting to make money and nobody is waiting for what you do. Which perhaps explains why the most adventurous novels – Günter Grass's *The Tin Drum*, Elsa Morante's *House of Liars*, Kingsley Amis's *Lucky Jim*, J.D. Salinger's *The Catcher in the Rye*, James Baldwin's *Go Tell It on the Mountain*, Nicholson Baker's *The Mezzanine*, Thomas Pynchon's *V.*, Marilynne Robinson's *Housekeeping* – are very often early works. Celebrity, it would appear, breeds conformity.

Pretty Violence

A handsome book just arrived on my desk. *War Is Beautiful*, the title declares. Surely not! Then I see the subtitle: "The *New York Times* Pictorial Guide to the Glamour of Armed Conflict". Ah, irony. An asterisk takes me to some tiny print at the bottom left of the cover: "(in which the author explains why he no longer reads *The New York Times*)". And who is the author? David Shields, the man who gave us *Reality Hunger* and many other thoughtful provocations. In fact, I now recall that a couple of years ago Shields, with whom I occasionally exchange an email opinion or two, and who was then on the lookout for a publisher, ran this project past me, and, although at the time I saw neither the book's title or its actual photographic contents, I endorsed his introductory essay with the quote: "Absolutely right, to the point and guaranteed to stir things up."

Basically, as Shields had promised, the book offers sixty-four very glossy war photos taken from the front page of the *New York Times* and arranged thematically: Nature, Playground, Father, God, Pietà, Painting, Movie, Beauty, Love, Death. The earliest picture is dated January 2002, from Afghanistan, the latest October 2013, from Pakistan. The accusation is that the newspaper does everything to make war glamorous and even, in some way, reassuring: "A chaotic world is ultimately under control," Shields observes. In an afterword, art critic David Hickey shows how consciously the photos reproduce well-known pictorial and painterly tropes:

There is a Magdalene in white clothing nodding onto the edge of the frame as she would in a Guido Reni. There is a Rodin of two kneeling marines in a flat field. There are warriors protecting children that echo imperial Rome, where war was an everyday fact, as the *Times* would seem to wish it now.

It's hard to deny, as you leaf through these photos, that they do indeed very deliberately aestheticize their subjects, and hence anaesthetize the viewer; these are glamour pictures to be admired rather than documentary images that give immediacy to violence and horror. "Connecticut-living-room trash" is how Hickey sums it up. In short, we are a long, long way from the more sober black-and-white images that chronicled the Vietnam War in the same paper.

All the same, an objection comes to mind: that this transformation of violence into beauty is hardly the reserve of the *New York Times*. In this regard, consider Luc Sante's fascinating article on the New York police photos of crime scenes taken in the early years of the twentieth century. These are stark images whose purpose was to provide legal evidence; nevertheless, there is a strong aesthetic element. "Not every one is a masterpiece," Sante observes, "but all display patient craftsmanship in their framing and lighting, making them seem lapidary, even definitive. Every picture is a tableau, complete unto itself." Except in very rare cases, it seems photographers and artists instinctively compose images in order to make the experience of looking at them dramatic, impressive and, above all, bearable.

And this has been going on for hundreds of years. Take the ugly subject of beheading. We have all expressed our shock over the Islamic State's habit of posting YouTube videos of their warriors decapitating hostages. Sometimes it has seemed that we are more shocked by the existence and availability of the videos – the mere fact that they tempt us to become witnesses to such violence – than by the act itself. Yet of course our "civilization" has a long history of depicting beheading. There is hardly a major art gallery in Europe or the United States without a *Judith and Holofernes*. From Caravaggio to Klimt, painters have enjoyed the drama of the beautiful woman hacking off the soldier's head. Salome and John the Baptist are another popular pair, the Baptist's head always decorously framed by the (usually silver) plate on which it is presented to the pretty dancer. In another Biblical episode, the courageous young David has no qualms about hacking off Goliath's head, and Donatello delights in showing a cute boy naked with the dead giant's beard under his foot. Of course, this is "art", not documentary, but it creates a habit of viewing violence in a certain way.

Nor is literature any less capable of turning such scenes into "beauty". "The program of the photos," Shields observes of the images he has collected together, "is the same as that of the *Iliad*: the preservation of power." How can one not be brought up sharp by that claim? If we stop reading the *New York Times* in protest at this glamourizing of war, do we stop reading the *Iliad*? *Beowulf*? *War and Peace*? Primo Levi complained that a great deal of Holocaust literature was guilty of making the suffering more palatable by sanctifying the victims. Aestheticizing horror can be a subtle process.

Then how are we to distinguish between images that are rendered with the worst intention – "the preservation of power", assuming we are agreed that that is not a legitimate aim – and those that are supposedly being used to expose this intention for the hypocrisy it is? Arguably, Kubrick's *Barry Lyndon* had this element of protest, but in the end it too produced some glamorous images of extreme violence. Likewise the many Vietnam War movies. Even Shields's book, as I am sure he is aware, invites ambiguous responses. The cover includes a score of quotes besides my own. "Fantastic, engrossing, and gruesome," says

Davis Schneiderman on the back cover of the book. "I love it." "A work of perilous ambiguity," Andrei Codrescu observes more soberly. For, of course, as soon as we have metabolized the criticism levelled at the *New York Times*, we do indeed settle down to enjoy these extraordinary photographs, which the publisher has been careful to present in as lavish a form as possible.

At which point the question arises: can we ever get away from this transformation that makes a beauty of the beast?

Let's go back to Homer, since Shields has mentioned him. In the *Odyssey*, when Helen and Menelaus are back in Greece, Telemachus visits them. All they want to talk about is Troy, the war; in the end Troy is the great focal point of their lives. But it's too painful. Menelaus will have to remember Helen's betrayal, Helen her dead lovers, Telemachus his dead friends and missing father, whom he assumes is dead. The truth is too ugly to be comfortable with.

Helen gets up, goes into another room, finds a drug she was given in Egypt and slips it into the wine. It's a drug, Homer says, "that would allow you to recount your brother's death with a smile on your face". And so it is. She and her husband and Telemachus have a wonderful evening going over all the unbearable violence of Troy – the drug has made it noble, glamorous – and then fall serenely asleep. Needless to say, that drug is literary form: rhyme, rhythm, art.

The *Inferno* does the same with hell.

> The many people and their ghastly wounds
> did so intoxicate my eyes
> that I was moved to linger there and weep.

Dante complains. But his guide, Virgil, insists he keep moving fast: "Let your talk be brief... We must not linger here." To stop and really look would be to risk being overwhelmed by suffering;

the rapid movement of the *terza rima* with its ever-reassuring rhymes takes the sting out it all. One can see why Dante's guide had to be a poet: only art can take you through hell, by making it beautiful. Endless descriptions of punishment and disfigured, mutilated bodies become weirdly attractive. Centuries later, Beckett, a Dante fan to the end, understood the game perfectly, and his novel *Watt* offers a sort of *reductio ad absurdum* of the Dantesque method:

> Personally of course I regret everything. Not a word, not a deed, not a thought, not a need, not a grief, not a joy, not a girl, not a boy, not a doubt, not a trust, not a scorn, not a lust, not a hope, not a fear, not a smile, not a tear, not a name, not a face, no time, no place, that I do not regret, exceedingly. An ordure from beginning to end.

Life's awfulness is rigidly organized into a nursery-rhyme pattern of chiming opposites. One hardly notices the suffering at all. Such is art, Beckett suggests.

One could list any number of writers who set out to write protests over the horrors of war and ended up glorifying it in their way. Tennyson's 'The Charge of the Light Brigade' is emblematic: a stupid communications error in the Crimean War had led six hundred cavalrymen to charge a line of cannons. The carnage was inevitable. Everyone was appalled. But Tennyson's poem transforms it into beauty:

> Cannon to right of them,
> Cannon to left of them,
> Cannon in front of them
>   Volley'd & thunder'd;
> Storm'd at with shot and shell,
> Boldly they rode and well,

Into the jaws of Death,
Into the mouth of Hell
  Rode the six hundred.

You might argue that Tennyson still lived in a time that wanted to believe in heroes, willing to acknowledge the bravery of the men despite the stupidity of the sacrifice. But what about the First World War poets? Take Wilfred Owen's 'Anthem for Doomed Youth':

What passing-bells for these who die as cattle?
– Only the monstrous anger of the guns.
Only the stuttering rifles' rapid rattle
Can patter out their hasty orisons.
No mockeries now for them; no prayers nor bells;
Nor any voice of mourning save the choirs, –
The shrill, demented choirs of wailing shells;
And bugles calling for them from sad shires.

It's true this reads like a serious protest; all the same I do not think today's warmongers would have much quarrel with a poem in which the soldiers' suffering has been so monumentally cast in poetic diction of the "hasty orisons", "wailing shells" and "sad shires" variety.

The truth is that the more apocalyptic modern warfare becomes, the more the opportunity for glamour presents itself. Curzio Malaparte, reporting on the German campaign in northern and eastern Europe during the Second World War, saw this very clearly. Beyond any desire for manipulation, he suggests in his masterpiece *Kaputt*, the very intensity of war, the emotions it arouses and the acts of cruelty and self-sacrifice it prompts make it impossible for us not to find art in it; if only because so much of our past art has depicted scenes inspired by similar emotions:

I looked at the sky, at the fiery tracks of the tracer bullets streaking the black glass of the night; they looked like coral necklaces hanging on invisible feminine necks... A Jewish Chagall sky.

The raucous voice, the neighing, the occasional sharp rifle shots... seemed also to have been engraved by Dürer on the clear cold air of that autumn morning.

At one point Malaparte describes how Russian cavalry horses flee an artillery barrage by plunging into a Finnish lake on the very night it freezes over for winter. The horses are all trapped, frozen, so that the "lake looked like a vast sheet of white marble on which rested hundreds upon hundreds of horses' heads. They appeared to have been chopped off cleanly with an axe. Only the heads stuck out of the crust of ice... The scene might have been painted by Bosch."

Is there any way out of this? Is there any way at all to represent war, even to ourselves, that would be free of this aestheticizing process? I'm not sure there is. *Guernica* is a beautiful painting. It has its wild glamour. But the painting is now more famous than the bombing it depicts and deplores, perhaps because it allows us to feel that being sophisticated and pacifist is one and the same. Which is gratifying. But there is no evidence it stopped any bombs.

Perhaps, beyond our immediate anger with the *New York Times* for its crass glamourizing of conflict, we need to go further and ask ourselves about the deep purpose of all representation of violence and war. Doesn't it shift our attention from the object itself to the form in which the object has been given to us, inviting a safe savouring of dangerous emotions, with the result that the whole ugly reality can continue exactly as it always has, thanks, at least in part, to the consolatory beauty with which it is evoked?

Leafing back and forth through Shields's book, considering how right Hickey is when he speaks of the allusions to celebrated paintings, one cannot help wondering whether art in general is not, as artists and art lovers would have it, part of the solution, but deeply complicit with the problem.

Leave Novelists Out of Fiction

Why do we have so many novels and films featuring writers and artists? Films abound – on Mozart, Picasso, Turner, Oscar Wilde, Neruda, Leopardi. In fiction we have, among others, Michael Cunningham's Virginia Woolf in *The Hours*, Colm Tóibín's Henry James in *The Master*. And now the English novelist Jo Baker has dramatized the war years of Samuel Beckett.

What is the attraction? With intriguing variations, the underlying plot is mostly the same and, in the end, not so unlike Joyce's autobiographical novel, *A Portrait of the Artist as a Young Man*. We savour the artist's growing awareness of his or her specialness, which becomes one with a particular, always unconventional vision of the world, a peculiar style of thought, an almost mythical superiority to run of the mill experience. And we marvel at society's obtuseness, its determination to obstruct this special sensitivity, which the reader at once admires and yearns to share, perhaps conceding a little of the same to the author of the new work – Tóibín, perhaps, or Cunningham – who thus borrows some glory from his or her more celebrated subject.

If there is a risk in a project like this, something the straightforward biographer need not worry about, it is the danger of being compared, as an artist, to the artist hero. A poem about Leopardi would very likely invite the reader to reflect that Leopardi was the finer poet. Likewise a novel that took, say, Hemingway as its hero. Always assuming, that is, that contemporary readers are sufficiently familiar with Leopardi's poetry

172

or Hemingway's novels. If they are not, there is the second problem that, unaware of the real achievement of the artist/hero in question, they may simply not appreciate why the subject is worth so much attention. They cannot pick up the allusions that link the great writer with his or her work.

In *The Master*, Tóibín has James notice a little girl performing an innocence that she doesn't perhaps truly possess. The reader is presumably supposed to realize, "Ah, so *that's* where *What Maisie Knew* came from!" If you've never read *What Maisie Knew*, it's hard to see what's so interesting. If you've not only read the novel, but reread it and admired it deeply, this kind of connection might seem simplistic. It's hard to see how a writer can get around this. Certainly this kind of novel is stronger when it dramatizes a pattern of behaviour in line with what we find in the novels, rather than merely image and incident.

Jo Baker's previous novel, *Longbourn*, was also a form of benign literary parasitism. Just as Tom Stoppard once focused on two minor figures in Shakespeare's *Hamlet* to give us *Rosencrantz and Guildenstern are Dead*, Baker dramatized the life of the servants who minister to the main characters of Jane Austen's *Pride and Prejudice*. But while Stoppard offered a sparkling absurdist play, Jo Baker's work is solid realism, insisting on the physical effort and sheer drudgery of those who served the privileged. Alongside the fun of recognizing events in Austen's novel, as seen and interpreted by the servants, there was also the satisfaction of agreeing that inequality of opportunity is an ugly thing and feeling mildly superior to the Bennet family and their time.

To move from this charming entertainment to dramatizing the life of the twentieth-century artist who, more than any other, insisted on his apartness, his reticence and privacy, a man who felt the traditional novel, and indeed language in general, was utterly inadequate to express experience – or, worse than inadequate, mendacious – suggests ambition of a different order. Both Henry James and Virginia Woolf had developed elaborate styles to mimic the unfolding of consciousness, suggesting how their own minds moved. This allowed Tóibín and Cunningham – great talents in their own right – to imitate those styles and achieve a certain authenticity for their imaginings; they seemed close in spirit to their literary heroes, as if their books were a natural continuation of the earlier authors' endeavours.

But Beckett did no such thing. He did not believe that words could express interiority, or really very much at all, and his work never presents conventional reality in a traditional manner. "It is indeed becoming more and more difficult, even senseless, for me," he observed, "to write an official English. And more and more my own language appears to me like a veil that must be torn apart in order to get at the things (or the Nothingness) behind it."

To attempt, then, to present this man as the hero of a traditional realist novel with an omniscient narrator who moves effortlessly in and out of the most intimate thoughts of both Beckett and his partner, Suzanne Déchevaux-Dumesnil, when they're enjoying or failing to enjoy love-making, fleeing the Germans or simply drinking with friends, inevitably suggests an abyss between the sensibilities of Baker and her hero. She ably describes a lanky, diffident, disconnected man who looks like the Beckett of the photographs and behaves as Beckett is described as behaving in the biographies, but the moment we become privy to his thoughts, it is very hard to imagine we are reading about Beckett at all. "How easy," wrote Emil Cioran, "to imagine [Beckett], some centuries back, in a naked cell, undisturbed by the least decoration, not even a crucifix." How much more difficult to think of him worrying that Suzanne will be upset if he stays out for another whisky or two.

Baker's title, *A Country Road, a Tree*, recalls the stripped-down stage directions that open *Waiting for Godot*. The idea of her novel is that it was Beckett's wartime experiences that took him from being a rather pathetic Joycean acolyte, seeking and failing to reproduce the richness of his mentor's work, to becoming an independent artist with a clear sense of a quite different project, to present experience in its most basic and irreducible manifestation, something very like the tired, broken, hungry, unwashed body of the many war refugees with whom he would share his life in these years. In reality, in the letter quoted above, written in 1937, Beckett had already remarked that he was headed in a very different direction from Joyce.

Baker begins her story with Beckett deciding to return to Paris and Suzanne after a holiday in Ireland, despite England's declaration of war on Germany, despite his widowed mother's desperation, despite having no apparent part to play in the forthcoming conflict. It then tracks the couple's confused movements first to the south of France, following Joyce and other friends – Joyce was to die shortly after reaching Switzerland – then back to Paris during the Occupation. At this point, Beckett gets drawn into the French Resistance, collecting and correlating information passed to him by different agents. It was a major step for one who had always had difficulty involving himself in any kind of collective enterprise. Baker gives us his supposed emotions and thoughts as he types out a message indicating a movement of warships that will very likely cause the British to bomb Brest:

His fingertips peck out the letters, and the letters strike on to the paper, and the letters cluster into words, and the words seethe on the page, and he can't bear this and yet it must be borne. He swallows down spittle, closes his eyes. All he can see is fire and blood and broken stone.

Eventually betrayed, he and Suzanne take refuge in safe houses, and are then helped to escape, not without various heart-in-mouth vicissitudes, south to Roussillon, in the so-called free zone above Marseille, where they live in a small community of like-minded exiles and in constant fear of further betrayal. Anxious not to be entirely passive, Beckett again becomes involved in the Resistance, storing explosives and helping to impede the German retreat. Returning to Ireland and his mother at the end of the war, he sees no hope of remaining, but at last experiences the revelation of the path he must pursue. The wild Joycean "hubbub", as Baker has Beckett imagine it, must be abandoned for the essential profile of a stark figure against the night. He goes back to France to work in a field hospital as part of the process of reconstruction, then finally heads for Paris and Suzanne, where, at last, he can sit down in peace and unburden himself of all he must write.

There is much opportunity for action and melodrama here. Hunger, terror, cold, pursuit, gunshots, rationing. Baker tells it in an emphatic, evocative style. Suzanne's face is "open as a wound". Beckett feels "a gut-punch of guilt". British Prime Minister Neville Chamberlain's voice "spools" from the radio and "tangles" across the floor. Moonlight "kicks off Perspex". A car "burns through scattered dwellings". A train "is peeling past". And so on.

Meanwhile, the images crucial for Beckett's future work are patiently gathered. A painting by Rouault where "trees stand like gibbets by the roadside" has Beckett raptly gazing; it's the setting for *Godot*. Hungry, Beckett sucks a stone, and the knowing reader looks forward to the hilarious sucking-stone routine in the later novel *Molloy*. During a conversation "soft words accumulate, like sand trickling through an hourglass. They are up to their knees in it and yet still they can't stop." One cannot, of course, be up to one's knees in an hourglass, but the mixed metaphor allows us to look forward to *Happy Days*, where the lead actress is slowly buried in sand. Feeling "shambolic. A broken-down old tramp. A mummy", Beckett himself metamorphoses into one of the battered figures in his later fiction.

It's all admirably earnest, but never convincing. Nor does Baker know what to do with the relationship between Beckett and Suzanne. Alternating between admiring facilitator and exasperated mother figure, adoring or nagging, Suzanne never emerges as the intellectual she was. She is shown despairing over the doodles Beckett made while trying to translate his early novel *Murphy* into French, but we hear nothing of her reaction to the utterly bizarre and quite wonderful novel, *Watt*, that Beckett wrote while waiting the war out in Roussillon. It is as if Baker herself had no idea how to put this strange achievement in relation to her hero's wartime life.

When Beckett and Suzanne are imagined waiting by a tree, as night falls, for a contact who is to take them across the border into the free zone, and begin to use, when the contact doesn't show up, almost exactly the words from *Godot*, the whole strategy is revealed as embarrassingly mechanical. Very likely, the war years did offer Beckett images and experiences that, stripped of context, he would make universally powerful, but speculatively reconstructing the context to then colour it with the melodrama Beckett assiduously pared away hardly seems a helpful exercise.

In an afterword, as if to justify her efforts, the author offers an uplifting moral gloss on her story. During the war, in "impossibly difficult situations, [Beckett] consistently turned towards what was most decent and compassionate and courageous... he grew, as a writer and as a man. Afterwards he would go on to write the work that would make him internationally famous, and for which he would be awarded the

Nobel Prize for Literature." What a happy formula: good-ness, personal growth through hardship, artistic fame. It is the *reductio ad absurdum* of this strange form of fiction that would have us consume our literary heroes in a conveniently palatable sauce.

"Work that still resonates powerfully with us today," Baker goes on to say, using the sort of pat phrase that had Beckett comparing conventional prose with a Victorian bathing suit. Not powerfully enough, one might object, if this is the novel it has led to. Here, by way of decontamination, is Beckett from *Watt*. Our eponymous hero has been struggling with the feeling that the word "pot" no longer seems quite right to denote, well, the thing he used to call a pot. The mismatch makes him anxious.

> Then, when he turned for reassurance to himself... he made the distressing discovery that of himself too he could no longer affirm anything that did not seem as false as if he had affirmed it of a stone. Not that Watt was in the habit of affirming things of himself, for he was not, but he found it a help, from time to time, to be able to say, with some appearance of reason, Watt is a man, all the same, Watt is a man, or, Watt is in the street, with thousands of fellow-creatures within call... And Watt's need of semantic succour was at times so great that he would set to trying names on things, and on himself, al-most as a woman hats. Thus of the pseudo-pot he would say, after reflection, It is a shield, or, growing bolder, It is a raven, and so on. But the pot proved as little a shield, or a raven, or any other of the things that Watt called it, as a pot. As for himself, though he could no longer call it a man, as he had used to do, with the intuition that he was perhaps not talking nonsense, yet he could not imagine what else to call it, if not a man. But Watt's imagination had never been a lively one.

So he continued to think of himself as a man, as his mother had taught him, when she said, There's a good little man, or, There's a bonny little man, or, There's a clever little man. But for all the relief that this afforded him, he might just as well have thought of himself as a box, or an urn.

Extraordinary how Beckett, taking an axe to the relation between words and things, conveys and entertains so much more than the novelist who confidently puts words to his inner thoughts. We should read our great authors, not mythologize them.

The Limits of Satire

What does satire do? What should we expect of it? Recent events in Paris inevitably prompt these questions. In particular, is the kind of satire that *Charlie Hebdo* has made its trademark – explicit, sometimes obscene images of religious figures (God the Father, Son and Holy Spirit sodomizing each other; Muhammad with a yellow star in his arse) – essentially different from mainstream satire? Is it crucial to Western culture that we be free to produce such images? Do they actually *work* as satire?

Neither straight journalism nor disengaged art, satire alludes to recognizable contemporary circumstances in a skewed and comic way so as to draw attention to their absurdity. There is mockery, but with a noble motive: the desire to bring shame on some person or party behaving wrongly or ignorantly. Its *raison d'être* over the long term is to bring about change through ridicule; or if change is too grand an aspiration, we might say that it seeks to give us a fresh perspective on the absurdities and evils we live among, such that we are eager for change.

Since satire has this practical and pragmatic purpose, the criteria for assessing it are fairly simple: if it doesn't point towards positive change or encourage people to think in a more enlightened way, it has failed. That doesn't mean it's not amusing and well observed, or even, for some, hilarious, in the way, say, witty mockery of a political enemy can be hilarious and gratifying and can intensify our sense of being morally superior. But as satire it has failed. The worst case is when satire reinforces the state of mind it purports to undercut, polarizes prejudices and

180

provokes the very behaviour it condemns. This appears to be what happened with *Charlie Hebdo*'s images of Muhammad.

Why so? Crucial to satire is the appeal to supposed "common sense" and a shared moral code. The satirist presents a situation in such a way that it appears grotesque, and the reader who, whatever his or her private interests, shares the same cultural background and moral education agrees that it is so. The classic example, perhaps, is Jonathan Swift's *A Modest Proposal* of 1729. Swift's target was Protestant England's economic policy in Catholic Ireland and the disastrous poverty this had created. After paragraphs of statistics on population and nutrition, we arrive at the grotesque:

> I have been assured... that a young healthy child well nursed, is, at a year old, a most delicious nourishing and wholesome food, whether stewed, roasted, baked, or boiled; and I make no doubt that it will equally serve in a fricasie, or a ragoust.

By selling their children for food, the pamphlet claims, the poor can save themselves an expense and guarantee themselves an income. Disoriented, every reader is made aware of a simple principle we all share: you don't eat children, even Irish children, even Catholic children. So, if those children are not to be left to starve, something else in Ireland will have to give.

This appeal to what we all know and share becomes more difficult when satire addresses itself to people from different cultures with different traditions. In this regard, the history of *Charlie Hebdo* is worth noting. It grew out of a left-wing magazine, *Hara Kiri*, later *Hebdo Hara Kiri* (where *Hebdo* is simply short for *hebdomadaire* – weekly), which was formed in 1960 to address national political issues and subsequently banned on a number of occasions. When it was banned in 1970 over a mocking headline about Charles de Gaulle's death, its editors reopened it under a different name to avoid the ban, calling it *Charlie Hebdo* to distinguish it from a monthly magazine, *Charlie*, that some of the same cartoonists were already running. Charlie was Charlie Brown, but also now, comically, Charles de Gaulle. Its focus was on French politics, and when it was felt to have overstepped the mark, the democratically elected French government was in a position to impose a temporary closure. It was a French affair.

Wound down for lack of funds in 1981, *Charlie Hebdo* was resurrected in 1991 when cartoonists wanted to create a platform for political satire about the first Gulf War. With this explicitly international agenda the relationship between satirists, readers and targets became more complex. The readers were the same left-wing French public, used to seeing fierce attacks on all things sacred, but the targets sometimes lay outside France or at least outside mainstream French culture. In 2002, the magazine hosted an article supporting controversial Italian author Oriana Fallaci and her claims that Islam in general, not just the extremists, was on the march against the West. In 2006, *Charlie Hebdo*'s cartoons of Muhammad and reprint of the Danish newspaper *Jyllands-Posten*'s controversial Muhammad cartoons led to the paper's selling 400,000 copies, rather than the normal 60,000 to 100,000. Popularity and notoriety had arrived through mockery of a target outside French culture, but with which an aggrieved minority in France now identified.

Sued by the Grand Mosque, the Muslim World League and the Union of French Islamic Organizations, the paper's editors defended themselves, insisting that their humour was aimed at violent extremists, not at Islam itself. Islamic organizations didn't see it that way. While President Chirac criticized satire that inflamed divisions between cultures, various politicians, Hollande and Sarkozy included, wrote to the court to defend the cartoonists, Sarkozy in particular referring to the ancient

French tradition of satire. Eventually the court acquitted the paper and freedom of speech was upheld. But the effect of the cartoons had been to inflame moderate areas of Islam. The ancient French tradition of satire was creating more heat than light. It was also uniting French politicians usually opposed to each other against a perceived threat from without.

It is said, by contrast, that Christian leaders have now grown used to their religion being desecrated and pilloried in every way. This is not entirely the case. In 2011, *Charlie Hebdo* noted that while Muslims had sued the paper only once, the Catholic Church had launched thirteen cases against it. In the 1990s, writing satirical pieces for the Italian magazine *Comix*, I had my own experience of the difficulties of attacking the Church through satire. In this case too an issue of cultural blindness was involved. Reacting to yet another Vatican condemnation of abortion, even in cases of rape, I suggested that if the Catholic Church really cared about abortion it might perhaps change its position on contraception and actually manufacture condoms with images of the saints, or perhaps even prickly hair-shirt condoms, or St Sebastian condoms, so that lovemaking would be simultaneously an indulgence and a penitence, and people would be mindful of their Lord even between the sheets. *Comix* refused to publish.

This was not, I believe, a question of self-censorship or lack of courage on the magazine's part. The editors of *Comix* were perfectly ready to attack the Church on issues of abortion and birth control. They just didn't think that the idea of people having sex with condoms showing their favourite saint was the right way to go about it. Too many of their readers – mostly Catholic by culture if not practice – would be offended; it would not help them to get distance and perspective on the debate. Knowing Italy and Italians better now, I reckon they were right. It was my Protestant background and complete carelessness about images of saints and virgins that made me unaware of the kind of response the piece would have stirred up.

Most likely, however, that same Italian public would have had no problem with the drawings of Muhammad that provoked the massacre at *Charlie Hebdo* last week; because they, like me, but unlike the vast majority of Muslims, set no value on the image of Muhammad. When I see *Charlie Hebdo*'s cartoon entitled "Muhammad overcome by fundamentalists", showing a weeping Muhammad saying "It's tough being loved by assholes", I smile and take the point. For a Muslim reader perhaps the point is lost in the offence of a belittling representation of a figure they hold sacred.

Where we're coming from and who we're writing to is important. Not all readers are the same. In *The Satanic Verses* (1988), Salman Rushdie includes a dream sequence where the prostitutes have the names of Muhammad's wives. There are also various provocative reinterpretations of Islam, but certainly nothing that would disturb a Western reader, and in fact the novel was on the shortlist for Britain's Booker Prize for Fiction without even a smell of scandal in the air. Only as publication was approaching in India and the paper *India Today* ran an interview with Rushdie did the controversy begin in earnest, with riots, deaths and eventually the Ayatollah Khomeini's *fatwa* calling for Muslims to kill Rushdie.

It is, in short, this mixing of cultures and immediate globalization of so many publications through the Internet that makes satire more problematic, as the Swiftian appeal to the values we share becomes more elusive. In the *Inferno*, Dante could imagine Muhammad in hell, his body obscenely split open – "from the chin right down to where men fart" – as fit punishment for his crime of religious schism. The *Divine Comedy* was not intended for publication in India. Needless to say any such representation of Christ would have been unthinkable.

The following questions arise: now that the whole world is my neighbour, my immediate Internet neighbour, do I make any concessions at all, or do I uphold the ancient tradition of satire at all costs? And again, is a culture that takes mortal offence when an image it holds sacred is mocked a second-rate culture that needs to be dragged kicking and screaming into the twenty-first century – *my* twenty-first-century, that is? Do I have the moral authority to decide this?

In his response to the attack on *Charlie Hebdo* in Paris, the cartoonist Joe Sacco makes the distinction between the right to free expression and the sensible use of it. One might be free, he says, to draw – as he does to illustrate – a black man falling out of a tree with a banana in his hand, or a Jew counting money over the entrails of the working class, but of what possible use are these images? And actually of course we're not free. In Italy and Germany it is illegal to display certain images that recall Fascism and Nazism. Denial of the Holocaust is a crime in France. In the United States and Britain, our freedom – in practice – to indulge in racist, anti-Semitic, misogynist and homophobic insults has been notably limited, at least since the late 1980s when notions of "political correctness" became increasingly pervasive. Even *Charlie Hebdo* fired a cartoonist for anti-Semitism. None of these restrictions have proved a great loss, at least for me.

Joe Sacco's take on the tragedy in Paris is smart. In raising the question of the usefulness or otherwise of a cartoon, rather than remaining fixated on the question of freedom of speech, he reminds us of the essentially pragmatic nature of satire. However grotesque and provocative its comedy, its aim is to produce an enlightened perspective on events, not to start riots. At this point, and notwithstanding a profound sense of horror for the evil and stupidity of the terrorist attack on the magazine's offices, one has to wonder about *Charlie Hebdo*'s pride in constantly dubbing themselves a "*journal irresponsable*". The current edition of the paper shows Muhammad in such a way that his white turban looks like two balls and his long pink face a penis. The Prophet is being dubbed a prick. He holds a *Je suis Charlie* placard and announces that all is forgiven. The print run was extended to five million copies after a first run of three million sold out; this up from a standard run of 60,000. Is it likely this approach will help to isolate violent extremists from mainstream Muslim sentiment?

Stifled by Success

Can a writer's original inspiration survive success?

Imagine you are Karl Ove Knausgaard at this point in his career. You have launched into a madly detailed, multi-volume exposure of your family life. You began the project in relative obscurity. The book was a major departure from the novels you had been writing before. The possibility that what you were writing would become a major national, then international literary "event" barely crossed your mind. There was simply the turmoil and excitement and hard work of putting new territory on paper.

Then the reviews began, the features, festivals and flattery, the interviews, the travel, the larger and larger advances, the requests for contributions to prestigious newspapers or quotes for the covers of other writers' books, an interminable stream of emails and phone calls. Of course you might be able to resist all this, but even resisting would change the tone of your life. A siege mentality would ensue. And why should you resist? Why not enjoy success? Why not accept that you are a genius, if people insistently tell you that you are?

One way or another, from this point on it will be hard to achieve the same concentration, the same *innocence*, when you return to the empty page and the next stage in a life story that is now radically transformed. Inevitably you will be tempted to write towards what the public has appreciated, laying the guilt and shame on thick, if it was the expression of guilt and shame that the critics admired. Or, conversely, you may now find yourself deliberately refusing to give the public what they were enjoying, precisely to avoid becoming their servant, to stay in control. Either way the atmosphere you work in has changed.

In 1874, Giovanni Verga, at the time a modestly successful society novelist, was invited to write a short story about Sicilian country folk. Something of a dandy himself, a man who had abandoned Sicily to be at the heart of a more modern and mundane Italy in Milan, Verga wasn't enthusiastic. But because he needed money to finance his fancy-clothes habit he wrote a story, 'Nedda', that entirely changed his life. Essentially it is the tale of how a country girl comes to grief, falling pregnant before marriage, then loses her husband-to-be in a farm accident. 'Nedda' was such a success that Verga, who now saw that he had stumbled upon something close to his heart, began a whole series of "country-folk" novellas, each more brilliantly constructed and devastatingly pessimistic than the next.

Constantly praised for the stories' implacable social realism, and again for his use of Sicilian dialect – or, to be more accurate, a rich mix of dialect forms and regular Italian that gave readers the illusion they were hearing Sicilian voices – Verga, who was rapidly growing wealthy from his sales, began to study in academic earnest the world he had hitherto written about only from memory and with great creative liberty. He began to think of himself as some kind of anthropologist involved in a vast Zola-like project of mapping out Sicilian society.

So he wrote the considerable novels *I Malavoglia* and *Mastro-don Gesualdo*. But to read these overly long, muddled works, cluttered with detail and packed with Sicilian proverbs, is to appreciate that both the public and Verga had misunderstood the qualities of the novellas. Their success had nothing to do with any commitment to social justice. Their achievement was to fuse an apparently collective narrative voice, as if the story were told by the community, with protagonists who accept and

even engineer their own downfalls, because, however scandal-
ously treated, they have completely internalized society's judgement of their predicaments and see nothing strange in their
"punishment". And all this happens very quickly and with a
devastating sense of inevitability. So Nedda, unable to support
her dying mother or feed her baby, hardly protests that her fellow Catholics are denying her charity because she had the child
out of wedlock. It seems entirely normal to her. The irony that
we all allow a hypocritical society to guide our most intimate
judgements was something Verga struggled with in his own
personal life and that he had now found a way of expressing
on paper. Which makes the fact that he was himself pulled off
course by public acclaim and the contemporary enthusiasm for
pseudo-scientific realism all the more ironic.

Of writers like Joyce, or Pavese, or Beckett, one might say
exactly the opposite. They did everything they could *not* to go
where the public pushed them. Joyce relentlessly made things
more and more difficult for readers, as if success actually prevented him from producing more of the same, so determined
was he to be nobody's servant. Hence the lucid and fluent *Dub-
liners* becomes the more difficult *Portrait of an Artist as a Young
Man*, then the far more difficult *Ulysses*, packed with passages
that many felt were obscene, and finally, when that brought
even more success, the completely indigestible *Finnegans Wake*.
Joyce would read sections of his "Work in Progress" to friends
to see how they responded; when he felt they had understood
too easily, he would go and make it more difficult.

Cesare Pavese was convinced that any literary success must
mean he had compromised his principles in some way, allowed himself to be contaminated. In 1950, shortly after winning Italy's major literary prize, the Strega, he killed himself,
aged forty-one. Reading Beckett's letters after the first produc-
tions of *Waiting for Godot*, one has the impression of a man

determined to deny fans and critics the profound significance they are convinced must lie behind the play. His increasingly cryptic later works look very much like a reaction against success, a determination not to let the public have its much craved symbolism, to, as he put it, "take away with a choc-ice at the end of the performance".

We can admire this determination not to surf a wave of public acclaim, but all the same, none of these writers is isolated from the consequences of success. Their work is clearly influenced by the attention it achieved. And since many admire a writer all the more for his intransigent refusal to cosy up to the reader, this hostile reaction actually feeds the public's interest and esteem. The more cryptic Beckett becomes in reaction to those readers after a meaning, the more he resembles the kind of author some readers are eager to adore, because meaning is always more profound when arrived at with effort. Indeed, the presence of the cryptic almost guarantees the seriousness of the meaning withheld. Someone who hides has something to hide.

Among more recent authors, Philip Roth has played endlessly with the critics' interest in the relationship between his fiction and his private life; in *Deception* he even has a character called Philip Roth announce, "I write fiction and I'm told it's autobiography, I write autobiography and I'm told it's fiction, so since I'm so dim and they're so smart, let *them* decide what it is or it isn't." These are games one can only play when one's previous work has created a certain notoriety; Roth never seemed worried that he was allowing his novels to be influenced by this noisy engagement with his own celebrity. Conversely J.D. Salinger and later Thomas Pynchon allowed celebrity to push them into long periods of silence, as if success had forced them to become austere. But whether happy to join the scrimmage or appalled by the idea of being contaminated, all these writers are inevitably changed by the reception of their work and removed from the atmosphere of their initial inspiration.

Let us add one more complication success brings: the illusion of predestination. In this regard I cannot help recalling a long conversation with V.S. Naipaul in which he insisted that he could not have failed as an author, and that recognition, even immediate recognition, of his genius was inevitable, simply because he was so good. I could not persuade him to accept that he only believed this because he had in fact been successful and that it must have been possible, given the world's perversity, for recognition to have eluded him. The conviction of predestination came after the event.

But whatever the exact psychology of the process, the present has a way of contaminating the past. And the writing will change accordingly. Turmoil and dilemma once experienced with a certain desperation may be seen more complacently as the writer reflects that through expressing them he has realized his inevitable and well-deserved triumph. The lean years of patient toil when no one paid attention may even begin to seem preferable to the present. The very thing you created in the heat of fierce concentration has destroyed the circumstances that made it possible. The writer is devoured along with his books.

The Books We Talk About
(and Those We Don't)

What is the social function of the novel? I'm not thinking about the pay-off for the author, who gets to develop a skill and earn a living from it and accrue a prestigious public image into the bargain. Nor about the rewards for the publisher, who may, or more likely may not, make a significant amount of money. Nor even the pleasure for the individual reader, who enjoys hours of entertainment and maybe feels enlightened or usefully provoked along the way. What I'm asking is, what's in it for society as a whole, or at least for that part of society that reads novels?

Conversation. A shared subject of discussion. Something complex for minds to meet around. This is particularly the case when we're talking to people we don't know well, people we meet, as it were, socially. Of course there are plenty of other topics available. The weather. Sports. Politics. But there's only so much that can be said about cloud formations, not everyone sees the fascinations of baseball, and politics, as we know, can be dangerous territory. Novels – or films or television dramas for that matter – offer a feast of debate and create points of contact: are the characters believable? Do people really do or think these things? Does the story end as it should? Is it well written? The way different people respond to Philip Roth's *American Pastoral*, or J.M. Coetzee's *Disgrace*, will tell you a lot about their personalities without anything personal needing to be said. Novels are ideal subjects for testing the ground between us.

When Laurence Sterne started publishing sections of *Tristram Shandy*, newspaper book reviewing was in its infancy. The novel's droll sexual innuendoes, its constant flirtation with incomprehensibility and obscenity, provoked excitement and consternation among more or less everyone who read books at the time. How could fiction be written in this way? What relation did Sterne's tale have to real experience, and indeed to other books? Did the unreferenced inclusion of work from other writers (Rabelais, Francis Bacon, etc.) amount to plagiarism? The debate was fierce. Sterne thrived on it, including reviewers' comments and his reactions to them in later parts of the book. Since *Tristram Shandy* was seven years in the publishing, other writers chipped in, offering unauthorized alternative versions, sequels and prequels. There was a snowballing effect. Enthusiasts invented *Tristram Shandy* recipes, set up graveyards with the tombs of the novel's characters and named racehorses after them. The book had become part of a national – and on occasion international – conversation. People understood their relations to each other by gauging how they related to the book.

More than a hundred years later, the debate was even more heated around the publication of Thomas Hardy's *Tess of the D'Urbervilles*, famously subtitled *A Pure Woman Faithfully Presented*. How could she be pure, reviewers demanded, when first she had an illegitimate child with a man, then lived with him as his mistress while married to someone else? It was a good question. But Tess was so attractive, so endearing and so incredibly unlucky. The divergence of opinion was so acrimonious that it became difficult to have supporters and detractors sitting side by side at society dinners. Essentially the novel had forced readers to reconsider received Victorian opinion on sexual mores, exposing the phobic side of polite society's moral rigour. Inevitably, the more people raged against the book the more it sold.

One could list any number of novels – *Hard Times*, *Uncle Tom's Cabin*, *Native Son* – that have provoked an intense level of public debate, usually because they combined a seductive plot with issues that mattered deeply to people in that particular time and place. A novel becomes a focus for such issues, provoking conversations perhaps only latent to that point, and these conversations then guarantee the work's further success and the writer's celebrity. Beyond a certain level of readability, however, the ultimate quality of the writing, or the "art" involved, is largely irrelevant, at least for this social function. A poorly written book, whether it be *What Is to Be Done?* by the nineteenth-century Russian intellectual Nikolay Chernyshevsky or E.L. James's *Fifty Shades of Grey*, can stimulate intense general conversation far better than an extraordinary but taxing piece of writing – Beckett's *Trilogy* or Robert Walser's *Jakob von Gunten* – or even a genre work that, however popular, raises no underlying issues: Simenon's Maigrets, Fleming's Bond books, le Carré's spy stories.

So as well as categorizing novels as well or poorly written, popular or unpopular, one could also, and perhaps more usefully, distinguish those that become part of *the conversation*, and those that do not. Jonathan Franzen's *The Corrections* became part of the national conversation; Lydia Davis's short stories, for all their brilliance, did not. In Europe, Michel Houellebecq is part of the conversation, like it or not (but not liking it intensifies the conversation); Peter Stamm, an author whose work I always look forward to, is not. Social issues and literary ambition may be important here, but are really not essential. Arguably there was a huge conversation generated around the Harry Potter saga that had nothing to do with social issues, but was perhaps very largely a discussion about the appropriateness of adults avidly reading stories written for children. Conversely, many writers who deliberately try to provoke a conversation by novelizing topical issues that are already at the centre of debate, often fail miserably. John Updike's *Terrorist* was arguably his least talked-about novel.

But whatever the content or quality of a novel, in order for a general conversation to take hold, people, or enough people, have to have read it. It is no good if everybody is reading brilliantly provoking, perhaps electrically interesting, but quite different books. How often have we been involved in conversations, at a party maybe, where four or five people ask what others think of this or that novel, only to find that no one else has read it? Even, or perhaps especially, among people who read a lot it is often difficult to find a single recently published book that we have all read. The conversation founders, literature fails to bring us together, no debate is provoked. Or to find a book to talk about we have turn to one of the blockbusters or media-hyped works of the day, something one almost feels authorized to talk about whether one has read it or not: *Underworld, The Girl with the Dragon Tattoo, Interview with a Vampire, My Struggle*. Regardless of quality, regardless even of sales, since Knausgaard's are nowhere near on a level with the others, these are books that have been as it were *chosen for the conversation*, perhaps precisely because it's often embarrassingly difficult to find a book we've all read to settle on. Instead of the conversation occurring "naturally" as with *Tristram Shandy*, or *Tess of the D'Urbervilles*, it is to a certain extent thrust upon us.

The extraordinary increase in the number of novels published each year, together with the internationalization of fiction, is in good measure responsible for this changed state of affairs. Victorian England produced a considerable number of novels, but at any one time only a limited number were being serialized in the major weekly and monthly magazines of the day. This guaranteed that those books had sufficient readers to generate a conversation. Novelists writing for the magazines knew who their readers were, more or less, and, reluctantly or enthusiastically, adapted their work accordingly. Since readers had much in common, it was more likely that a piece of fiction would open up issues that animated conversation and since there was far less journalism available than today, difficult topical issues would often be tackled only through novels.

But how does a book enter the conversation today? The serialized novel has been replaced by serialized television fiction that has become so successful at generating discussion that those of us who didn't follow *The Sopranos* or *The Wire* were often made to feel left out. Meantime, in the bookshops, readers choose from literally thousands of recently published titles. In the countries of western Europe a good fifty per cent of those books will come from abroad; so people's reading is not focused on the society they live in, and the stories read are often set elsewhere. In 2011, when I ran a little survey in a Dutch bookshop on the kind of novels people were reading, younger readers in particular said they often chose to read popular foreign authors, particularly American or English – Dan Brown or Ian McEwan or Philip Roth or Zadie Smith – so that they would have a common subject of conversation when meeting other young people during their summer travels. Their choices seemed random and were taken regardless of quality. Rather than a situation where people are naturally finding themselves reading the same thing and then talking about it, some readers are responding to celebrity in the hope that what they read will enable them to join an international conversation.

And yet it still does happen that quite unexpectedly a book, a writer, becomes successful beyond the wildest dreams of their publishers, and perhaps in the absence of publishers at all, causing people to read things they wouldn't normally read and to talk together about things they wouldn't normally talk about. I've recently read and reviewed two authors who have had this extraordinary fortune, E.L. James and Haruki Murakami, the one accused of writing trashy soft porn, the other praised for his evocation of everything disorienting and surreal.

Is it possible that two such different authors have anything in common, anything that drew this level of attention to their work and created such animated polemics around them? For while Murakami is sometimes touted for the Nobel, he is also frequently attacked for poor writing, adolescent sensibility and deliberately seeking a dislocated global public. (I was recently invited to speak at a conference whose sole purpose seemed to be to attack Murakami.) And E.L. James, though dismissed by the literati, found her work reviewed in the most serious literary papers and attracting a readership far broader than has ever before occurred with a work of soft erotica.

Both authors, it seems to me, in their quite different ways are fascinated by the same thing: the individual's need to negotiate the most intimate relationships in order to get the most from life without losing independence and selfhood. If *Shades of Grey* had any seriousness, it was in asking these questions: how is sexuality to be negotiated in a couple? How can I give the other what he/she wants and remain myself? In a sense, how can I control what appears uncontrollable? In an infinitely more sophisticated and certainly more mystical fashion, Murakami invariably asks: how can I avoid being overwhelmed on the one hand by others, on the other by loneliness? Where is the middle way?

Of course there are many other authors whose work deals with these issues. But how many books can the world be talking about at any one time? A dozen, twenty? It's hard not to feel that a certain amount of the merest chance is involved.

References, Please

In the age of the Internet, do we really need footnotes to reference quotations we have made in the text? For a book to be taken seriously, does it have to take us right to the yellowing page of some crumbling edition guarded in the depths of an austere library, if the material could equally well be found through a Google search? Has an element of fetishism perhaps crept into what was once a necessary academic practice?

I have just spent three days preparing the text references for a work of literary criticism for Oxford University Press. There were about two hundred quotations spread over 180 pages, the sources being a mix of well-known nineteenth- and twentieth-century novels, very much in the canon, some less celebrated novels, a smattering of critical texts and a few recent works of psychology. Long-established practice demands that for each book I provide the author's name, or the editor's name in the case of a collection of letters or essays, the translator's name where appropriate, the publisher, the city of publication, the date of publication and the page number. All kinds of other hassles can creep in – when a book has more than one volume for example, or when quoting from an essay within a collection of essays, perhaps with more than one editor, more than one translator, more than one author. Since the publisher had asked me to apply the ideas I develop in the book to at least one of my own novels, there are even three quotations to be referenced from *Cara Massimina*, a noir I wrote way back in the 1980s.

As it turns out, I don't have a copy of *Cara Massimina* in the flat I am presently living in, so while writing my critical book I bought a copy on Kindle to find the quotations I needed, using the electronic search facility to pick up key words in half-remembered sentences. Easy. But now that I'm preparing the footnote, where am I going to get the bibliographical information, which notoriously Kindle doesn't give? From the Internet of course. My publisher's website, or Amazon, or any number of other sources. So there's no need to get hold of the book itself, the paper version that is. Good.

Ah, but what about the page numbers? The Kindle edition doesn't give page numbers, though some e-books now do and some newer Kindle devices apparently have a way to reveal them. For a moment this seems an insuperable problem. Would I have to order a paper copy of my own book? No. I typed the first of my quotations out in Google Books, and in a twinkling there it was. With the page number! My reference was complete: Tim Parks, *Cara Massimina* (London: Vintage, 1995), p. 11.

Excellent. So now any reader who wishes to see if I am quoting correctly from my own book can buy or borrow a copy of *Cara Massimina* – assuming, of course, they get hold of the same edition I cite, in this case the Vintage paperback published several years after the original – go to page 11, scan the page and check the words. Or they can stick it in Google and get there in two seconds.

This is the point. And this is what made these three days' labour so galling.

Footnotes of course come in all shapes and sizes. Throughout the eighteenth and nineteenth centuries there was an admirable push to use properly referenced citations to allow greater precision, in particular in relation to historical texts. Sources would be meticulously listed; where there were pirated and often corrupted editions of older texts, the most authoritative version would be identified. In *The Footnote: A Curious History* (1999), Anthony Grafton traces this aspiration back to Pierre Bayle's 1697 *Dictionnaire historique et critique*. By referring to an authority, the author could both invite a sceptical approach on the reader's part – I don't want you to accept anything I say on trust – while simultaneously suggesting that possible objections had already been met by reference to a previous text. Anyone reading academic texts, however, will know how wearisome this strategy has become in recent scholarship. Too often, writers will use it to mention as many other texts as possible, covering their backs even where cover is hardly necessary (an academic journal recently forbade me from using the term "postmodern" without a supporting reference to a definition of the concept); or alternatively, with the hope that with so many references and notes no one will actually check that the texts referred to do not cover their backs at all. Chuck Zerby's *The Devil's Details: A History of Footnotes* offers curious examples of what you can find if you do go and check up the texts referred to.

Never mind. It is not to the "appeal to authority" footnote that I am talking about, but the exhausting overkill of information when nailing down a citation. Do readers need to know that Yale University Press is based in New Haven and Knopf in New York? How does this add to their ability to track down a quotation? Once one has the title and the surname of the author, do we really need the author's initials or first name (Oxford University Press wants the full first name, which can sometimes be very difficult to find when the author him or herself prefers to use initials)? But the real question is: are we never going to acknowledge that modern technology has changed things?

Almost twenty years ago I wrote a much longer, more elaborate academic book, *Translating Style*. On that occasion the job of adding the citations took a whole week and was extremely laborious. But I do not recall feeling irritated about the effort at all. It was obviously necessary. There was no way readers could access a literary quotation and check the work I had done if I didn't provide them with adequate references. They needed to know the edition and the page number, because there might be different page numbers in different editions. However, with this new book I was acutely aware that one reason I was preparing the references more swiftly than in the past was precisely because rather than going to my shelves to pull out the various books I was using Google. So any reader could do this too, and my careful notes were completely unnecessary.

Of course there are objections. For many texts Google Books has stopped giving page numbers. For example, in one chapter I had included quotations from Claire Tomalin's biography of Dickens – which I had read on Kindle. The fact is, when you are reading a novel in view of an eventual essay, an e-book has the advantage of being rapidly searchable, while any notes I make on my portable Kindle are immediately synchronized with the app on my computer and easier to browse while writing than notes scribbled on paper. The snag being, again, the absence of page numbers.

Needless to say, Google Books had Tomalin's book, and when I typed in the quotations I wanted they came right up, but without the page numbers. This occurred with three or four other recent publications. Presumably in alliance with the publishers, in order to force those of us who need to prepare footnotes to buy paper editions, Google has stopped giving page numbers. Of course, since the reader could always check the quotation on Google without knowing the page number, you might ask why publishers still insist we put the numbers in? And in fact I am asking that. Obviously they are necessary with paper. It can take for ever to find a quotation if you don't know the page number. But where there are electronic texts online, particularly in reliable online libraries like Project Gutenberg, I'm not sure we need page numbers.

I decided to ask my contacts at the Oxford University Press about this and did get one concession. Where a novel was famous and the final text not a matter of dispute, we would just give author, book title and chapter number. This eliminates the need to mention editions and page numbers. It has to be said, though, that some chapters of Dickens are very long, while it's a matter of dispute whether *Ulysses* has chapters at all. Never mind, the method worked wonderfully well with Hardy and Lawrence. There is no need for the same notation to be used with all books.

Of course it will be objected that Google is not always accurate and does not yet include everything. Who would disagree? Though my experience with literary texts is that Google Books, or again Project Gutenberg, or the online University of Adelaide Library are accurate in an overwhelming majority of cases. But if they are not, let's insist they become more accurate and more comprehensive, particularly with all works that are now out of copyright.

Simply, it's time to admit that the Internet has changed the way we do scholarship and will go on changing it. There is so much inertia in the academic world, so much affection for fussy old ways. People love getting all the brackets and commas and abbreviations just so. Perhaps it gives them a feeling of accomplishment. Professors torment students over the tiniest details of bibliographical information, when anyone wishing to check can simply put the author name and title in any Internet search engine. A doctoral student hands in a brilliant essay, and the professor complains that the translator's name has not been mentioned in a quotation from a recent French novel, though of course since the book is recent there is only one translation of the novel and in any event anyone checking the cited edition will find the translator's name in the book.

There is, in short, an absolutely false, energy-consuming, nit-picking attachment to an outdated procedure that now has much more to do with the sad psychology of academe than with the need to guarantee that the research is serious. By all means, on those occasions where a book exists only in paper and where no details about it are available online, then let us use the traditional footnote. Otherwise, why not wipe the slate clean, start again and find the simplest possible protocol for ensuring that a reader can check a quotation. Doing so we would probably free up three or four days a year in every academic's life. A little more time to glean quotes from Barthes, Borges and Derrida...

Raise Your Hand if You've Read Knausgaard

Is there any consistent relationship between a book's quality and its sales? Or again between the press and critics' response to a work and its sales? Are these relationships stable over time or do they change?

Raise your hand, for example, if you know what the actual sales are for Karl Ove Knausgaard's *My Struggle*. This mammoth work of autobiography – presently running at three five-hundred-page volumes with three more still to be translated from his native Norwegian – is relentlessly talked about as an "international sensation and best-seller" (Amazon) and constantly praised by the most prestigious critics. "It's unbelievable... It's completely blown my mind," says Zadie Smith. "Intense and vital... Ceaselessly compelling... Superb," agrees James Wood. Important newspapers (the *New York Times* for one) carry frequent articles about Knausgaard and his work. A search on the *Guardian* website has ten pages of hits for articles on Knausgaard, despite the fact that the first volume of *My Struggle* wasn't published in the UK until 2012. In a round-up of authors' summer-reading tips in the same newspaper, the academic Sarah Churchwell remarks that after sitting on the jury for the Booker Prize she looks forward to being "the last reader in Britain" to tackle *My Struggle*.

One could be forgiven, then, for imagining that this is one of those books which periodically impose themselves as "required reading" at a global level: Umberto Eco's *The Name of the Rose*, Jostein Gaarder's *Sophie's World*, Peter Høeg's *Smilla's Sense of Snow*, Jonathan Franzen's *Freedom* all spring to mind, literary equivalents of internationally successful genre works like Stieg Larsson's *The Girl with the Dragon Tattoo*, Dan Brown's *The Da Vinci Code* and E.L. James's *Fifty Shades of Grey*.

Well, as of a few days ago UK sales of all three volumes of Knausgaard's work in hardback and paperback had barely topped 22,000 copies. A respectable but hardly impressive performance. In the US, which has a much larger market, that figure – total sales of all three volumes (minus e-books) – stood at about 32,000. This was despite the fact that, with Knausgaard's growing reputation, the powerful Farrar, Straus and Giroux stepped in to buy the paperback rights from the minnow Archipelago and bring its own commercial muscle to bear. On the Amazon best-sellers ranking, *A Death in the Family*, the first and most successful volume of the *My Struggle* series, is presently 657th in the USA and 698th in the UK, this despite a low paperback price of £8.99.

So what is going on here? Should we be reassured that critics are sticking loyally by a work they admire regardless of sales, or bemused that something is being presented as a runaway commercial success when in fact it isn't? Wouldn't it be enough to praise Knausgaard without trying to create the impression that there is a huge international following behind the book? Or do the critics actually assume that everyone *is* buying it because they and all their peers are talking about it?

The truth is that one can only get hold of accurate statistics by subscribing to an organization called Nielsen BookScan. The figures in this article were obtained by pestering friends in companies who hold such subscriptions. Even BookScan isn't entirely reliable, since it doesn't take in all independent booksellers. So actual sales will be slightly higher than those I have given, though independents notoriously do not account for a large slice of the market. In general, however, the public are only given hard figures when they are impressively high. It's a reticence that encourages hype, especially in an age in which we have come to expect that these huge international best-sellers will happen, the publishers in particular treading water and looking around themselves like surfers hoping to catch the next monster wave.

Of course we have seen the same assumption of worldwide success with any number of novels that are presented as fol-low-ups to a previous international bestseller – Eco's novels after *The Name of the Rose*, Rushdie's after *The Satanic Verses*, Franzen's *Freedom* after *The Corrections*. Initial reviews of *Free-dom* in particular were wildly over the top, the *Guardian* even giving the book a preview in prime position on its home page with the critic pronouncing the novel a major work while ad-mitting that he hadn't yet received a copy. We're used to this kind of thing. But *Freedom* did sell 68,236 in hardback in the UK, rather fewer in paperback, about half of what *The Correc-tions* sold. Rushdie's *Joseph Anton*, a memoir telling of his years in hiding after the *fatwa*, commanded enormous column space in the press, understandably given the subject matter, but UK sales were just 7,521 in hardback and only 1,896 in paperback. However, in these cases, as soon as the wave doesn't happen the critical buzz quickly subsides.

The curiosity with Knausgaard, then, is that the impression of huge and inevitable success was given not with the precedent of previous international success, but solely on the basis of the book's remarkable sales in the author's native Norway. Norway, however, is a country of only five million people – a population that is half the size of London's – and of course the whole tone and content of *My Struggle* may very well be more immediate and appealing for those who share its language and culture: it is their world that is talked about. So the great success was announced before it happened and continues to be announced as it continues not to happen. At the level of public perception, in a way, it *has* happened. People *believe* the book is a major best-seller. Let us try to get the situation into some kind of perspective.

When I was growing up in the Sixties and Seventies, we were given to believe that there was a distinction between literary fiction and popular or genre fiction. The latter would sell better than the former but would not be reviewed; at most, thrillers and romance novels would receive a brief notice. They might also be advertised at the expense of the publisher. Apparently no one felt the need to talk about a book just because it sold a lot of copies. Publicity was left to publicists. Works of literary fiction on the other hand would be earnestly reviewed with no reference to their commercial success or otherwise.

In reality this distinction was already breaking down. Literary authors like Graham Greene and Muriel Spark in the UK, or Updike and Roth in the US, were achieving very considerable sales in their own countries, and genre authors like John le Carré or Isaac Asimov were justly noted for their literary qualities. As early as 1950, the Italian novelist and critic Cesare Pavese was worrying about the blurring of lines between the trivial and the serious, complaining that the commercial was being presented as literary and the literary made as commercial as possible – indeed that literariness itself was becoming a genre. Literary prizes, he believed, were not immune; eager for winners to reach a wide readership and bring the prize more attention, juries would be encouraged to choose popular winners, and writers would begin to write towards this mix of popularity and easy prestige.

Certainly now, for better or worse, almost all distinction between the way different kinds of novels are presented has largely disappeared. Newspapers review Dan Brown, Alice Munro, J.K.

Rowling and Orhan Pamuk with equal solemnity, attention being driven by the sense that the writer is winning prizes or moving copies or being pushed as the book of the season by a major publisher, not by a lucid curiosity for whatever may be written between the covers. At the same time, serious publishing houses have discovered the trick of packaging genre fiction as if it was great literature; one thinks of the prestigious Italian publisher Adelphi reissuing all seventy-five of Simenon's Maigret novels in very much the same format and with the same €15 price tag as their editions of Thomas Bernhard, Sándor Márai or Nabokov. Even the academics have joined in, with whole conferences dedicated to, for example, the "problem" of translating the character names in the Harry Potter saga. No one wants to be left out of a global success.

Meantime, since most newspapers have gone online and many have their own online bookshops, a certain confusion seems to be developing between reviewing and sales promotion. Best-seller lists sit beside reviews on every webpage, as if commercial success were an index of quality, while one can often click on a link at the end of a review to buy the book. Literary novels come complete with stickers announcing them as international best-sellers, as if this were a part of their literary achievement. In Europe publishers never forget to tell readers in how many countries the author's work is published.

Although readers tend to prize writers for their independence from influence, they also seem eager to buy the works of writers who have attracted the highest number of readers; at the same time, it's hard to imagine that the writer him- or herself will not be influenced by the confirmation that commercial success brings. Would J.K. Rowling have written seven Harry Potters if the first hadn't sold so well? Would Knausgaard have written six volumes of *My Struggle*, if the first had not been infinitely more successful (in Norway) than his previous novels? Sales influence both reader and writer – certainly far more than the critics do.

In general I see nothing "wrong" with this blurring of lines between literary and genre fiction. In the end it's rather exciting to have to figure out what is really on offer when a novel wins the Pulitzer, rather than taking it for granted that we are talking about literary achievement. But it does alert us to the fact that, as any consensus on aesthetics breaks down, best-sellerdom is rapidly becoming the only measure of achievement that is undeniable.

Or put it another way: a critic who likes a book and goes out on a limb to praise it may begin to feel anxious these days if the book is not then rewarded by at least decent sales, as if it were unimaginable that one could continue to support a book's quality without some sort of confirmation from the market. So while in the past one might have grumbled that some novels were successful only because they had been extravagantly hyped by the press, now one discovers the opposite phenomenon. Books are being spoken of as extraordinarily successful in denial of the fact that they are not.

I can only encourage others (and myself, for I'm by no means immune) to hold on to the idea that what matters about a book for the reader is our experience reading it, not the number of copies it has sold. However, given that it is unlikely that critics, publishers and retailers will ever stop using commercial success as a tool of persuasion, let us at least have easy access to the real sales figures. I might for example have picked up Knausgaard's *Struggle* precisely to be able to talk about it with others, only to discover that the others hadn't read him. But then I suppose we have all read the reviews. We can talk about those.

My Life, Their Archive

Today's successful author will sooner or later be invited to sell his or her personal papers. Sooner rather than later most likely, and not just papers, manuscripts, typescripts, notebooks, but electronic data too, emails, chat messages, the lot. Everything you have written, then, but also everything you will write. Your emails to your children, your grandchildren, great-grandchildren, your ex-wife or husband, present partner, future partner, lovers, ex-lovers, dying parents, estranged cousins, needy friends, your application for this or that grant, your fencing with would-be publishers or agents, your self-promotional lobbying for the Pulitzer or the Booker, deluded dreams of the Nobel, half-truths for the taxman, heated exchanges with magazine editors when payment is delayed.

Of course, assuming an author didn't take preventive action and was still highly regarded at death, much of this material would eventually have been gathered in public archives anyway. The interest in private papers goes right back to the ancient world. Many authors have sold or bequeathed their manuscripts to appropriate archives. The letters of D.H. Lawrence (in eight volumes) or Virginia Woolf (in six), have come to seem as much part of the authors' oeuvres as their novels. What has changed is the predictive and competitive nature of the acquisitions, with writers being selected on the basis of a few years' celebrity or a prestigious literary prize and invited to sell their correspondence even before it is written. What makes this easier is that now we all use email we get to keep what we write, rather than consigning our letters to someone else's hands. The only problem is preserving all the damn things.

For the author, needless to say, the lure is money. Large sums can be involved. The Harry Ransom Center at the University of Texas reputedly paid $1.5 million for J.M. Coetzee's papers. The British Library more modestly gave £110,000 for the manuscripts of novelist Graham Swift, announcing as a special attraction "a tape recording of the answerphone messages he received on the night he won the Booker Prize". We all love a winner.

But not only money. Any organization that spends a considerable sum on you will also have an interest in promoting your reputation. They don't want to be accused of having thrown cash at a lemon. So there will be exhibitions, seminars, features of archived material. You will be talked up. Everything will be done to transform ephemeral celebrity into durable literary glory. With your papers now declared part of the world's cultural heritage, you have an edge over your rivals and are paid into the bargain. "Unto he that hath shall more be given" is a logic that always holds in the art world.

My agent mentions this possibility to me, and immediately I'm enthusiastic. In these days of falling advances and general publishing crisis, how many writers would not welcome the arrival of a major injection of liquidity? And how nice, frankly, to be shot of those yellowing manuscripts gathering dust in the attic. "The Jim Crace Papers," warns the Harry Ransom Center website, "include a small amount of material that was exposed to moisture and suffered minor mould damage… Patrons may consider wearing gloves and a dust/mist respirator while handling this material." I remember the last time I moved my boxes of unpublished manuscripts they were full of silverfish. Turning insect-ridden papers into cash has to be a good idea.

And privacy?

No problem. An author can stipulate which correspondence must not be released before you are, as it were, safely dead. Or before your wife/husband/partner is dead. (It might be wise to avoid telling your spouse about this clause.) Some arrangements will even admit to the existence of material so toxic it must not be released until a hundred years after the author's ashes have been scattered in the rose garden.

So what could possibly be wrong here?

I imagine sealing such a deal. From now on everything I write has a public. Everything I dash off is to be a legitimate object of scrutiny for some future researcher. Someone somewhere will one day become an expert in all my prevarications, give his life to understanding how I screwed up mine. And, knowingly or otherwise, any person I correspond with is also, in a sense, party to that publication, that exposure, could be promoted or damaged by his or her dealings with me. Immediately I fear a drastic reinforcement of my superego. Surely I will hold myself back in these altered circumstances, as when my mother used to warn me that God saw everything I did and even thought, so that one of the reliefs of losing faith was the recovery of a little privacy.

Or alternately I might deliberately start writing all kinds of outrageous things in order to impress. I'll be dead – who cares? – this will wake up the balding scholar with his gloves and respirator; this will get them talking about me in the twenty-second century.

Or more likely I'll find myself making a huge effort *not* to change the way I write and relate to others just because the stuff is destined for the archive. No, that future expert, future notoriety is not going to psyche me out. I'm going to remain exactly as I was. In fact, now I see the possibility of a fascinating Ph.D. thesis that examines the extent to which authors' correspondence changes once they sign their archive agreements.

Or doesn't change, perhaps; some authors always thought their every word worthy of inspection. Departing on a first trip to Paris, aged twenty, Joyce told his brother Stanislaus that if anything should happen to him his papers should be sent to all the great libraries of the world.

But needless to say, the day will come when I want to write some letter so mean or libidinous or just downright evil that I wouldn't want others to know about it, however dead I am, ever. If one is vain enough to want every pen mark to be an object of study, one is doubtless also sufficiently self-obsessed to want something to remain hidden. I imagine opening an email account that the archive isn't aware of to start a scabrous correspondence that will be all the wilder for the rush of adrenalin arising from my being free at last of those professorial minders, as yet unborn.

Then I feel guilty. They paid for everything. What am I doing trying to hold a bit back? What if they find out? Could the person I am writing to now blackmail me by threatening to expose this subterfuge? Or alternatively try to sell correspondence that has escaped the archive? If he/she does so, could the archive that bought the whole caboodle claim that the work was theirs and illegally sold?

Or what happens if I change my mind? If suddenly the idea of a cult of me becomes an atrocious burden. I want to burn everything, delete everything, not to pollute the planet in any way, not leave any footprint at all. Such changes of heart are not unthinkable. Dickens burned his correspondence. It is harder to think of a man vainer than Dickens. Likewise Thomas Hardy. Perhaps one day I will suddenly be overwhelmed by the realization that it really isn't healthy for anyone to be wasting his life going through the peelings of mine. Isn't there simply so much private material now floating around on the Internet, much of it apparently inerasable, that to add to the miasma seems vulgar and disheartening? After all, deep down one knows that if there were no money involved, one would definitely hold on to the stuff to the end and make the decision then, even if it's only the decision to let posterity do as it will.

Meantime, stepping back a little, isn't it extremely odd that the academy, which generally frowns on "biographism", should so solemnly endorse this vast accumulation of memorabilia: Graham Swift's correspondence with Ted Hughes, the British Library tells us with evident enthusiasm, "includes tips for fishing the River Torridge in Devon, together with Hughes's handwritten sketches marking 'fish traps' along the river". Public money well spent, no doubt. On the other hand, it may also seem a little paradoxical that someone like myself, who has always believed that life and work cannot be separated, should feel so circumspect about the phenomenon.

But no. It is *because* life and work are as seamless as mind and body that one has to sit up and pay attention here. Alter the terms of an author's relationships with others and inevitably you alter his or her work. Perhaps it now seems that an email or text message requires as much craft as your novels. Clearly this shift of creative effort is already occurring on Twitter. But a tweet is of its nature in the public domain, while the recipient of an email has a right (or doesn't he/she?) to imagine the exchange is private, that you are not inserting elements for the admiration of others or excluding elements to hide them from others. How ironic to have fought government surveillance all one's life only to allow it by a cultural institution.

Going back to my own dusty boxes, while I would definitely be glad to see the back of the manuscripts and their silverfish, I can't help wanting to reserve the right to a good bonfire of the correspondence. Or deletion of the email account. But perhaps I will think differently if an offer is large enough.

Book Fair Hype

It's one world, we're one community, and so we must all read the same books. Otherwise how could we talk about them to one another? Thus the logic of globalization: ever larger numbers of people worldwide reading the very best (or best-promoted?) authors. It's good news for those authors and their publishers, not so encouraging for the increasing number of people who would like to make a living from writing. And of course it raises the intriguing question: even when well translated, can we really understand what other cultures are talking about? Will a housewife in Tibet (assuming there are "housewives" in Tibet) make sense of Jonathan Franzen's St Paul, Minn.? Can other people truly get the hang of Bulgarian etiquette or courtship in Laos or street life in the Philippines? Are we interested? Does it make sense to be interested? In short, do all good books travel?

Certainly the authors travel. It isn't enough to publish: to become part of the global conversation, you have to promote yourself worldwide. Even if you're not enthusiastic yourself, your publishers will be pushing you to get on the move; after all, they earn a lot more from every sale than you do, especially if you still have an advance to earn out. And the places you travel to are likely to be literary festivals, the growth of which is more or less contemporary with the globalization process. Likewise the international literary prizes. They are part of the felt need to establish a worldwide conversation about books. I'm of two minds about their worth – whether for me as a writer, or in general as a way of promoting good writing. All the same, this summer I'm going to two: in Edinburgh and Melbourne. Why? Because festivals can be fun, especially if you travel in company. Because I'm not immune to the megalomania that drives so many authors and artists. And because there is no better place to assess the aspirations, fragility, heroism and hypocrisy of the book world than at a major literary festival.

The International (of course) Edinburgh Book Festival is one of the biggest. Staged during the last two weeks of August, it plays host to more than 800 writers from more than 55 countries at more than 700 events held in smart white pavilions in a genteel garden square in Georgian Edinburgh. About 220,000 visitors rise to the bait. Tickets average around £10, and just £5 for the children's events. You can't say that's not reasonable. However, since the book festival runs simultaneously with the more general Edinburgh International Festival ("Welcome, World" the website announces), finding a hotel room in town is tough and paying for it tougher still. One of the main *raisons d'être* of any festival is to support local business; writers as well as readers become part of that project when they agree to go to a certain place to pursue their interests. The more of us who attend, the more hotel and restaurant prices rise. So if an author complains that he gets only £200 for his performance (Edinburgh pays the same to all writers), the festival organizers can point out that at least he's getting a free trip to Edinburgh, though actually it is the publisher, not the festival, who will pay for that.

We're well meaning and we're winners. That's the message that comes across loud and clear from the festival catalogue, and indeed from all festival catalogues. The Edinburgh one is ninety-seven pages long with about sixty words per event, a short book in itself. The mix and the rhetoric are fascinating and tell us all we need to know about the role literature is being assigned in the politics of globalization. "Imagine Better" this year's edition is titled, which means (as the director, Nick Barley, explains) asking ourselves how we can "share our ideas and envisage a better world". Events on refugees, human trafficking, genocide and persecution sit side by side with celebrations of *Finnegans Wake* and Shakespeare, Ezra Pound and Samuel Beckett. Discussions of feminism and socialism, Brexit and Europe rub shoulders with readings from crime novels, fantasy novels, graphic novels and poetry. The "programme partners" of the festival include cultural organizations from a good twenty countries, all represented by an author or two: the Icelandic poet and novelist Sjón, the Belgian prize-winner Peter Terrin, the New Zealand-born Kirsty Gunn and so on. From Mexico, "Diego Enrique Osorno tells stories of teenage prostitution, Sergio González Rodríguez describes systematic violence against women, and Emiliano Ruiz Parra recounts a good man's assassination".

And of course, perhaps more understandably, there is Scotland: discussions about Scotland's past, present and future; readings from Scottish novelists and Scottish poets; presentations by Scottish sportsmen and Scottish entertainers. That seems altogether right. We're in Scotland: we want to hear the Scots. The curious thing is the amount of crossover between the various themes and genres. One main event is a theatre adaptation of Alice Munro's stories about her Scottish ancestors migrating to Canada. A Scottish historian discusses his country's role in the slave trade. This is not intimate Scotland, at home with itself, but Scotland as part of world drama. Novels are frequently described as discussing wars, crises and dramatic political events all over the globe, while non-fiction works are presented as narratives: the "award-winning *New York Times* journalist Anjan Sundaram has an astonishing story to tell. *Bad News* is his eyewitness account of events in Rwanda today."

All in all, it's hard not to feel that fiction and poetry are allowed to exist only in so far as they are willing to be subsumed into a liberal, international, "forward-looking" agenda. They are telling stories as part of a project to imagine a better world, championing mental health issues, transgender issues, human rights issues. With great frequency they set their stories in times and places that have become clichés of the collective imagination, moments of particular turmoil when particular well-defined problems were on the agenda: Tudor England, nineteenth-century Britain, terrorism in 1970s Rome, Nazi Germany, Paris in 1968, the various killing fields of the twentieth century and many more. One non-fiction writer joins a novelist to explore "How Writers Live through War". Another looks at "writers and the spying game". All of them are concerned that we learn from history and from our mistakes.

And all of them are "brilliant". We thank "the brilliant authors and their courageous publishers, as well as everyone who buys tickets and books", the introduction says. The dynamic is clear enough. These writers are "good" in both senses. They write about serious issues, and they are celebrities. The novelist Rupert Thomson "is on the journey to literary superstardom"; Philip Howard and David Greig "enjoy stellar careers"; Kate Tempest is "a rising star of British literature". The "UK-Iranian Shappi Khorsandi is a star of stand-up who has mined her comic talent to unearth a witty, sometimes shocking debut novel". About a teenager "battling her addictions". An important issue.

I don't mean to be critical of the organizers. I doubt I would do things much differently myself. All festival catalogues are like this. They have to be. But that is the point. The public wants to meet wonderfully talented people with their hearts in the right place. It makes sense. And of course this is how people all over the globe can be drawn into the same bookish conversation. We won't get the rich specificity of Mexican

Spanish, the endless ways Rwandans share being Rwandan, the tones and gestures of China, the complex family relationships of Thailand. Instead, each country is an exotic backdrop for an easily recognizable drama: *The Boy Who Never Was*, for instance, "is a moving depiction of a young gay man's experience in 1918 Iceland". Set in a home for sick children in Vienna, *The Chosen Ones* describes "brutality and tenderness in the Nazi era". Et cetera. I think of one of my favourite authors, Barbara Pym, of her extraordinary ear for a certain kind of dialogue in a very specific social milieu. *A Few Green Leaves*, *Quartet in Autumn* – these are novels whose characters require readers with a shared awareness of fine nuance and infinite shading. I do not think a writer of this kind would be invited to today's global debate.

After Brexit

"How will literature be affected by Brexit?"

This was the question four authors, myself included, were asked at a recent London bookshop event with the rather curious title: "European Fiction in the United Kingdom: In or Out?" It was evident that we were expected to find Brexit detrimental. "We believe that the cultural voice was largely ignored during the referendum campaign," the event's moderator, Rosie Goldsmith, had observed in her preamble. A greater awareness of European culture, she felt, might have encouraged people to make a wiser decision. Ninety-seven per cent of those working in the creative arts – she had the statistic on hand – had supported the Remain camp.

Authors of course live largely by their imaginations; all the same, none of us were quite able to conjure up the required predictions of post-Brexit literary decline. The British writer, illustrator and Francophile Joanna Walsh came the closest. She suspected European funding for literature would surely drop off, though admitted she had no figures. She used the expressions "cultural networks", "university networks" and "cultural foundations", all of which she supposed would suffer. Then aware, perhaps, that all this might seem underwhelming to our attentive audience, she fielded the notion that the European Union has been largely responsible for peace in Europe over the last six decades. In this regard the Brexit scenario was, she thought, frightening.

The hint of war upped the stakes considerably. But could it really be literature we were worried about at this point? Is one concerned about the production and circulation of quality fiction when the sabres start to rattle?

Antoine Laurain – a Parisian novelist in his forties, splendidly droll and non-committal – declined to take up the melodramatic scenario. He really could not see, he said apologetically, or not yet, how Brexit might affect literature. Nor did he suppose that British literature would suddenly cease to influence European writers or vice versa. Since he was struggling to say more, I interrupted and wondered how on earth a nation's political decision to leave a trade organization could affect the literary scene. Had the European Union as such made any significant contribution to literature or the arts over its sixty-year history? Not that I knew of. Had British readers become "European" in their tastes during the country's forty-year membership? Hardly. Why would literature decline as a result of this development?

No doubt my intervention betrayed my impatience with this kind of conversation, although, looking back, the more pertinent question would have been: why would we suppose that literature and political liberalism are mutually sustaining, the implication being that only a "healthy" or well-behaved nation produces and consumes good literature? Can that possibly be true?

The fourth writer offered the first interesting answer. Very tall, handsomely unshaven and seductively gloomy, the Romanian Claudiu Florian had more reason than the others of us to be positive about the EU's influence on culture. His novel *The Ages of the Game – Citadel Street* was a recipient of the 2016 European Union Prize for Literature, which, over three-year cycles (since 2009), rewards one emerging writer from each member country, encouraging translation of his or her work throughout the European Union.

Florian is a diplomat who has worked at Romanian embassies and cultural institutes in Germany and Switzerland. It was hence predictable that he would begin by stressing what a good thing the EU was, though he then went on to tell us how traumatic it had been for Romania to adapt to the organization's many rules and requirements. There was some consternation when Florian explained this by remarking that there were strong similarities between the European Union and the Soviet bloc's Comecon in the way they allocated distinct economic roles to different countries. But as for Brexit's affecting literature, he suddenly observed, as if stumbling across an evident truth, it could very likely have a positive influence, because of course writers were stimulated and inspired by conflict and upheaval. Dramatic events are good subject matter.

Here an abyss opens. Writing may require a minimum of stability and comfort for the actual business of getting the words down on the page, but the truth is it thrives on discomfort. "Emotion recollected in tranquillity" was Wordsworth's formula. You need the tranquillity, but it will be no use to you if you haven't had the emotion. And so often that emotion will mean conflict, betrayal, sickness and breakup. Like the jackal, the writer feeds on corpses. Western literary culture begins with the carnage of the *Iliad*. It proceeds with such savage tales as Aeschylus's *Oresteia*, the *Aeneid*, *Beowulf*, with the sins and torments of Dante's *Inferno*, the violence of *Tamburlaine* and *Macbeth*. *War and Peace* speaks for itself. Likewise *Crime and Punishment*. Where would Hemingway be without his First World War experiences, without the bullfights and the hunting parties? How could Curzio Malaparte have written the extraordinary *Kaputt* without his time on Hitler's Eastern Front? Even where the conflict is less bloody it can nevertheless be extremely cruel: *Madame Bovary*. *The Good Soldier*. *Women in Love*. *The Trial*. Long before funding, fiction feeds on strife.

As if to demonstrate this truth, we four authors now each read out a short piece of writing. Joanna Walsh's short story, from her collection *Vertigo*, begins with the striking line: "A friend told me to buy a red dress in Paris because I am leaving my husband." The cryptic observations that follow, on shopping in Le Bon Marché, are all galvanized by the pain and turbulence that underlie this unhappy rite of passage, something Walsh conveyed quite disturbingly with the peremptory brittleness of her delivery, as of someone struggling to keep a grip on difficult emotions.

Antoine Laurain's reading from his novel *French Rhapsody* was, like his comments on Brexit, wryly laconic: essentially, an artist reflecting on his new installation – a huge inflatable model of his own brain – is primarily interested in outdoing his rivals and frustrating his critics. Though he knows it is expedient to talk piously about dialogue and dialectic, in reality everything is experienced in terms of self-promotion and rivalry. It made uneasy listening for anyone who likes to believe that artists are for the most part good and wise.

My own piece, from the novel *Thomas and Mary*, told of a woman with a talent for giving her husband and offspring hilarious if demeaning nicknames; they all have to call one another by the names she invented. In adolescence the children finally rebel, and following their example the husband too at last insists on being called by his own name, a moment that marks the beginning of the end of the marriage. So a little comedy masks a thirty-year power struggle.

But it was the Romanian who had the strongest material. Far from being funded when it mattered, he described how he had written his novel in pencil during his morning and evening train commutes while working in Berlin. The story it allusively tells, in the voice of a little boy listening uncomprehendingly to his parents' conversations through the 1970s, is that of Romanian history in the twentieth century, a long chronicle of war, revolution and betrayal. Once again, the message that came across from the reading is that while life is dangerous and full of strife, art unashamedly transforms it into something engaging and even charming: we may not know how to live, but we certainly know how to talk about it.

Which is not to say that one wishes Brexit would lead to conflict just so as to promote more fiction. After all, the referendum itself was conflictual enough. The day before this literary event, a friend had told me of a wedding planned for the Saturday after the vote. When it became clear the Remainers had lost, the bride sent a tweet to say that if any of the wedding guests had voted for Brexit they were uninvited. Imagine, I immediately thought, if in the secret of the ballot box the groom himself had been so bold. Not a bad short story, perhaps.

God's Smuggler

Does someone want to silence us? Are we at war? Nothing is more exhilarating for a writer than to feel that simply putting pen to paper is an act of courage and a bid for freedom. Remember this novel?

> The thing that he was about to do was to open a diary. This was not illegal (nothing was illegal, since there were no longer any laws), but if detected it was reasonably certain that it would be punished by death, or at least by twenty-five years in a forced-labour camp. Winston... dipped the pen into the ink and then faltered for just a second. A tremor had gone through his bowels. To mark the paper was the decisive act. In small clumsy letters he wrote: April 4th 1984.

And nothing is more galvanizing for readers than to feel that they are collaborators in this bookish heroism, that reading itself is a revolutionary act. I remember in my early teens unwrapping a Christmas present from my evangelical parents to find a copy of *God's Smuggler*, by Brother Andrew, an account of a Dutch Christian's adventures smuggling Bibles into the Soviet bloc. It was 1967. The idea my parents no doubt wanted to get across was that our own daily Bible reading was a brave act of subversion in a heathen world. And I must say I enjoyed *God's Smuggler* rather more than the Bible. I enjoyed Brother Andrew's miraculous escapes from brutal soldiers, and at thirteen I believed in the power of prayer that blinded the eyes of his persecutors. Very soon, though, to read Sade's *Justine*, I took the precaution of hiding the book under the bedclothes. My mother was not so easily bamboozled as those Soviet soldiers. And though she never actually confiscated anything, she would burst into tears whenever I was found to be "siding with the Devil". In the years to come, Lawrence, Beckett, Genet and Sartre were all best kept out of sight.

Meantime, through the late 1960s and '70s, we read Solzhenitsyn and other Soviet-bloc dissidents with a sense of awe. For them writing really was a brave and dangerous thing. We imagined that in reading their books we were playing our part in a great ideological struggle. I remember my father in his unbuttoned, after-lunch ease with a copy of *Cancer Ward* on his lap. We rejoiced when our hero was given the Nobel. It seemed right that the prizes should go to those who took risks for their freedom and their beliefs, those who spoke out: Nadine Gordimer, Gabriel García Márquez, Naguib Mahfouz. Perhaps we even felt a certain naive envy of artists from countries unhappier than our own. The struggle was so clear for them, the path to glory so obvious.

Why mention this now?

In the months I have been writing these essays for the *New York Times* (of which this is the last), I have been drawn, almost against my will, to notice the intensifying politicization of the literary world and, hand in hand with that, a predilection for melodrama, for prose that stimulates extreme emotions – in good causes of course. The cause justifies the melodrama. The melodrama serves the cause. This past year's winner of the Man Booker International Prize, *The Vegetarian*, by the Korean writer Han Kang, was emblematic. A young woman is abused and victimized when she chooses to stop eating meat. Food is forced down her throat. She is raped. A patriarchal, carnivorous society cannot accept her modern sensibility. It is very hard for readers to get their allegiances wrong in this kind of narrative, hard not to feel that in buying the novel and reading and talking about it, one is doing one's bit for freedom and emancipation worldwide.

The year's political upheavals contributed to this growing sense of embattlement. At a conference called European Literature Days in Wachau, Austria, in early November 2016, participants were explicitly invited to rally against the centrifugal forces threatening to break up Europe. Any who felt that Brexit was not such a bad thing in the end would have been wise to keep such heresy to themselves. There was definitely a new excitement in the air. People were anxious, but not perhaps unhappy. Writers were suddenly more relevant. Over lunch, a Swiss writer, Jonas Lüscher, described a spat with his fellow Swiss novelist Peter Stamm. Stamm – whose wry, spare fiction I can't recommend highly enough – had given a speech insisting on the necessary separateness of art from politics; to introduce the topical and overtly political into fiction, he thought, was a form of impoverishment, or even worse, of opportunism and self-promotion. Lüscher had replied by insisting on the dignity and indeed importance of the artist's political engagement. On the last evening of the conference he read from his first novel, *Barbarian Spring*, an account of the grotesquely extravagant wedding party of two London traders in a luxury tourist resort in Tunisia at precisely that moment in 2008 when world finance began to fall apart. It was satire in flamboyant style, and it was a rousing success with the public. We all felt pleasantly superior to those crass and irresponsible bankers. British to boot.

Then Donald Trump was elected president and PEN America began to send me frequent requests to donate to their campaign to defend freedom of speech in America. Trump's election, their premise went, marks the beginning of a new war. On home territory. Very soon Americans might be presented with the kind of struggles our Soviet-bloc heroes faced. Then they too would have their path to glory. One request, oddly enough, was signed by J.K. Rowling and arrived on my screen as if sent personally to me by the great lady herself. How flattering. Exhorting me to donate, Rowling (who lives in Edinburgh) wrote, "We will not go quietly and we are Louder Together!"

It is the enthusiasm, the militancy, that is disturbing, not the goal. Those sharing my unease might want to take a look at David Attwell's discussion of J.M. Coetzee's 1983 novel *Life & Times of Michael K*, in *J.M. Coetzee and the Life of Writing*. Coetzee had imagined a poor man caught up in conflict and racial hatred, whose only ambition is to settle down and tend a garden. But was his hero "ever going to take to the hills and start shooting"? Coetzee worried in his notes as he wrote the book. It seemed the obvious direction for the story to take; it was what readers would want; it was desirable and logical. But Michael is inexplicably reluctant. To the extent to which he is the author's alter ego – in an earlier draft Michael had been a poet, not a gardener – he simply could not go there. He did not want to be "louder together".

Reviewing Coetzee's novel, Nadine Gordimer recognized it was "a marvellous work that leaves nothing unsaid… about what human beings do to fellow human beings in South Africa", but then claimed that, in showing "a revulsion against all political and revolutionary solutions" and denying recognition to the black struggle, it distorted "the integral relation between private and social destiny… more than is allowed for by the subjectivity that is in every writer". Replying, indirectly, in a talk given in 1987, Coetzee complained that novelists were "a tribe threatened with colonization" by those who would have them "address what are called problems and issues". Curiously, these are the very terms in which Stamm replied to Lüscher's criticism: we are all being herded towards the big controversies, he complained. It's a loss of imagination, not a gain.

In the months ahead, this debate will heat up. Both as readers and as writers, each of us will react in a way congenial to our temperament. It is impossible to imagine Coetzee writing like Gordimer, Lüscher like Stamm, or vice versa of course. My own position is this: let us by all means defend our freedom of speech when and if it is threatened, but let us never confuse this engagement with our inspiration as writers or our inclination as readers. Above all, let us not get off on it.

Gained and Lost in Translation

In the Tumult of Translation

In a recent letter to the editor, Leon Botstein, the head of Bard College, scolds the *New York Review of Books* for not mentioning translators. As a translator myself, I'm all too familiar with the review that offers a token nod to the translation, announces it good, bad or indifferent, perhaps offering one small example to justify praise or ignominy. But although not specifically singled out by Botstein, I fear I am one of the culprits. My review of Levi's *Complete Works* did not name the translators or discuss their work.

The fact is that much space is required to say anything even halfway serious about a translation. For example, the three volumes of Levi's *Complete Works* include fourteen books and involved ten translators. There is the further complication that the three best-known books – *If This Is a Man, The Truce* and *The Periodic Table* – had already been translated, the first two by Stuart Woolf, the third by Raymond Rosenthal. *If This Is a Man* appears here in a "revised" version of the 1959 translation, Woolf himself having carried out the revision more than a half-century after his original. However, *The Truce* appears in an entirely new translation by Ann Goldstein. One can only imagine what negotiations lay behind this odd arrangement; Levi's writings are still under copyright, which presumably allowed Woolf or his publisher to dictate terms. Ann Goldstein also offers a new translation of *The Periodic Table*, and is the translator of *Lilith and Other Stories*, another book in the *Complete Works*.

We should say at the outset that while Levi liked to describe himself as a writer with a determinedly plain style, the truth is rather different. Often a direct speaking voice shifts between the colloquial and the literary, the ironically highfalutin and the grittily scientific. It's true that there are rarely serious problems of comprehension, but the exact nature of the register, which is to say the manner in which the author addresses us, the relationship into which he draws us, is a complex and highly mobile animal. It is here that the translator is put to the test.

Stuart Woolf, later to become a distinguished professor of Italian history, was in his early twenties when he met Levi in 1956 and worked with him on the translation of *If This Is a Man*, which would appear to have been his first book-length translation. "It is opportune to recall," he remarks in his translator's afterword, "that half a century ago the complexities, ambiguities, and compromises that have become inherent in the expression of one culture in the language of another were not yet discussed." This is not true. There was a rich body of reflection on translation long before the invention of translation studies, and Italy, a country that translated more novels than any other throughout the first half of the twentieth century, has a particularly strong tradition in this area.

Angela Albanese and Franco Nasi recently published *L'artefice aggiunto, riflessioni sulla traduzione in Italia: 1900–1975*, an anthology of writings on translation in Italy before the invention of modern translation studies. Going further back in time, Leonardo Bruni, Melchiorre Cesarotti, Ippolito Pindemonte, Ugo Foscolo, Giovanni Berchet, Pietro Giordani, Niccolò Tommaseo and, most wonderfully, Giacomo Leopardi all offered fascinating accounts of "complexities, ambiguities, and compromises". In any event, Woolf's afterword mainly describes his own relationship with Levi, gives no examples of translation from the text, and does not discuss his criteria for revision, leaving us with the elusive remark: "I have made what I believe to be improvements in the translation, and I owe thanks to Peter Hennig for sending me a substantial list of alternative words and phrases, some of which I have adopted..."

Here are some of the changes I have found. In this first passage, Levi is describing his days as a new arrival in the camp. Here is the 1959 edition:

And it is this refrain that we hear repeated by everyone. You are not at home, this is not a sanatorium, the only exit is by way of the Chimney. (What did it mean? Soon we were all to learn what it meant.)

Here is the 2015 edition:

And it is this refrain that we hear repeated by everyone. You are not at home, this is not a sanatorium, the only way out is through the Chimney. (What does that mean? We'll soon learn very well what it means.)

Levi's original gives:

Ed è questo il ritornello che da tutti ci sentiamo ripetere: non siete più a casa, questo non è un sanatorio, di qui non si esce che per il Camino (cosa vorrà dire? lo impareremo bene più tardi).

The Italian here is entirely standard, plain and colloquial, with just a little touch of drama in the capitalization of "Camino" ("Chimney") and again in the closing parenthesis. Given the awfulness of what is being discussed, this downbeat style is remarkable and hence should be preserved at all costs.

The 1959 version shows all Woolf's inexperience. Can we really imagine the camp inmates saying: "the only exit is by way of the Chimney"? The Italian *di qui non si esce che* (literally, "from here one doesn't go out but by") suggests something like, "the only way you'll get out of here is through the Chimney". In the 2015 edition "exit" has been replaced with "way out", which is certainly an improvement. In the following parenthesis, the verb has been shifted from past to present – "What does that mean?" – which livens things up a little. However, the Italian uses a future tense – *cosa vorrà dire?* – which gives the sense "what is that supposed to mean?" The 1959 solution, "we were all to learn", is shifted in 2015 to "we'll soon learn", respecting the new tense sequence but leaving "learn", where a more standard English idiom might use "know" or "find out".

I include the first part of my quotation, which remains the same in both texts – "it is this refrain that we hear repeated by everyone" – to suggest Woolf's difficulties with the syntax. A more idiomatic translation might have given "that we hear everyone repeating" (the Italian doesn't use a passive here, so why should the translation?). "Refrain" too – though literally it has the same sense as *ritornello* – has a rather more elevated feel; Italians often use *ritornello* disparagingly to suggest a trite phrase mindlessly repeated – something we don't do with "refrain". All in all, a translator wishing to get the fluent directness of the original might offer:

> Everyone keeps repeating the same thing: you're not at home now, this isn't a sanatorium, the only way out of here is through the Chimney (what's that supposed to mean? We'll soon find out).

In general, Woolf's revisions to his 1959 translation are very light. In a second example, the camp inmates are so determined to be on time for their meal that they are unwilling to stop to pee. Levi has:

Molti, bestialmente, orinano, correndo per risparmiare tempo, perché entro cinque minuti inizia la distribuzione del pane, del pane-Brot-Broit-chleb-pain-lechem-kenyér, del sacro blocchetto grigio che sembra gigantesco in mano del tuo vicino e piccolo da piangere in mano tua.

Woolf's 1959 text gave:

Some, bestially, urinate while they run to save time, because within five minutes begins the distribution of bread, of bread-Brot-Broid-chleb-pain-lechem-keynér, of the holy grey slab which seems gigantic in your neighbour's hand, and in your own hand so small as to make you cry.

Why we have "some" (which would be *qualcuno* or *alcuni* in Italian) rather than "many" is not clear. *Bestialmente* can be used in Italian to mean simply "like an animal". "Bestially" sounds rather like a criticism of these desperate folk. And do we usually invert verb and subject: "begins the distribution of bread"? Wouldn't we normally put an article – "of the bread"? Again, the Italian is entirely standard here, by which I mean that one could hardly think of a simpler way of putting this. However, if the translator uses a more standard English – "Because in five minutes the bread distribution begins" – he will have a problem with the phrase in apposition immediately afterwards ("of bread-Brot-Broid-chleb, etc."). Since this needs to be tagged directly onto the word "bread", Woolf decides to leave the Italian structure intact. Of course, this solution is entirely possible in English, but gives the feeling of something rather more elaborate and less spoken than the Italian. In the end, the only things revised here in the 2015 edition are the English spelling ("gray", "neighbor"), the use of "which" rather than "that" and the repetition of the word "hand".

My own sense of Levi's original might go like this:

> To save time many are urinating as they run, like animals, because in five minutes they'll be handing out the bread, Brot-Broid-chleb-pane-pain-lechem-keynér, that sacred grey slab that looks so huge in the hands of the man next to you and so small you could cry in your own.

I've risked a little confusion using two "they"s with different referents in the first line, though in the context of the paragraph the sense will be clear enough. Italian has no other word but *distribuire* for the idea of distributing, but English has "handing out". Why go for the more formal "distribute" for this rather brutal process of handing over slabs of stale bread? I've introduced *pane* into the list of words for bread, since it seems strange to eliminate Italian from the languages the inmates are speaking. I've also used the straightforward "looks" instead of "seems" (again Italian has no choice here), and I've speeded up the end "so small you could cry in your own" in line with Levi's extremely condensed *piccolo da piangere in mano tua*. Meanwhile, *il tuo vicino* is a tricky problem. It means "the person next to you", hence also "your neighbour". So it could take on a Biblical ring. But it is also absolutely the word you would use for the guy standing next to you in a line at a bus stop. The question is: how much attention do we want to draw in the English to a word that draws none at all to itself in Italian?

Sometimes Woolf's revisions actually make things less clear. Here, after the men get their bread and return to their dormitory block, the 1959 edition tells us that, "the Block resounds with claims, quarrels and scuffles". In the new version this becomes, "the block resounds with claims, quarrels, and flights".

Flights? On reading this I confess it took me a moment to grasp what was meant. Levi is explaining that in the camp bread is the only form of currency for trading, hence the moment the men get their bread is payback time. If someone owes you something, you need to get his bread off him now, before he can eat it. The Italian gives:

Il Block risuona di richiami, di liti, e di fughe.

Richiami could indeed mean "claims" or "protests", but would more usually indicate "calls", "shouts", "cries"; in particular it is used to refer to the noises animals make calling each other, something that links back to *bestialmente* and indeed the whole theme introduced by the title *If This Is a Man*; *liti* means "quarrels", or even "fights". *Fughe* is "flights" in the sense of people running for it. Again, it's a word in common use in Italian; we could talk of the *fuga* of a football player who breaks free of his defender, or a thief running from the police. In English the word is barely comprehensible here, and even if we do understand, it takes us back to a usage of long ago in a higher register – the flight from Egypt, perhaps – or something metaphorical: "The Flight from Conversation", a recent *New York Times* article was headlined.

I can find no example in English of "flights" used in the plural in this sense without a qualification of who is fleeing from what or whom. This no doubt is why Woolf avoided the word in the 1959 version. Introducing it now in the new edition, presumably for correctness, since *fughe* definitely does not mean "scuffles", he disorients the reader. The upward jolt to the register reinforces the slightly literary tone of "resound" ("the block resounded"), which, like "refrain", has a more elevated feel than the word it is translating, in this case *risuona*, which again is standard Italian fare. The whole thing might have been delivered as:

> The Block is filled with the noise of cries, quarrels, men running for it.

I spoke of a play of registers in Levi's writing, but so far have only given examples of his plain prose. Needless to say, if your translation of the plain prose sounds anything but plain, it will be difficult to indicate a change of gear when you shift up a register. That said, Woolf is more convincing with the high register. There is a tough moment near the beginning of the book where, having heard that they are to be deported to Germany the following morning, a group of Jews in a detention centre, Levi included, spend a sleepless night, at the end of which

> *L'alba ci colse come un tradimento, come se il nuovo sole si associasse agli uomini nella deliberazione di distruggerci.*

In 1959 Woolf translates the first sentence fairly freely. "Betrayal" (*tradimento*) becomes "betrayer", the idea of the sun joining up with *gli uomini* – "men/mankind" – in the determination to "destroy us" is somewhat paraphrased:

> Dawn came on us like a betrayer; it seemed as though the new sun rose as an ally of our enemies to assist in our destruction.

In 2015 he moves closer to the original in the first part of the sentence, cuts the unnecessary and cumbersome "seemed as though" and offers a different paraphrase of the second part:

Dawn came upon us like a betrayal, as if the new sun were an ally of the men who had decided to destroy us.

This sounds pretty good, but still loses the impact of Levi's use of *gli uomini* in the general sense of all men or, in a higher register, mankind, not a specific group of enemies. Again, this usage fits in with the book's questioning of what it means to be a man, to be part of the human race. Here the Jews are being treated as if they didn't belong among men. So more accurately we might have:

Dawn came upon us like a betrayal, as if the new sun were joining forces with men in the determination to destroy us.

If you wanted to stress this point, it would be acceptable to give "as if the sun were joining forces with mankind". That is the kind of decision you might take on your nth reading of the whole translation, when you have the voice firmly in your mind. At the moment it seems a little too "loud" to me.

Let's move a few lines further on for our last example. With the dawn comes action; the hiatus of the night is over; Levi winds up the register with some archaic terms and images:

Il tempo di meditare, il tempo di stabilire erano conchiusi, e ogni moto di ragione si sciolse nel tumulto senza vincoli, su cui, dolorosi come colpi di spada, emergevano in un lampo, così vicini ancora nel tempo e nello spazio, i ricordi buoni delle nostre case.

In 1959 Woolf drops the *senza vincoli* (literally, "without constraints"), presumably in order to keep the English tight, though the real problem in this sentence is Levi's rather mysterious use of the verb *stabilire*, which in the translation appears as the noun "decision". As for the archaic *conchiusi* ("concluded", "finished") it is hard to see how it could be rendered in English.

> The time for meditation, the time for decision was over, and all reason dissolved into a tumult, across which flashed the happy memories of our homes, still so near in time and space, as painful as the thrusts of a sword.

What decision or decisions could people have been taking, since their destiny is now entirely out of their hands? There has been no mention of decisions to be made. Woolf doesn't clarify this in his 2015 translation, but recovers the idea of *senza vincoli* in "unrestrained tumult" and rearranges the second part of the sentence for fluency:

> The time for meditation, the time for decision was over, and all reason dissolved into an unrestrained tumult, across which flashed, as painful as the thrusts of a sword, the happy memories of our homes, still so near in time and space.

This works well enough, though a phrase like "as painful as the thrusts of a sword" still has a wearisomely translationese feel to my ear. But let's put some pressure on that word *stabilire*. Usually this verb takes an object: "to establish/fix/set/decide" *something*. But what can it mean if there is no object, and in the generally portentous lexical mix Levi has concocted here? People have spent the night reflecting on their destiny. They have meditated. They have, literally, "established". But now that time is over. Now reason, or rather every *moto di ragione* (literally, "movement of reason"), dissolves (*si sciolsero*), and we have a tumult that is unrestrained (*senza vincoli*).

There is an evident polarity here between reasoned construction of some kind of response (what people have tried to "establish" through the hours of the night), and confused, ungovernable dissolution, as the fateful day begins and a tumult of emotions takes over, robbing people of their human dignity. It's a polarity that, when linked to the idea of "the time for this and the time for that", cannot but remind us of Ecclesiastes. And indeed Italian annotated versions of the text suggest a reference to "a time to break down and a time to build up".

How to get this across in translation? If one offers "the time for gathering thoughts (or coming to terms with things) was over", one perhaps gets something of the idea and a proper contrast with thoughts that are then scattered, but still the strangeness of Levi's usage would be lost. I offer a version I'm not happy with, but it's the best I can do:

> The time to meditate, the time to settle, was over and every effort of reason dissolved in this unrestrained tumult through which the happy memories of our homes, still so close in time and space, stabbed painfully as sudden sword thrusts.

To sum up, in 1956 Woolf had the intuition that Levi's book, then largely unrecognized, was an important work, worthy of translation. Bravely, he translated it on spec, without a contract; later an American publisher, Orion, got in touch with him and eventually published it. We owe Woolf our gratitude and admiration for having introduced the book to the English-speaking world when it mattered in a highly serviceable, if undistinguished translation. Unfortunately, that is the version we still have, since the 2015 "revision" amounts to little more than a light edit.

Why then, you might ask, has this translation (in both its manifestations) been widely praised? It is a fascinating question that I will try to answer in my next piece.

A Long Way from Primo Levi

Perhaps inevitably when reading translations, from time to time one comes across a strange word: "ankylosed", for example. "Nor was it easy to understand how he had survived in Auschwitz," we read in Ann Goldstein's new translation of Primo Levi's *The Truce*, "since he had an ankylosed arm." If we turn back to Stuart Woolf's 1965 translation of what was Levi's second book, we get the same word with a different spelling, "anchylosed".

This strange word is, of course, the English cognate of Levi's original: *anchilosato*. But the two words are hardly equivalent in effect. If we type "an ankylosed arm" into a Google search of the entire English-language Internet, we get just five hits, three of them from surgical texts published a century ago; the remaining two are *The Complete Works of Primo Levi*, in which Goldstein's translation appears, and a long online discussion of King Philip II of Macedon's ankylosis, "a stiffness of a joint due to abnormal adhesion and rigidity of the bones of the joint".

On the other hand, if we ask Google to search "*un braccio anchilosato*" we get 477 results (and we remember that Italian, being less widely spoken than English, usually has far fewer hits for equivalent phrases – "concentration camp", 7.5 million, "*campo di concentramento*", 581,000). This time the results are mainly from journalism and popular fiction, including one of Emilio Salgari's famous novels for young adults.

If, in the changing room after my yoga class, in Milan, I complain that my *braccio* feels all *anchilosato*, no one will be surprised. They know I'm feeling stiff. It's a commonplace (and a common condition, alas). So much so that you can use it metaphorically. The Italian bureaucracy is *anchilosata*, observes *Corriere della Sera*. As a result of the financial crisis, the real-estate business is *anchilosato*, complains the other leading newspaper, *La Repubblica*.

If, finally, we look more carefully at those Italian usages in Google, we also discover, curiously enough, that quite a few came from translations of works originally written in English. So what was the English that prompted the Italian *anchilosato*? I tracked this down, from James Frey's *How to Write a Damn Good Novel*: where would Hank Aaron have been, asks James rhetorically, "had he had a withered arm"? And this from *The Lost Wife* by Alyson Richman: "the thought of my [as yet unborn] grandchild possibly not making it or having a limp arm for the rest of his or her life… terrified me".

These are clearly more extreme cases than my stiff arm after yoga. But the Italian translators are right both times. The word *anchilosato* is understood to cover a range of experiences from a serious medical condition to a more banal feeling of rigidity. Crucially, it is not a word that draws any attention to itself in Italian. Not so in English. The same would be true, say, of "quintals". "*Dalla ricca campagna circostante arrivavano i carri dei contadini con quintali di lardo e di formaggio,*" writes Levi. "From the rich surrounding countryside arrived the peasants' carts with quintals of lard and cheese," translates Goldstein. Woolf's earlier translation gave "tons", recognizing that "quintals" is not a standard English term for expressing abundance or excess, as is *quintali* (the plural of *quintale*, which literally means a weight of one hundred kilograms).

In my previous piece in this space, discussing Stuart Woolf's 1959 translation of Levi's first memoir, *If This Is a Man* (lightly revised by Woolf for the 2015 *Complete Works*), I observed that, although mostly serviceable as a translation, the English is frequently a little stilted or simply odd where the original is fluent and standard; this seems to have been a result of Woolf's staying close to Italian syntax or having difficulty getting the lexical choice that fits Levi's overall register. Why then has the book, and indeed the translation, been so admired?

The first answer, as you might expect, is the extraordinary content and quality of Levi's memoir; the experience of Auschwitz, as Levi narrates it, is so extreme that no ordinary reader would focus on some hiccups in the translation. But there is more to it than this.

I said it was curious that Google's hits for "*un braccio anchilosato*" referred in quite a few cases to novels translated from English. However, when one remembers that about seventy per cent of novels published in Italy are translated and of those about seventy per cent are translated from English, it isn't perhaps so strange at all. And since the Italians, like most other Europeans, read so many foreign books, there is more awareness of the process of translation and a general determination on the part of the publishers to produce fluent translations in standard Italian.

This has its drawbacks. Often books with very particular stylistic qualities come out of the translation machine (there is a great deal of translation editing in Italy) as entirely ordinary Italian. Where there is "interference" from the original English – that is, English words and syntax are imposing themselves at the expense of standard Italian – it may be because the pressure of English on Italian is now so great that usages once considered unusual are now being accepted in the language. For example, when I arrived in Italy thirty-three years ago, the verb *realizzare* did not mean "to realize" in the standard English sense of "to become aware", but only in the sense "to realize an investment/dream/goal". Now the Italian word is freely used in exactly the way English speakers use "realize". Right or wrong, people simply fell into the habit.

The situation could hardly be more different with translations *into* English. In the USA and the UK fewer than four per cent of published novels are translations, and there is no particular country that publishers are buying from. Aside from very occasional best-sellers – Stieg Larsson's *Millennium* trilogy, for example – most of these books are in the more literary area of the market, with small prestigious publishers like Archipelago, which only publishes translations, or New Directions, which publishes a great many, actually making a significant contribution to the overall number of translations coming into the US.

The result – or so I have the impression – is that a certain credit or self-esteem now attaches itself to reading translations; it is something that intelligent, broad-minded people do. Above all, it is understood that the books will be literary and challenging, perhaps with something of their exotic origins still clinging to them.

In short, the American reader of translated novels is predisposed to read a rather different, non-standard English. No one need be anxious that "quintals" or "ankylosed" might force themselves into standard vocabulary; rather, they will remain pleasant curiosities, or perhaps even pretentious markers, catering to a self-consciously "informed" reader of foreign novels. The website of a young American translator from the Italian speaks of offering "accurate" translations that nevertheless retain "the flavour" of the Italian. If, by "flavour", he means the tone of the book, its register, the whole feeling it conjures up for Italian readers, then I am with him one hundred per cent. But I fear he doesn't mean that. I suspect he means that he will encourage an awareness that the book was written in Italian, by seeking to retain in some way the accents of Italy, or the sound of Italian to an English person.

But is this actually possible? We know what it sounds like when an Italian speaks English with an Italian accent. But how can we possibly recognize the flavour of written Italian in written English, if we can't read in Italian? How can we distinguish it – in English – from the flavour of Spanish or French or Russian or Czech? What can we experience beyond a muddled exoticism?

Here, for example, in *The Truce*, Levi is talking about refugees on a train who can't work out where they're going. Goldstein's translation gives: "There existed only two or three maps, relentlessly argued over, on which we had trouble following our problematic progress." "Existed" is a little surprising here; in English its use is normally reserved to indicate not so much the presence of an object in a given situation – "There is a book on the table" – but the existence of an object at all: "Does alien life exist on Mars?" Italian, on the contrary, frequently uses the verb *esistere* not only in "there is" statements but in all kinds of other situations. For example, if you want you can exclaim, "*Non esiste!*" to mean, "It can't be true!" Rather than falling back on the cognate then, one would normally translate Levi's sentence as "There were only two or three maps" or "We had only two or three maps between us".

So, does the American reader understand Goldstein's "existed", together with the endless other slightly inappropriate Latinate words that tend to creep into Italian translations, as the flavour of Italian? Or does he or she suppose that the translator is responding to an equally unexpected word in the original text, a word conveying something thematically relevant; this, after all, is how literature often works, drawing our attention with an unusual usage. If we accept that there is no significance in the unusual word, merely a bit of "Italian flavour", how can we distinguish that from moments when our author did write something significantly out of the ordinary in Italian, something we should be paying attention to as theme and not as "flavour"?

Let's consider the following examples from Levi's *The Truce*. They are simply places where, when reading Goldstein's translation, the English sounded distinctly odd, or where I felt that there was some interference from the Italian original. In almost all cases, the effect is to shift the register upwards, making the book sound more quaint, literary and Latinate. Interestingly, Woolf, who translated this text many years after his 1959 translation of *If This Is a Man*, is more flexible here, more aware of the need really to get the book into English. Since it seems unfair to criticize others without offering up something of one's own to be shot down, I'll give you my version too. Not that I imagine there will be anything "perfect" about my rendering; I just want to suggest what, after so many years in Italy, most of them teaching translation, I hear in the original, its pitch and voice. In short, I will try to give you the original without any "Italian flavour".

Here, at the beginning of the book, Levi is talking of the last days of Auschwitz as a concentration camp:

Perciò tutti i prigionieri sani furono evacuati, in condizioni spaventose, su Buchenwald e su Mauthausen, mentre i malati furono abbandonati a loro stessi.

Woolf:

Thus all healthy prisoners were evacuated, in frightful conditions, in the direction of Buchenwald and Mauthausen, while the sick were abandoned to their fate.

Goldstein:

Thus all the healthy prisoners were evacuated, under frightful conditions, to Buchenwald and to Mauthausen, while the sick were abandoned to themselves.

Parks:

So all the healthy prisoners were moved out in appalling circumstances to Buchenwald and Mauthausen, while the sick were left to fend for themselves.

"Abandoned to their fate" is a standard expression in English, in a fairly high register. The Italian makes no mention of fate. "Abandoned to themselves", a literal rendering of the Italian, is now rather archaic (Google's leading hits come from *The Gentleman's Magazine* in the early 1800s, theological tracts, quotations in history books). Of course we do use "abandoned" in modern English – an abandoned house, a novel the writer abandoned years ago – but we wouldn't say, as a young Italian might of an ordinary evening out, "then my friends went off together and I was abandoned to myself". We would say "left alone". Or, depending on the situation, "left to fend for myself". Because *abbandonare* is common in everyday Italian, and precisely the genius of Levi's style is to sound straightforward and everyday about even the most terrible events. Aside from this, it's worth noting here how Goldstein tends to repeat prepositions ("to Buchenwald and to Mauthausen"), something that is again ordinary practice in Italian, but unnecessary in English, introducing a slightly emphatic effect.

Shortly after leaving the camp, Levi is struck down by illness. As in *If This Is a Man*, there is a frequent contrast between the animal and the human, with illness here presented as a wild beast:

Pareva che la stanchezza e la malattia, come bestie feroci e vili, avessero atteso in agguato il momento in cui mi spogliavo di ogni difesa per assaltarmi alle spalle.

Woolf:

It seemed as if the weariness and the illness, like ferocious and cowardly beasts, had waited in ambush for the moment when I dismantled my defences, in order to attack me from behind.

Goldstein:

It seemed that the weariness and the illness, like fierce, vile beasts, had been lying in wait for the moment when I was stripped of every defense to assault me from behind.

Parks:

It felt as though illness and tiredness had been lying in wait like fierce, treacherous beasts to attack me from behind the moment I let my defences drop.

The Italian *vili* (plural of *vile*) is tricky here. It does not mean "vile" in the English sense of rude or repulsive. Woolf is right that it means "cowardly", but specifically when someone commits an act of aggression in an underhand, cowardly way. It's difficult to fit this idea neatly into the English, where we usually reserve "cowardly" for humans, not animals. Elsewhere, Woolf's "dismantled my defences" is bizarre. Goldstein tries to keep the idea of "undressing" (*mi spogliavo di ogni difesa* – literally "I undressed myself of every defence") with "stripped", but makes the notion passive ("I was stripped of every defence"), as if someone else had taken his defences away, whereas the Italian is more like "I shed/let go of my defences". In short, the relief of freedom has led to a lapse in Levi's determination to defend himself, and he falls ill.

This illness is serious, but after a month Levi begins to turn:

Verso la fine di febbraio, dopo un mese di letto, mi sentivo non già guarito, ma stazionario.

Woolf:

Towards the end of February, after a month in bed, I was not yet cured, and indeed began to feel but little improvement.

Goldstein:

Toward the end of February, after a month in bed, I felt not recovered but stable.

Parks:

Towards the end of February, after a month in bed, I felt stable if not actually recovered.

Woolf's version is confusing and wordy here. It seems odd "to begin to feel but little improvement". Surely "begin" should precede a change, not a stable situation. But Goldstein is equally disorienting. Type "I felt not recovered" in Google and you will find only one entry, Goldstein's translation. Nobody says this.

Meantime, in the infirmary, Levi has met Noah:

Noah si aggirava per le camerate femminili come un principe d'oriente, vestito di una giubba arabescata e variopinta, piena di toppe e di alamari. I suoi convegni d'amore sembravano uragani.

Woolf:

Noah wandered around the feminine dormitories like an oriental prince, dressed in an arabesque many-coloured coat, full of patches and braid. His encounters were like so many hurricanes.

Goldstein:

Noah wandered through the women's rooms like an oriental prince, wearing a varicolored jacket with an arabesque design, covered with patches and braid. His love meetings were like hurricanes.

Parks:

Noah wandered through the women's dormitories like an oriental prince, in a multi-coloured jacket full of patches, loops and arabesque patterns. His amorous couplings shook the roof.

Woolf ducks out of the lovemaking, while Goldstein's "love meetings" has a very odd sound (at least to my ear). The Italian *convegni d'amore* is slightly archaic and hence ironic here – not standard usage. Levi is making fun. However, *uragano* ("hurricane") is commonly used to describe anyone whose energy causes a disturbance and is very often applied affectionately to children: "Little Giovanni is a real *uragano*!" Since we don't often raise people to hurricane force in English (with the notable exception of Rubin "Hurricane" Carter), it seemed appropriate to look for another image to get the idea.

Here, describing a doctor, Levi playfully uses a word – *pococurante* – that, though it sounds Italian, doesn't exist in that language, but is borrowed from French or English:

> *...un medico, Pjotr Grigorjevič Dancenko, giovanissimo, gran bevitore, fumatore, amatore e pococurante;*

Woolf:

> ...a medical doctor, Pyotr Grigoryevich Danchenko, extremely young, a great drinker, smoker, lover, a negligent person;

Goldstein:

> ...a doctor, Pyotr Grigorievich Dancenko, who was very young, a great drinker, smoker, and lover, and indifferent to the job;

Parks:

> ...a doctor, Pyotr Grigorievich Dancenko, extremely young, a great drinker, smoker and lover, but not much of a medic.

The joke is that in Italy a GP can be referred to as a *medico curante*, literally a doctor who "takes care" or "cures". Levi plays on this, using *pococurante*, which to an Italian reader will have the sense of "little-caring", and is also close to the word *noncurante*, meaning "careless of" or "heedless to". So a great lover, but not a great doctor. There is no question of his being "indifferent to the job" or "a negligent person". The terms here are amused rather than critical. My version fails to get the humour of Levi's playfulness, but avoids missing the point and changing the tone.

Here Levi talks about another concentration-camp inmate:

Sopportava male la fatica e il gelo, ed era stato ricoverato in infermeria infinite volte...

Woolf:

He painfully endured the fatigue and the cold, and had been sent to the infirmary countless times...

Goldstein:

He didn't tolerate hard work and cold well, and had been admitted to the infirmary many times...

Parks:

He found the work and the cold hard to handle and had been admitted to the infirmary any number of times...

Even when they are not using a cognate, Woolf and Goldstein still choose Latinate words, "endured" and "tolerate" to translate *sopportare*, the verb Italians use on a daily basis for our "put up with", "stand", "handle" or "deal with" (e.g. *non lo sopporto più*: "I can't stand it any more"). As a result, the tone of the book becomes more solemn and literary. Then, if one wants to use these verbs, why not organize the syntax with a little more care: "He found the cold hard to endure", "He couldn't tolerate the cold" (but as soon as we start trying to imagine this sentence with "tolerate", we realize that this verb is usually used to indicate impatience – "I won't tolerate this behaviour!" – not endurance). Meantime, Levi's *infinite volte* has become merely "many times" in Goldstein's version.

Now let's focus on Galina, a young girl working in a Russian transition camp. Levi writes:

Di fronte a Galina mi sentivo debole, malato e sporco;

Woolf:

Face to face with Galina I felt weak, ill and dirty;

Goldstein:

In front of Galina, I felt weak, ill, and dirty;

Parks:

Around Galina I felt weak, ill and dirty;

Di fronte a does not mean "in front of". It's a "false friend" and a straight red mark when correcting a translation. In what way would Levi be "in front of" Galina? They are not standing in line! In purely positional terms *di fronte a* has the sense of "opposite" or "facing", which is why Woolf gives us the rather odd "face to face". More generally it can be used to put two things in relation or comparison. "*Di fronte a* ('confronted with') this new situation, I decided to resign." In Levi's example, it just means that when they were together and comparison was possible, he felt dirty, etc.; "next to Galina", or "in Galina's presence" would also work.

In translations, much is said about the virtues of faithfulness and literalness, though in these examples it is very often the awkward element that actually departs from the original. Indeed, the list of inappropriate cognates in Goldstein's *Truce* is so long and their cumulative effect so ponderous that one sometimes wonders whether the translator has spent much time living and thinking inside the Italian language. In any event, the moral of the tale is that what all we translators most need, aside from a thorough grounding in the language we are working from and a matching resourcefulness in the language we are working towards, is a damn good editor, someone who will go through our work meticulously, pointing out all interferences and awkwardness, inviting us to reconsider and reflect. This was always my first request when agreeing to do a translation: give me someone who can stop me from writing translationese. However well the kind of "ankylosed" prose we find in Goldstein's translation may be received among an English-reading literary public, it is a long way from the fluency and intimacy of Primo Levi.

The Translation Paradox

Glory, for the translator, is borrowed glory. There is no way around this. Translators are celebrated when they translate celebrated books. The best translations from the Italian I have seen in recent years are Geoffrey Brock's rendering of Pavese's collected poems, *Disaffections*, and Frederika Randall's enormous achievement in bringing Ippolito Nievo's great novel *Confessions of an Italian* into English. Brock, who has also given us an excellent version of *Pinocchio*, finds an entirely convincing English voice for the troubled Pavese. Randall turns Nievo's lively, idiosyncratic pre-Risorgimento prose into something sparklingly credible in English. However, neither of these fine books became the talk of the town, and their translators remain in the shadows.

The Complete Works of Primo Levi, which contained the work of ten different translators, offered an example of the general situation in microcosm. Levi is remembered above all for his Auschwitz memoir, *If This Is a Man*, and to a lesser degree for *The Truce*, an account of his return from the camps, and *The Periodic Table*, an engaging collection of autobiographical essays drawing on his work as a chemist. These three books, whose translations I discussed in the previous posts in this series, have monopolized critical comment on the *Complete Works* and inevitably brought prestige to their translators, Stuart Woolf and Ann Goldstein. But they amount to fewer than 600 of almost 2,800 pages. The other writings – comprising about 1,600 pages of stories and essays, 150 pages of poems, a novel, *If Not Now,*

When?, and a fiercely controversial reflection on concentration-camp survivors, *The Drowned and the Saved* – have received at best generous nods and asides from the critics, while their eight translators were fortunate if they were named at all.

In her editor's introduction to the three-volume edition, Ann Goldstein remarks on "the obvious difficulty... of many voices attempting to represent the voice of a single writer". This was a problem she previously faced when she worked as an editor (together with Michael Caesar and Franco d'Intino) and copy editor, as well as one of the translators, for the recent English-language version of Giacomo Leopardi's *Zibaldone*, an intellectual notebook from the early nineteenth century of immense vitality and complexity; the translation ran to more than 2,500 pages and involved a team of seven translators. Here as there, there is talk of a "uniform editorial standard" and the claim that it has resulted in a "consistently recognizable" tone. Here as there, this is not the case. The English *Zibaldone* alternated some brilliant, highly readable translations of Leopardi's strenuous thinking with pages so laden with Latinisms and lost in the poet's challenging syntax as to be illegible for anyone but the most dedicated academic. *The Complete Works of Primo Levi* likewise offers both sprightly and wooden performances. Ironically, the three books everyone is most interested in fall into the second category, while some of the least read works are brought to the page with exemplary freshness.

Jenny McPhee and Nathaniel Rich, both novelists in their own right, offer lively translations of texts that would likely never have been republished were it not for the great memoirs that preceded them and our consequent interest in Levi. Here is McPhee, translating 'The Versifier', a playful short story in which a professional poet, rhymester and copywriter invites a salesman to demonstrate a "poetry machine": feed this amiable contraption a subject, line length and metre, and it will quickly produce a (terrible) poem. Invited to ad-lib a poem, however, it shows a poignant interest in the poet's secretary:

> *Una ragazza da portare a letto*
> *Non c'è nulla di meglio, mi hanno detto.*
> *Non mi dispiacerebbe far la prova*
> *Per me sarebbe un'esperienza nuova:*
> *Ma per lei, poveretta, che tortura!*
> *Quest'intelaiatura è troppo dura.*
> *Ottone, bronzo, ghisa, bachelite:*
> *Tende la mano ed incontra una vite;*
> *Tende le labbra ed incontra una brossa;*
> *Mi stringe al seno, e si prende la scossa.*

McPhee gives:

> A girl worth taking to bed:
> There's nothing better, it's said.
> I wouldn't mind trying it, too,
> For me it would be something new:
> But for her, poor thing, what torture!
> My frame is rock hard, that's for sure.
> Bronze, cast iron, Bakelite, brass:
> She offers her hand and is met by things crass;
> She offers her lips and is met by a grock.
> She hugs me to her breast and gets quite a shock.

Of course McPhee has the advantage that in the general satire of the machine's rhyming capacities, the worse it sounds the better, so she can cheerfully get away with "for sure" rhyming with "torture", and simply invent the term "grock" where Levi introduces the obscure factory jargon *brossa* – a metallic brush – a word neither the poet or his secretary know. The poem is fun and McPhee gives us the feel of it, and indeed of the work as a whole.

Nathaniel Rich is equally energetic in his rendering of Levi's 1978 fictional work *The Wrench*. Here a talkative crane-fitter, Tino Faussone, tells the book's Levi-like narrator a series of stories taken from his working life around the world. The opening lines run thus:

Eh no: tutto non le posso dire. O che le dico il paese, o che le racconto il fatto: io però, se fossi in lei, sceglierei il fatto, perché è un bel fatto. Lei poi, se proprio lo vuole raccontare, ci lavora sopra, lo rettifica, lo smeriglia, toglie le bavature, gli dà un po' di bombé e tira fuori una storia; e di storie, ben che sono più giovane di lei, me ne sono capitate diverse. Il paese magari lo indovina, così non ci rimette niente; ma se glielo dico io, il paese, finisce che vado nelle grane, perché quelli sono brava gente ma un po' permalosa.

That *Eh no* announces the book's colloquial register with great determination. Rich gives:

No way – I'm not going to tell you everything. Either I tell you about the country or I give you the facts: if I were you, I'd take the facts because they're pretty good. Then, if you want to pass the story on to someone else, you can work it over, straighten it out, hone it, file off the burrs, flatten it with a hammer – and that way you'll make it your own. You know, I might be younger than you, but I've got lots of stories. Okay: maybe you'll figure out what country I'm talking about, that wouldn't be the worst thing in the world. But if I tell you its name – the country, that is – I'll get in trouble, 'cause the people there are nice, but a bit sensitive.

This is simply light years away from the "ankylosed", cognate-rich world of Goldstein and Woolf. It's true there are mistakes. Faussone doesn't want to reveal the name of the country in which the events took place. This is the sense of *tutto non le posso dire* – "I can't tell you everything". And he clarifies: "*O che le dico il paese, o che le racconto il fatto*" – literally: "Either I tell you what country, or I tell you what happened." There is no question of telling "*about* the country" and *il fatto*, an idiomatic usage, has the sense of the event, what happened – not, as Rich has it, "the facts". Towards the end of the paragraph, Faussone acknowledges that the narrator may guess the country: "*magari lo indovina, cosí non ci rimette niente*" – literally, "maybe you'll guess it, that way you don't lose anything", or more fluently, "that way you'll have it all". In difficulty with this expression, Rich invents: "that wouldn't be the worst thing in the world".

These are issues an editor should have picked up. After all, Goldstein's introduction had promised us "a rigorous degree of accuracy". That said, Rich has an admirably light touch that captures the playful tone of the book, and he is resourceful when it comes to dealing with its endless references to complex engineering equipment. Certainly if the book never achieves much celebrity, it will not be the translator's fault.

With time and energy one could place all the other translators in the Levi *Complete Works* project on a line between the two extremes of Woolf and Goldstein, on the one hand, and McPhee and Rich, on the other, pointing out who is more or less mistake-prone on the way. Alessandra and Francesco Bastagli, relative novices, would be nearer Goldstein; Antony Shugaar, Michael F. Moore, two extremely experienced translators, nearer the two novelists. Anne Milano Appel's contribution, the least significant in terms of number of pages and content, stands out as near perfect; she does not foreground zest and vitality as McPhee and Rich do, but is quietly brisk, which is just right for

Levi. She doesn't switch things around when they don't need it, but she knows how to make everything English. And she doesn't make mistakes that I can find. Here is Levi imagining a young girl who is developing wings:

Da parecchi giorni Isabella era inquieta: mangiava poco, aveva qualche linea di febbre, e si lamentava di un prurito alla schiena. I suoi dovevano mandare avanti la bottega e non avevano molto tempo da dedicare a lei. – Si starà sviluppando, – disse la madre; la tenne a dieta e le fece frizioni con una pomata, ma il prurito aumentò. La bambina non riusciva più a dormire; applicandole la pomata, la madre si accorse che la pelle era ruvida: si stava coprendo di peli, fitti, rigidi, corti e biancastri. Allora si spaventò, si consultò col padre, e mandarono a chiamare il medico.

Milano Appel's translation takes flight quite unobtrusively. Everything sounds right:

For some days, Isabella had been agitated: she was barely eating, was running a slight temperature and complained that her back itched. Her parents had the shop to run and didn't have much time for her. "She must be developing," her mother said. She kept her on a diet and rubbed her back with ointment, but the itching grew worse; the girl was unable to sleep. Her mother, applying the ointment, noticed that the skin felt rough: it was covered by a dense layer of short, stiff whitish hairs. Then she got frightened and discussed it with Isabella's father, and they sent for the doctor.

So the translations in the *Complete Works* range from excellent to pretty poor. But how much of this has emerged in the critical response to the book? This is the question I want to raise here. How much, or how little, did the polish, or lack of it, of the various renderings *matter*? James Wood in the *New Yorker* remarks that Levi's "best-known work has already benefited from fine English translation", this despite all the evident problems in Stuart Woolf's versions of *If This Is a Man* and *The Truce* that I laid out in an earlier article (though Wood does go on to criticize Michael Moore, rightly, for translating *avventura* as "ordeal" in *The Drowned and the Saved*). James Marcus, in *Harper's*, himself a translator, speaks of Goldstein in her editorial responsibility as having "finessed" the work of the different translators, entirely accepting her claim to have created a "consistent" tone and quality. True, he goes on, in a footnote, to point out a couple of embarrassing errors, and then in a separate blog post discusses further errors, all lexical, all from Goldstein and Woolf, but never the very evident problems of style. In general his whole attitude, like that of most other reviewers – indeed of most other reviews of any major work in translation – was one of automatic congratulation. Chunks of Levi are quoted in various publications, often with embarrassing infelicities, and nothing is said.

Of course, one explanation for this would be space. In my original *New York Review* essay on the *Complete Works* there seemed so much to say about Levi that I decided not to tackle the translations. I wanted to focus on the unevenness of the books themselves and what that tells us about Levi. Another explanation is a default diplomacy: so-and-so is generally spoken of as a superb translator so let's repeat the formula, thereby satisfying the translators' lobby who are always waiting to pounce on a reviewer who omits to mention the translator or translators. Some reputations are never questioned. We move in a small world where it's just not wise to say what you think. Of course, once a translated book has had commercial success, the publishers have an interest in talking up the translator, however little influence that person's work may have had on sales. In particular, when a major investment has been made in a project like Levi's *Works* or Leopardi's *Zibaldone*, the publishers inevitably seek to encourage our inveterate eagerness to pat ourselves on the back for our love of culture, our desire to believe that we now possess the author in our language and so on.

All this is understandable. Who wants to be the spoilsport to stand up and say that many pages of the *Zibaldone* were miserably translated, and that to an extent the project was a missed opportunity? But I believe the question goes deeper than this and is perhaps symptomatic of the time we live in and the diminishing importance of the written word, and in particular of literature, in our society. Simply, many readers, many critics, *don't notice*. Or if they do, don't particularly care. They read for content. The clamour of idioms about us has become so loud that we hardly notice when a translation, or indeed any piece of prose, is cluttered with incongruities. In fact, the writer whose work was above all an achievement of style and linguistic density, an exploration of what could be done with the language, directed at a community who could understand the nature of the experiment – Joyce, Woolf, Gadda, Faulkner – is largely a creature of the past. And where, as in the case of the *Zibaldone*, the reader or critic finds sentences that are unreadable and quite likely skips or abandons the book, they imagine that this is because the original was of this nature and the translation necessarily impenetrable. They may even admire the translator for having got it into English at all.

I remember in the 1990s a friend at a major Italian publishing house telling me that he and other editors had received a corporate directive instructing them to reduce the price paid for translations, because their market research had shown that the public couldn't tell the difference between good and bad translators. I was indignant. I was young. These days experience tells me that from the merely commercial point of view they were right. There are many poorly translated books that are highly praised and widely sold, in the US as in Europe.

So does translation matter? Does the choice of translator matter? Some translators' associations (in Germany for example) insist that a translator ought to be paid a royalty for the translation and share in the commercial success of the work, as if the individual translator had the same impact on the work as the author. This is nonsense. Umberto Eco was better translated by Geoffrey Brock and Richard Dixon than by William Weaver, but *The Name of the Rose,* which Weaver translated, was an infinitely better book than *The Mysterious Flame of Queen Loana* (Brock) or *Numero Zero* (Dixon). Why should the one translator grow rich and the others not? J.K. Rowling, Stieg Larsson and E.L. James are not difficult authors to translate. Would it really make sense to skew translators' earnings by giving vast amounts of money to those doing work that is immeasurably easier than, say, Jonathan Galassi's translations of Montale, or Anne Milano Appel's 2012 translation of Claudio Magris's impossibly convoluted novel *Blindly?* To introduce royalties would be to encourage the finest translators to drop literary work altogether and concentrate on genre novels.

Translation matters for those who want to be brought as close as possible to the original inspiration of books that matter (a group that does not necessarily include publishers' accountants). The choice of translator is crucial when a text is of such a nature that a very special affinity and expertise is required. The problem is that it is hard for the wider public or even the critics really to know whether they have been given a good translation, and not easy even for the editors who have the duty of choosing the translator, fewer and fewer of whom have appropriate second-language skills. So the inclination is to consign the book to a translator who has some reputation, deserved or not, and be done with it. In particular, there is a tendency to privilege those who gravitate around the literary world, as if this were some kind of guarantee of linguistic competence. It is not.

Some years ago, I gave an evening course in Milan for English-language translators working in the city who wanted to move from technical, business, legal and medical translations to literary translation. I was hugely impressed by their work. One woman in particular, who translated for AGIP, the Italian oil giant, gave excellent renderings of a range of Italian authors. In general, these were all people who knew Italian to a fault and who were daily involved in getting it into English. None of them would have been guilty of the clumsiness I pointed out in my previous pieces on the Levi translations.

Yet these translators were hardly given the time of day when they wrote to English and American publishers asking for work. Perhaps their years of business translations were considered a stigma. All the same, I suspect that Milano Appel is so good, so true in her pitch, because she has done such a wide range of non-literary translations in business, advertising and marketing, work that obliges one to become aware of how the language is used on a day-to-day basis. If I myself learnt how to translate more or less well it was because of the fifteen years spent translating just about every kind of document a society produces, from shoe fashion magazines to instructions for manufacturing diesel filters. My first literary translation, Alberto Moravia's *Erotic Tales*, which I was given before I had published any fiction of my own, seemed infinitely easier and more congenial than the daily fare of tourist brochures and quarrying-plant manuals.

So why, in her seventies now, is a fine translator like Milano Appel not better known? Because glory, for the translator, is borrowed glory. No book she has translated has captured the public imagination.

Raw and Cooked

How can I judge a translation if I don't know the original language? Time and again fellow reviewers have raised this question with me. We can tell if a book is fluent or not, elegant or not, lucid or not, but how do we know if the original is like this?

Conversely, if we can't judge the translation, how can we arrive at an opinion about the book itself? It seems poorly written, but perhaps that is just the translator. Or vice versa, of course. Are we reduced simply to saying that we like or don't like the package, without any notion of whom we should praise or blame?

This would seem to have been the conclusion of those who designed the new Man Booker International Prize. Until recently given for a lifetime's literary achievement to any author whose work is available in English, this year the rules changed and the prize is now awarded to a single foreign novel translated into English, the money involved – £50,000 – being shared equally by author and translator. 155 books were in the mix for this edition, representing, the organizers claimed, "the finest in global fiction". Orhan Pamuk, Elena Ferrante and Kenzaburō Ōe were all on the shortlist. The winner, however, *The Vegetarian*, came from outsider Han Kang, a Korean woman in her forties, and was translated by Deborah Smith, who is English. In an interview, Smith explains how, having completed a degree in English literature, she decided to become a translator. Monolingual until then, she chose Korean "pragmatically", because she had heard there was a lively literary scene in Korea and far fewer translators than for European languages. She herself proposed *The*

Vegetarian to an English publisher, who accepted it. It is the first novel she has translated.

None of the judges for the prize appear to know Korean. Nor do I. So the novel provides an excellent opportunity for asking whether we can get any separate impressions of the achievements of writer and translator.

A premise. The Hogarth edition of *The Vegetarian* comes complete with thirty-four endorsements and review quotations to prime us, as it were, before we tackle the text. We are told that the book is "gracefully written", "elegant", "assured", "poetic", "beguiling", "understated", "spellbinding", "precise", "spare" and "devastating". Playwright Deborah Levy praises its "cool, still, poetic but matter-of-fact short sentences, translated luminously by Deborah Smith, who is obviously a genius", while author James Morrow tells us that "Han Kang's slender but robust novel addresses many vital matters – from the politics of gender to the presumptions of the male gaze, the conundrum of free will to the hegemony of meat – with a dark élan that vegetarians and carnivores alike will find hypnotic, erotic, disquieting, and wise".

It all sounds very promising.

Unable to compare translation and original or even to check single English words against the corresponding Korean, since I cannot distinguish one Korean character from another, I have but one resource. I must consider the relationship between content and style in the English translation. In a literary text, a certain content manifests itself in a certain style. There is no separating the two. The difficulty with translation is always to reconstruct that relationship. The danger is that one winds up with a voice that may be fluent, but that sits uneasily with the content.

The Vegetarian is divided into three sections initially published as separate stories and written in quite different styles. Each has a simple plot. The first is narrated by a crass young man who has deliberately chosen for himself a plain, quiet, obedient wife in line with his limited but determined business ambitions. He is entirely happy with his choice until, one morning, he finds her throwing out all the meat from the fridge. Following an ugly dream, she has decided she will never again eat or cook meat. Unwisely, our narrator drags her to dinner with his business associates, who treat her with contempt. This part of the novel ends with a dramatic encounter with the wife's family during which her father first tries to force meat into her mouth then slaps her violently. She cuts her wrists.

The reader's sympathies of course are entirely with the wife, who is a victim of a rigid, uncaring, unthinking society, suffocating in its ancient traditions. We learn that she was beaten as a child by her ignorant, patriotic father, a Vietnam veteran. All in all it is a savage indictment of Korean culture. Oppressed by unhappy memories and denied all sympathy, the wife stops speaking and eating altogether. At one meal she "didn't so much as stick her chopsticks into the mouth-watering salad". It seems strange that our intensely carnivorous narrator, who is generally uninterested in his greens, should describe the salad as "mouth-watering".

The voice of the story, the unpleasant husband's, is stiff and formal, in line with this traditional and conventional mindset that his wife experiences as a straitjacket (along with her vegetarianism she also refuses to wear a bra, because she finds it constricting). So we have phrases like "Ultimately, I settled for a job where I would be provided with a decent monthly salary in return for diligently carrying out my allotted tasks". There is a rather nineteenth-century ring to it, as if we were reading an old translation of a Chekhov short story. Combining this stiffness with a determination to keep the prose "spoken" and idiomatic leads to some uneasy formulations. "However late I was in getting home," the husband tells us, "she never took it upon herself to kick up a fuss."

"To take something upon oneself", the *Cambridge Dictionary* tells us, is "to accept responsibility for something without being asked to do so". Does this make sense next to the idea of "kicking up a fuss" about a husband's later return? Is this Han Kang indicating the husband's limited grasp of idiom, or a translation issue? There is always a danger, when translating a spoken voice, of opting for the idiomatic at the expense of precision. During the unpleasant dinner with the husband's business associates, for example, we are told that "awkward silences… were now peppering the conversation". One can imagine a conversation peppered with obscenities, perhaps, but aren't silences just too long to be peppery? Earlier, complaining of his wife's reading habits, the narrator talks of her "reading books that looked so dull I couldn't even bring myself to so much as take a look inside the covers". Is that "looked"/"look" repetition in the original? And the overkill of "even bring myself to so much as look at"?

Sometimes this mix of the uptight and the colloquial creates an awkwardness at the limits of comprehensibility. Here the narrator is regretting that he didn't marry his healthy, meat-eating sister-in-law:

Taking in her nicely filled-out figure, big, double-lidded eyes, and demure manner of speaking, I sorely regretted the many things it seemed I'd ended up losing somehow or other, to have left me in my current plight.

Do old-fashioned literary formulas like "demure manner of speaking", "sorely regretted" and "current plight" correspond to the Korean here? Is the original equally muddled syntactically? I am honestly not sure how the grammar works at the end of the sentence. Despite the wife's "vulgar curses" in response to his attempts at lovemaking, the narrator tells us, in what now seems a caricature of insensibility, that finally "I managed to insert myself successfully". However, a few lines later he speaks of his wife remaining mute at breakfast "as per usual", a specifically English (rather than American) idiom from quite a different register, contemporary and ironic rather than formal and old-fashioned.

If these things look to me like translation niggles, other incongruities are more likely the author's responsibility. When the narrator finds his wife alone in the kitchen at night, he first describes what she is wearing and how she is standing ("ramrod straight"), then, confusingly, tells us the kitchen was "pitch black". So how did he see her? After which "Her profile swam toward me out of the darkness". This swimming out of darkness seems rather more literary and poetic than we would expect of our small-minded husband. A little later we hear of her retreating figure being "swallowed up beyond the door", when in fact she has simply gone into a room and closed the door.

This occasional concession of a novelistic, sometimes even poetic tone to the boorish husband is most blatant when the wife grabs a knife and attempts suicide in her family's presence:

> Blood ribboned out of her wrist. The shock of red splashed over white china. As her knees buckled and she crumpled to the floor, the knife was wrested from her by [her sister's] husband, who until then had sat through the whole thing as an idle spectator.

The fancy metaphor of blood "ribboning" seems totally out of line with our narrator's expressive abilities. Was it there in the Korean? As for the detail of the "shock of red" splashing on the white china, the less said the better. "Buckled", "crumpled", "wrested from" all seem standard novelese. How puzzling, though, to see the common and critical collocation "idle spectator" applied to the brother-in-law, who, understandably, has not been involved in the argument between the wife and her parents. Wouldn't "spectator" be enough?

Perhaps the explanation is that Han Kang hungers for melodrama so that the constraint of the narrating voice she has chosen sometimes seems as uncomfortably tight for her as bras seem for the wife. Indeed, the husband's story is sporadically interrupted by brief sections in italics that we take to be the wife's internal monologue, her dreams, her memories.

Try to push past the meat, there's no end to the meat, and no exit. Blood in my mouth, blood-soaked clothes sucked onto my skin.

In that barn, what had I done? Pushed that red raw mass into my mouth, felt it squish against my gums, the roof of my mouth, slick with crimson blood.

Sometimes these thoughts seem to go well beyond what we would expect of the wife, as she has been described, an ordinary young woman with a limited cultural background and no experience at all of expressing herself in words:

A sound, the elasticity of the instant when the metal struck the victim's head... the shadow that crumpled and fell gleams cold in the darkness.
They come to me now more times than I can count. Dreams overlaid with dreams, a palimpsest of horror. Violent acts perpetrated by night.

And so it goes on, a repository of melodramatic cliché. This can hardly be the translator's fault. (Though at the end of this section of the novel, after the husband has dreamt he is killing someone, he reaches out to his wife – the two are in the hospital – and touches her "philtrum". Is it just me, or is that word as rare as I suspect? In any event I had to look it up: it means the groove between upper lip and nose. Again it would be interesting to know if the Korean word used here was equally unusual.)

We could easily continue with example after example from the second and third parts of the novel, where a third-person narrator tells first how the wife's artist brother-in-law paints flowers and plants all over her naked body in an attempt to see the birthmark on her buttocks, and second how her sister despairs as the Vegetarian starves herself to death in an attempt to become a plant herself (often standing on her head imagining shoots emerging from her crotch). But there would be little point.

Looked at closely, the prose is far from an epitome of elegance, the drama itself neither understated nor beguiling, the translation frequently in trouble with register and idiom. Studying the thirty-four endorsements again, and the praise after the book won the prize, it occurs to me there is a shared vision of what critics would like a work of "global fiction" to be, and that *The Vegetarian* has managed to present itself as a candidate that can be praised in those terms. Ideologically, it champions the individual (woman) against an oppressive society (about which we know nothing, except that it seems "worse" than our own). Emotionally, it allows us to feel intense sympathy for a helpless victim, which is always encouraging for our self-esteem. Aesthetically, it offers moments of surrealism – typically in the wife's heated and unhappy imaginings, or the brother-in-law's fantasies of vegetable couplings – which we can see as excitingly exotic and a guarantee of a lively imagination. In this regard, the slightly disorienting effect of the translation can actually reinforce our belief that we are coming up against something new and different. But above all the writing must be *accessible*. The foreignness and exoticism must in no way present a barrier to easy reading; "matter-of-fact short sentences," Deborah Levy said. Some element in the work that allows the word "erotic" to be dropped in can only be positive.

Once it has been decided that the book fits the bill, all evidence of its unevenness and opportunism is set aside, and thirty-four authoritative quotations are placed as guardians front and back, defying the reader to disagree. And of course if the novel is the real thing then the translation must also be excellent, instead of just perhaps OK. Curiously, this barrage of praise and prizes begins to feel, for the independent reader, rather like the straitjacket of conformity that Han Kang's unhappy heroine is determined to throw off.

When Not to Translate

We live in a time of retranslation. New versions of the classics appear fairly regularly, and of course, as soon as the seventy years of copyright following an author's death runs out, there is a spate of new translations. So Proust and Thomas Mann have recently been retranslated into English, while writers like F. Scott Fitzgerald, Virginia Woolf and D.H. Lawrence are all reappearing in new versions in Europe.

The logic behind this phenomenon is clear enough. A translation inevitably reflects the language and style of its time. For later generations, a translation seems more reminiscent of our own past culture than the culture the work originated in. Consider Pope's *Iliad*:

> Achilles' wrath, to Greece the direful spring
> Of woes unnumber'd, heavenly goddess, sing!

How can one think of anything but eighteenth-century British poetry? How can one not feel it will be easier to read in Ian Johnston's 2010 rendering:

> Sing, Goddess, sing of the rage of Achilles, son of Peleus –
> that murderous anger which condemned Achaeans to
> countless agonies.

Or compare the Reverend Cary's *Inferno*, published in 1805:

In the midway of this our mortal life,
I found me in a gloomy wood, astray
Gone from the path direct

with Robert Hollander's from 2000:

Midway in the journey of our life
I came to myself in a dark wood,
for the straight way was lost.

In both these cases we feel an impediment to reading has been removed. Our translator is working directly from the older text into a modern idiom, albeit with a respect for the text's age and distance.

But are new translations always better, or always feasible, even? Some time ago I was asked to do a retranslation of the *Decameron*. Such a commission is an honour and a responsibility. And a huge investment of time. The Penguin Classics edition runs to more than one thousand pages. So before giving an answer I thought I'd try translating a couple of passages for myself. Here is a passage from the fourth story of the first day. A young monk, guessing that his lovemaking with a girl smuggled into his cell has been observed by his abbot, contrives to have the abbot find the girl there alone, in the hope that he will commit the same sin. I translated:

Seeing the abbot come in, the girl lost her head and started to cry, afraid she would be disgraced. Looking her over and finding her fresh and pretty, the abbot, old as he was, immediately felt the same hot carnal urge his young monk had felt, and began to say to himself: "Well, why not enjoy yourself while you can, trouble and strife are always on offer, if that's what you want. She's a pretty girl and no one knows she's

here; if I can get her to give me a good time, I can't see why
I shouldn't. Who will know? No one, ever, and a sin hidden
is half forgiven. You're hardly going to get a chance like this
again. Then, it's only wise, I'd say, to enjoy what the Good
Lord sends your way."

This was as close to the semantics of the original as I could
manage, but seemed drained of all its fourteenth-century energy.
Expressions like "hot carnal urge", "trouble and strife" or the
proverbial "a sin hidden is half forgiven" seem somewhat fake,
or simply quaint rather than authentic and vigorous. I checked
various other modern translations to see if they felt notably
different. Let's look at just one, G.H. McWilliam's 1972 translation, which is still the current Penguin Classics version:

When she saw the Abbot coming in, the girl was terrified out
of her wits, and began to weep for shame. Master Abbot, having looked her up and down, saw that she was a nice, comely
wench, and despite his years he was promptly filled with
fleshly cravings, no less intense than those his young monk
had experienced. And he began to say to himself: "Well, well!
Why not enjoy myself a little when I have the opportunity?
After all, I can have my fill of sorrow and afflictions whenever I
like. This is a fine-looking wench, and not a living soul knows
that she is here. If I can persuade her to play my game, I see
no reason why I shouldn't do it. Who is there to know? No
one will ever find out, and a sin that's hidden is half forgiven.
I may never get another chance as good as this. It's always a
good idea, in my opinion, to accept any gift that the Good
Lord places in our path."

There are 174 words here as opposed to my 137. And it's easy to
see why. In an attempt to rediscover the energy of the original,

McWilliam hams things up. "*La giovane… tutto smarrì,*" Boccaccio wrote, meaning the girl was quite lost or disoriented, not "terrified out of her wits." Nor did she weep for shame. She wept *temendo di vergogna,* afraid of shame, afraid she would be disgraced. Of course McWilliam prefers pat phrases whenever he can find them because the *Decameron* has the reputation of being colloquial and idiomatic. So we have "fine-looking wench" for *bella giovane* in the Italian. Or "play my game" for *fare i piacer miei* (literally, "do what I want/give me pleasure"). The strategy reaches its climax in "any gift that the Good Lord places in our path", where neither gifts nor paths are mentioned in the original. It all sounds dangerously close to Christmas pantomime.

The problem is that much of the pleasure of reading the *Decameron* in Italian comes from feeling the language's distance from, but also closeness to modern Italian, feeling how surprisingly straightforward, almost brusque it is. There is no quaintness in it at all. Here is the original:

La giovane vedendo venir l'abate tutta smarrì, e temendo di vergogna cominciò a piagnere. Messer l'abate, postole l'occhio addosso e veggendola bella e fresca, ancora che vecchio fosse sentì subitamente non meno cocenti gli stimoli della carne che sentiti avesse il suo giovane monaco; e fra se stesso cominciò a dire: «Deh, perché non prendo io del piacere quando io ne posso avere, con ciò sia cosa che il dispiacere e la noia, sempre che io ne vorrò, sieno apparecchiati? Costei è una bella giovane e è qui che niuna persona del mondo il sa: se io la posso recare a fare i piacer miei, io non so perché io nol mi faccia. Chi il saprà? Egli nol saprà persona mai, e peccato celato è mezzo perdonato. Questo caso non avverrà forse mai più: io estimo ch'egli sia gran senno a pigliarsi del bene, quando Domenedio ne manda altrui.»

149 words. It's all very rapid, and flexible, and when it does move towards the bawdy (*veggendola bella e fresca*) or the proverbial (*peccato celato è mezzo perdonato*), it all seems to fit. It even rhymes. The language, the content, the sentiments mesh. I went to check a version in modern Italian – because as with Chaucer there are modern versions – and immediately had the same impression that I had with my own attempt: it was correct enough, but all the energy was gone. However, what finally decided me not to accept this commission was my discovery of the very first translation of the same passage in John Florio's 1620 edition.

Florio, we remember, was the first translator of Montaigne; his Italian father had been a Franciscan friar, and some people have made a case for claiming that he was actually William Shakespeare himself. Here he is:

> But finding it to be the Lord Abbot, shee fell on her knees weeping, as fearing now to receive publike shame, by being betrayed in this unkinde manner. My Lord Abbot looking demurely on the Maide, and perceiving her to be faire, feate, and lovely; felt immediately (although he was olde) no lesse spurring on to fleshly desires, then the young Monke before had done; whereupon he beganne to conferre thus privately with himselfe. Why should I not take pleasure, when I may freely have it? Cares and molestations I endure every day, but sildome find such delights prepared for me. This is a delicate sweete young Damosell, and here is no eye that can discover me. If I can enduce her to doe as I would have her, I know no reason why I should gaine-say it. No man can know it, or any tongue blaze it abroade; and sinne so concealed, is halfe pardoned. Such a faire fortune as this is, perhaps hereafter will never befall me; and therefore I hold it wisedome, to take such a benefit when a man may enjoy it.

Reading this, I experienced exactly the pleasures I feel reading Boccaccio in Italian. Albeit nearly three hundred years after the original was written, Florio still moves in a world where the whole thing makes sense, doesn't need to be quaint. And he is a supreme stylist too. He can find exactly the idiom in the English of his time. However good a translator might be today, I doubt whether the same level of conviction is possible. Certainly, I didn't feel I could achieve it.

Perhaps this perception of mine is false, due to my inability to judge language written so long ago. But I think not. I suspect what it suggests is the importance of finding the right translator for the first translation of a literary work, one who has a genuine affinity with the style of the original and, above all, can root it into our own literature in a moment when it makes sense, when the culture can really receive it in its own idiom. In Italy, with the lapse of copyright on Faulkner's writing, there have been a number of new Faulkner translations that are doubtless more semantically accurate than those made back in the Forties and Fifties. And yet those old translations – made when a modernist work was still a matter of excitement rather than an aesthetic museum piece – seem more aware of the energy and spirit of the original and certainly a better read than more recent academic efforts.

A No-Nonsense Machiavelli

"Why did you translate Machiavelli, if you didn't see the point of translating Boccaccio?" Since I wrote about my decision not to retranslate *The Decameron,* a number of readers have asked me this question. I had explained that I turned down the invitation to retranslate Boccaccio's wonderful stories because it seemed impossible in modern English to give the text the life and credibility it has both in the original, but also in John Florio's marvellous version from 1620. Not only was Florio himself a genius, but one senses that the English of his time was closer than ours to the spirit of the events described; it was drenched in religious reference, and he was able to say things easily that seem forced or false in our idiom today.

Matters are rather different with Machiavelli, or at least Machiavelli's *The Prince*. First, it isn't fiction. He is not intent on evoking the amours of ageing abbots or the confessions of witty usurers. Machiavelli, in exile after a long political career and living in the most turbulent times, wanted to say something clear and comprehensible about how power is won and lost – in short, to turn politics into a science. One sentence in particular from his opening dedication to Lorenzo de' Medici (not Il Magnifico, but a later Lorenzo) reads as both guidance and encouragement for all future translators:

I haven't aimed for a fancy style or padded the book out with long sentences or pompous, pretentious words, or any of the irrelevant flourishes and attractions so many writers use; I didn't want it to please for anything but the range and seriousness of its subject matter.

This doesn't mean, of course, that there aren't all kinds of rhetorical strategies in *The Prince*, or that the text shouldn't be entertaining. But the sense comes first; the language must not get in the way of the argument.

Yet when we turn to the original, language *does* get in the way, and not just for the foreigner who acquired his Italian in his twenties. Written in 1513, *The Prince* is not easily comprehensible to Italians today. The obstacle is not so much the vocabulary, most of which is still standard in Italian; rather it has to do with extreme compression of thought, obsolete and sometimes erratic grammar and, above all, a syntax in which subordinate and pre-modifying clauses abound in ways the modern reader is simply not used to.

If you settle down with the original and immerse yourself in it, you do begin to make sense of the author's claim to straightforwardness. Machiavelli has a spoken, flexible, often brusque voice; but these qualities manifest themselves in ways that seem disorienting to us today. In Chapter 21, for example, Machiavelli observes that if your state has two larger neighbours and those neighbours go to war, it is a mistake for you to remain neutral. You have to take sides. Here is Edward Dacres's 1640 translation, the first to be published in English:

A prince is also well esteemed when he is a true friend or a true enemy; when without any regard he discovers himself in favour of one against another; which course shall always more profit than to stand neuter: for if two mighty ones that are thy neighbours, come to fall out, or are of such quality, that one of them vanquishing thou art like to be in fear of the vanquisher, or not; in either of these two cases, it will ever prove more for thy profit, to discover thyself, and make a good war of it: for in the first case, if thou discoverest not thy selfe, thou shalt alwaies be a prey to him that overcomes, to the contentment and satisfaction of the vanquisht; neither shalt thou have reason on thy side, nor anything else to defend or receive thee. For he that overcomes will not have any suspected friends that give him no assistance in his necessity: and he that loses, receives thee not, because thou wouldst not with thy arms in hand run the hazard of his fortune.

It is all comprehensible enough, but hard work, and it is impossible not to be distracted by old English usages, which drain energy from the argument. At the tricky core of the passage is the moment when Machiavelli says of these neighbouring powers: "*o sono di qualità che, vincendo uno di quelli, tu abbia a temere del vincitore, o no.*" Literally, he is saying that the neighbouring countries

either are of qualities that, winning one of those, you ought to fear the winner, or not.

Dacres has it:

or are of such quality, that one of them vanquishing thou art like to be in fear of the vanquisher, or not.

If we turn to more modern translations, things improve, but not dramatically. Here is W.K. Marriott's highly respected 1908 version:

they are of such a character that, if one of them conquers, you have either to fear him or not.

This is neither straightforward nor elegant. George Bull's 1961 translation for Penguin Classics, which I was being invited to replace, gives:

> either they are such that, if one of them conquers, you will be in danger, or they are not.

This is a little closer to modern prose, yet you still can't help feeling that nobody trying to get this idea across in English today would introduce the second part of the alternative as Bull does by tagging "or they are not" onto the end of the sentence after the interpolation of an "if" clause. If we follow Bull's general structure, but move the "if" clause to the end – "either they are or they aren't such that if one of them conquers, you will be in danger" – the sentence gains in fluency, but still seems unnecessarily fussy where the original feels brutally direct. I remember looking at this sentence a very long time before appreciating that if one shifted the alternative aspect towards the verb "fear" and away from a description of the two states, the idea remains the same, but can now be expressed much more tersely:

> you may or may not have reason to fear the winner.

Some time later, the whole paragraph would come out like this:

> A ruler will also be respected when he is a genuine friend and a genuine enemy, that is when he declares himself unambiguously for one side and against the other. This policy will always bring better results than neutrality. For example, if you have two powerful neighbours who go to war, you may or may not have reason to fear the winner. Either way it will always be better to take sides and fight hard. If you do have cause to fear but stay neutral, you'll still be gobbled up by the

winner to the amusement and satisfaction of the loser; you'll have no excuses, no defence and nowhere to hide. Because a winner doesn't want half-hearted friends who don't help him in a crisis; and the loser will have nothing to do with you since you didn't choose to fight alongside him and share his fate.

Rightly or wrongly, I fell for the challenge of seeking out these reformulations, looking for every possible way to make the sentences sharp and direct while delivering exactly the sense of the original and keeping the no-nonsense tone. Rather than a liberty, this seemed right in line with Machiavelli's desire that the work be free of all "irrelevant flourishes".

But there are other challenges for a translator of *The Prince*. Written, an English cardinal claimed, "by Satan's finger", and put on Pope Paul IV's Index of Prohibited Books in 1559, Machiavelli's little treatise would be blamed for more or less every act of political ruthlessness in Europe over the following two centuries, not least Henry VIII's dissolution of the monasteries and the St Bartholomew Day's massacre in France in 1572. Very soon "Machiavelli" would be a popular term of denigration; Mach Evil and Mach-a-villain were typical English corruptions. By the end of the sixteenth century, "Machiavellian" was firmly established in the language as an adjective describing cold, clever, immoral calculation.

The result is that translators come to *The Prince* with prejudices; one is tempted to play to the reader's expectations, laying on Machiavelli's supposed cynicism at the expense of the text's surprising subtlety. Let me give a banal example from Bull's generally very faithful 1961 translation. At the end of Machiavelli's account of the rise and fall of the ruthless Cesare Borgia, having explained how he lost power when his father, Pope Alexander, suddenly and unexpectedly died and a pope hostile to Borgia was elected, Machiavelli writes: "*Raccolte io adunque tutte le azioni del duca, non saprei riprenderlo.*" Literally: "Having gathered then all the actions of the duke, I would not know how to reprimand/find fault with/reproach him."

Bull gives: "So having summed up all that the duke did, I cannot possibly censure him."

Here the word "censure" has a strong moral connotation, and the statement is made stronger still by the introduction of "can't possibly", which seems a heavy interpretation of the standard Italian formula: "I wouldn't know how to". In Bull's version it seems that Machiavelli is making a point of telling us that he has no *moral* objections to anything Cesare Borgia did, this in line with the author's reputation for cynicism.

But if we read the opening line of the next paragraph, it's clear that Machiavelli is not thinking in moral terms at all: "*Solamente si può accusarlo nella creazione di Iulio pontefice, nella quale lui ebbe mala elezione.*" Literally: "The only thing Borgia can be accused of is his role in the election of Pope Julius, where he made a bad choice"; that is, as far as his own interests were concerned, Borgia backed the wrong man, the man who destroyed him. And this brings us to the true nature of the "scandal" of *The Prince*: it is not that Machiavelli advocates or glorifies immoral behaviour; it is that he ignores morality altogether. He is entirely focused on the simple question of how to achieve and hold power, by whatever method. So with *The Prince* more than with any other text I can remember, it was important never to bring in one's own moral position, or reaction to Machiavelli's refusal to assume a moral position, into the translation.

But let's finish on a lighter note. While translators have played up Machiavelli's cynicism, they have also been rather prudish about any sexual reference. Machiavelli was a notorious womanizer, and in *The Prince* he believed he was addressing an audience of men who had no worries about political correctness. At the end of his book, discussing the way different personalities will mesh positively or negatively with different circumstances, he observes that there is no one type of person suitable for every situation. All the same, there are certain attitudes that are generally more successful than others; and he comes out with the famous – or infamous – line, "*la fortuna è donna, et è necessario, volendola tenere sotto, batterla et urtarla*". Literally: "fortune is woman, and it is necessary, wanting to keep her underneath, to beat her and shove her".

Clearly the image is a sexual one. Why else would he write "keep her underneath"? *Battere* and, particularly, *urtare* were both used colloquially to describe sex, from the male point of view. Like it or not, this is Trump territory. Machiavelli isn't talking about wife-beating. But many translators are hesitant; Marriot, very cautiously and literally, gives: "fortune is a woman, and if you wish to keep her under it is necessary to beat and ill-use her". Bull has: "fortune is a woman and if she is to be submissive it is necessary to beat and coerce her". The sex is gone.

Let me conclude, then, with the whole passage as it came out after endless revisions. No doubt if he were alive today, Machiavelli would see Trump's triumph as an extraordinary demonstration of the soundness of the advice he gives here:

To conclude then: fortune varies but men go on regardless. When their approach suits the times they're successful, and when it doesn't they're not. My opinion on the matter is this: it's better to be impulsive than cautious; fortune is female and if you want to stay on top of her you have to slap and thrust. You'll see she's more likely to yield that way than to men who go about her coldly.

The Expendable Translator

Is a translator effectively the co-author of a text, and if so, should he or she be paid a royalty as authors are?

After presenting a book of mine – or rather, its German translation – in Berlin, I found myself in a bar discussing this question with two experienced translators, Ulrike Becker and Ruth Keen. Rather than the nature of a translator's co-authorship itself, our discussion was kicked off by the fact that very few translators actually receive major benefits from royalties – even in Germany, where publishers are obliged to grant them. Over a long career, Ruth just once received a handsome €10,000-plus when a book about Napoleon's march on Moscow unexpectedly took off. Ulrike once received a couple of thousand when a literary novel made it onto the best-seller list. Otherwise, it's peanuts.

Why is this?

As in most countries, German literary translators are paid for their work on the basis of its length; something that, in this case, is calculated at a rate of around £15–20 a page. Not a lot. In the US or England, far fewer literary works are translated, and rates vary a great deal. But if a royalty is granted at all (and I for one was never given a royalty in the US), the initial payment based on length is usually considered an advance against it. Hence, if a translator has been paid, say, £6,000 for a book and granted a royalty of one per cent on a cover price of £15, the book would need to sell 40,000 copies before the royalty brought in any additional money. And 40,000 copies is an unusually big sale.

However, as Ruth explains to me, German law has been generous to translators, and a recent court ruling ordered that the initial payment must *not* be offset against royalties. What the ruling didn't do, however, was prevent the publishers from establishing a threshold below which royalties would not be paid, usually set at 5,000 or 8,000 copies, while the royalty will be as low as 0.8 per cent, or even 0.6 per cent. Since in Germany few books sell more than 5,000 copies, the result is that few translators see any money from these arrangements.

All the same, the occasional jackpot is surely better than none at all. So you would think. Ulrike tells me the story of Karin Krieger, who became a translators' hero when, in 1999, she took the publisher Piper to court over a royalty question. Krieger had translated three novels by the Italian writer Alessandro Baricco. When these began to sell well, she tried to get the publishers to honour a rather vague contractual clause granting her "a fair share of the profits" (royalties were not mandatory at that time). The publisher responded, unexpectedly and quite unusually, by having the books retranslated by another translator with a contract more favourable to the publisher.

After five years' litigation, Krieger eventually won her case and the money she was owed, but the sequence of events suggests the essential difference between translators and authors: Piper could never have tried to deprive Baricco of his royalties, since without him there would have been no books and no sales. He was not replaceable. But, however fine Krieger's translations, the publisher felt that the same commercial result could be achieved with another translator. It's not that translation work is ever easy; on the contrary. Simply that it rarely requires a *unique* talent. Krieger wasn't *essential*. She could be replaced.

At this point it's worth remembering why royalties were introduced in the first place. Before the eighteenth century, writers would sell a work to a printer for a lump sum, and the printer would make little or much, depending on how many copies they managed to sell. Writers, seeing printers grow rich (or some printers), wanted a share of the wealth they felt that they, more than anyone else, had created; hence in the early eighteenth century the first move, in Britain, to concede that writers owned what later came to be called "intellectual property" – their writing – and therefore had a right to a percentage of the income for every copy sold.

It could be argued that while this was "fair" as an arrangement between printers and authors, it hardly meant that a writer's income would reflect the quality of their writing and the work put into it – would, that is, be fair in some absolute sense. Today a blockbuster that sells globally – Dan Brown, Stephenie Meyer – will make its author many millions, while a fine work of poetry might bring in just a few hundred dollars. If anything, one could say that royalties were an invitation to writers to aim their work at the largest possible audience able to afford a mass-market paperback.

That said, whatever is in that paperback really is the author's creation. He or she will have had to sit down and write a substantial piece of work, not knowing how it will come out, not knowing for sure whether a publisher will buy it or whether, having bought it, they will be able to sell it. In short, the author has to fill an empty space, to create something where there was nothing. The translator, on the other hand, is in most cases commissioned to do a job. It could be the blockbuster, it could be the poetry. Sentence by sentence, the work is already there. However difficult it may be bringing it into another language, translators do not have to start from scratch, and they rarely have much choice, at least at the beginning of their careers, as to what kind of work they are translating. Certainly, in my own experience, nothing could be more different than settling down to a day's writing as opposed to a day's translating.

Two ideas drive the now decades-old campaign to extend royalty payments to translators. The first is practical: since publishers have tended to resist paying rates that would constitute a decent income for translators, one that corresponds to the professional skill and long hours involved, introducing a royalty clause into the contract ensures that, at least in cases where a translated book makes serious money, the translator will get some share of it. The second is conceptual: every translation is different, every translation requires a degree of creativity – hence the translation is "intellectual property" and as such should be considered authorship and receive the same treatment authors receive.

The problem with the first of these ideas is that, in so far as a translator's income is royalty-based, it will depend entirely on how publishers distribute the translations they commission. If, for example, we imagine two German translators with the same qualities and one is commissioned to translate *Fifty Shades*, Part V, and the other a book of short stories by a first-time New Zealand writer, one will make a fortune and the other very likely a pittance. Of course, the same is true, as we said, for the authors. If both receive ten per cent per copy, E.L. James will grow fabulously rich and the New Zealand short-story writer, however brilliant, would be well advised not to leave his regular job. Yet royalties are not a divisive issue among writers for the simple reason that, whatever one thinks of the qualities of a work like *Fifty Shades*, no one disputes that E.L. James was the person who had the idea for the book and took the risk of writing it. It is her work; it reflects her mind. Let her have her ten per cent.

The same is not true for the translator, for whom translating *Fifty Shades* with a royalty is simply a huge windfall for a task that may even be easier than translating far less remunerative books. What's more, one can safely disclaim all responsibility for the embarrassing content! At this point the institution of royalties threatens to divide translators. An Italian translator told me how all Dan Brown's translators had been brought together in Europe to receive the novel *Inferno* and be briefed on various translation issues. The French translator was in an excellent mood, since France, like Germany, now compels publishers to grant royalties. Others were bound to reflect that they would be receiving only a few thousand dollars for the whole six hundred pages, no matter how well their translation of the book sold.

The second, conceptual argument is more interesting, but no less problematic. That translation requires creativity is indisputable. As a translator myself, I have no desire to undermine the dignity of the craft. But is this creativity of a kind that constitutes "authorship"? Here are four versions of the opening lines of Dostoevsky's *Notes from the Underground*:

I am a sick man... I am a spiteful man. I am an unattractive man. I believe my liver is diseased. However, I know nothing at all about my disease, and do not know for certain what ails me. I don't consult a doctor for it, and never have, though I have a respect for medicine and doctors. Besides, I am extremely superstitious, sufficiently so to respect medicine, anyway (I am well-educated enough not to be superstitious, but I am superstitious). No, I refuse to consult a doctor from spite. That you probably will not understand. Well, I understand it, though.

– Constance Garnett, 1918

I am a sick man... I am an angry man. I am an unattractive man. I think there is something wrong with my liver. But I

293

don't understand the least thing about my illness, and I don't know for certain what part of me is affected. I am not having any treatment for it, and never have had, although I have a great respect for medicine and for doctors. I am besides extremely superstitious, if only in having such respect for medicine. (I am well educated enough not to be superstitious, but superstitious I am.) No, I refuse treatment out of spite. That is something you will probably not understand. Well, I understand it.

– Jessie Coulson, 1972

I am a sick man... I'm a spiteful man. I'm an unattractive man. I think there is something wrong with my liver. But I cannot make head or tail of my illness and I'm not absolutely certain which part of me is sick. I'm not receiving any treatment, nor have I ever done, although I do respect medicine and doctors. Besides, I'm still extremely superstitious, if only in that I respect medicine. (I'm sufficiently well educated not to be superstitious, but I am.) No, it's out of spite that I don't want to be cured. You'll probably not see fit to understand this. But I do understand it.

– Jane Kentish, 1991

I am a sick man... I am a wicked man. An unattractive man. I think my liver hurts. However, I don't know a fig about my sickness, and am not sure what it is that hurts me. I am not being treated and never have been, though I respect medicine and doctors. What's more, I am also superstitious in the extreme; well, at least enough to respect medicine. (I'm sufficiently educated not to be superstitious, but I am.) No, sir, I refuse to be treated out of wickedness. Now, you will certainly not be so good as to understand this. Well, sir, but I understand it.

– Richard Pevear and Larissa Volokhonsky, 1993

One can make all kinds of distinctions between these translations. "Spiteful", "angry", and "wicked", in the opening line, suggest three rather different qualities; which is right, or at least closer to the original? Why do three of the translations later cite this same quality – "spite", "wickedness" – as the reason why the narrator has not sought a treatment for his illness, while one, the translation that uses "anger", does not? We can only assume that the original uses the same word twice, but one translator has chosen not to respect that repetition. Two of the translations have a generic "know nothing at all" or "the least thing" about the narrator's illness, while one has "cannot make head or tail", introducing an image that risks getting confused with the anatomy, while the most recent translation oddly gives the most old-fashioned idiom, "don't know a fig".

Where two translations have a "Besides", and one a "What's more", the other has nothing. One translation introduces a "sir" – "No, sir", "Well, sir" – while the others do not; is it possible that all the other three translators would eliminate this "sir" if it were there? And why do two translators offer interesting nuances in the previous sentence – "you'll probably not see fit to understand this", "you will certainly not be so good as to understand this" – as if understanding were a matter of disposition rather than intellect, while the other two just give "you probably will not understand"?

There is simply no end to drawing fine distinctions between translations, discussing them in relation to the original and the cultural setting of the language of arrival or their own internal consistency. Yet all four of these translations are recognizably the same text. And Dostoevsky's main stylistic strategies emerge powerfully in all of them, above all the narrator's pleasure in parading his own perversity, his habit of qualifying everything he says in unexpected ways, of undermining received ideas (is it really superstitious to respect doctors?), of engaging, challenging and mocking the reader, and so on. Indeed, the more translations we have, the more we appreciate how overwhelmingly the text depends on Dostoevsky's unique authorship. Does it make sense, then, to talk of the translator's "co-authorship"? Why does translation have to be *likened* to something it is not? One might argue, of course, that Dostoevsky being long dead and his work out of copyright, the publishers could afford to pay a royalty since they are not paying one to the author. But that is a practical rather than a conceptual issue. Four translations of almost any text, ancient or contemporary, would yield the same results.

Some days after our meeting in Berlin, Ruth Keen emailed me the results of a questionnaire on earnings conducted by the German Translators Union. Five hundred and ninety-eight people had responded, and there were plenty of intriguing statistics: that almost sixty per cent of books translated had come from English, for example; that though around eighty per cent of translators were women, men tended to earn about £0.85 more per page; that work considered difficult was paid only marginally more per page than work considered easy (this despite the fact that the extra time taken over a difficult text might amount to a multiple of two or three, or even ten). But most of all, having presented a battery of statistics on royalties, the report lamented that low sales and high thresholds before royalties kicked in meant that it was extremely unusual for translators to benefit from them.

Where do these reflections leave us when it comes to pay and recognition for the wonderful work translators do? My own feeling is that the problem is less difficult than everyone pretends;

that it surely would not be impossible to bring together editor, translator and, say, an expert in translation from this or that language to establish how demanding a text is, how much time will be involved in translating it and what would be a reasonable payment for doing so. Perhaps it is time for translators and translators' associations to focus on putting such arrangements in place, without getting bogged down in the vexed question of authorship and royalties.

Gained in Translation

"But isn't it all just subjective?"

The scene is a Translation Slam, so-called. Two translators translate the same short passage and discuss their versions with a moderator in front of an audience of other translators. "Slam" suggests violent struggle and eventual victory or defeat. In reality, it's all very polite and even protective. There will be no vote to decide which version wins. Nobody is going to be humiliated.

All the same, the question of which choice is better comes up again and again. Right now, we're looking at the difference between "group" and "phalanx" in the phrases "commander of a group of loyal knights" and "commander of a phalanx of faithful men" – both translations of the Italian *comandante a una schiera di fedeli*.

The translator who has used "knights" explains that, since the "commander" in question is King Arthur, the *fedeli* or "faithful" whom he commands would surely be the Knights of the Round Table. The translator who has used "phalanx" explains that the Italian word *schiera*, as he sees it, means men arranged in a particular formation or order. And a phalanx would be such a formation.

What about "faithful" and "loyal"? "Faithful" alliterates with "phalanx". "Loyal" commonly collocates with "knights", and perhaps borrows a corroborating aura from its assonance with "royal".

We discuss all this for some time, until someone in the audience objects, "Isn't it all just subjective?" Meaning, this debate is pointless. *De gustibus non est disputandum*. Once the literal meaning has been more or less respected, a translation choice, or indeed any literary usage or style, is merely a question of personal taste. You like it or you don't.

The objection is persuasive, but is it true that aesthetic preferences are "just subjective"? We need to put some pressure on this idea. Does such a description match our experience of books, theatre, films and music? Not all our dealings with books are arbitrary. Young children tend to like a certain kind of story, a certain manner of storytelling, then they "grow out of it". This or that narrative formula begins to seem too simple, perhaps. Adolescents might enjoy romance or fantasy fiction, then their accumulating experience leads them to look elsewhere.

Two facts seem obvious here. Any element of choice is limited. The child cannot help first liking such and such a story, then eventually putting it aside. When your mother reads you *Where the Wild Things Are*, you are immediately hooked. Or not. So it's true that one simply likes or doesn't like something. You can't choose to respond positively to "Earth has not anything to shew more fair" if it doesn't grab you. And if you like *Fifty Shades of Grey*, you like it, even though it might be convenient to say you don't.

But it's also true that when preferences shift they do so *for a reason*, if not as a result of reasoning. Growing up, one brings more context and experience, more *world*, to one's reading, and this "more" changes one's taste. We might even say this new experience changes the person and with the person the book. At this point, earlier preferences will likely be disparaged, or fondly set aside.

From this observation, it's a small step to the idea of education and learning. I deliberately, systematically increase my experience and knowledge in order to have a richer encounter with what I read. The appropriateness of this approach is obvious when, say, reading in a second language: I know enough French to read *Bonjour Tristesse*, perhaps, but not enough to appreciate Proust. Or when reading things from other times: I pick up *The Faerie Queene* and am soon aware that the experience would be less frustrating if I knew more about the period and the genre. Our responses and preferences are not arbitrary: they depend on what we bring to what we read or watch.

Does this mean we can say that this preference is better than that? Or that this critical reading is superior to another? Let's go back to the Translation Slam. The passage we're looking at is the opening, three short paragraphs, of *L'isola di Arturo*, by Elsa Morante, which was a major best-seller when it was published in 1957. The first thing that strikes the reader is the way a highly elaborate style, packed with parentheses, subordinates and rhetorical outbursts, has been placed in the mouth of someone remembering what it was like to be a little boy. Here is an unapologetically literal translation of the first paragraph, to give you an idea:

> One of my first boasts had been my name. I had soon learnt (it was he, it seems to me, who was first to inform me of it) that Arturo is a star: the fastest and brightest light of the constellation of Boötes, in the northern sky! And that what's more this name was also borne by a king of ancient times, commander of a band of loyal men: who were all heroes, like their king himself, and by their king treated as equals, like brothers.

As an evocation of childhood, this is hardly *Huckleberry Finn* or *The Catcher in the Rye*. Or even *David Copperfield*. How to deal with it? One of the translators felt that the challenge of the Slam was to translate the passage in isolation, so he hasn't, he tells us, looked up the novel or read any further. In the Italian, he finds the style over-elaborate in places; it needs reining in, he feels, because English doesn't do these things.

The other translator says she initially felt disoriented by this extravagant voice and so found a copy of the novel and read on. What did she find? The narrator tells of his lonely boyhood on the island of Procida off the Bay of Naples. His mother died giving birth to him. His father – who turns out to be the "he" of the second sentence – is mostly absent. Aided by a couple of elderly peasant folk, Arturo grows up in a house mysteriously known as the House of Rascals, in the company of a cheerful dog. The house is full of classical literature, myths and heroes and epic wars, which become the boy's only education; so he spends his days in a fantasy world imagining grand exploits, beside his dog, in his Mediterranean paradise, yearning for the presence of a father, who, Ulysses-like, is always travelling. Alas, with time Arturo will discover that the reality behind the House of Rascals and his father's absence is depressingly squalid. The book ends as he abandons his boyhood island for the continent of adulthood.

The elaborate nature of the style aligns with pleasurable illusion, pretensions, posturings and boyish boasts that are inflated only to be later deflated and disappointed. Looking at the translations, one of the slammers has talked about being "proud of my name"; one has kept the idea of boasting. One has talked about Arturo being "the name of a star"; one has stayed closer to the original and said "Arthur is a star". One has simplified and shortened the paragraph; one hasn't. Perhaps we can't decide which of these two brief translations is better in absolute terms, as a passage in English, but we might begin to sense which is more in line with the book's pattern of inflated illusion followed by disillusionment. And if we want to translate a book because we admire the original, perhaps that pattern is worth keeping. Fortunately, to warn us what she has in store,

Morante gives us the emotional cadence of her story in minia-ture right on the first page. Thus the second paragraph, again in merely literal translation, begins:

> Unfortunately, I later came to know that this famous Arturo king of Britain was not definite history, just legend; and so I left him aside for other more historical kings (in my opinion legends were childish things).

It is exactly the learning process we mentioned before. Discovery of the problem of historicity has altered Arturo's appreciation of his name. But no sooner has the Camelot boast been shot down than the boy launches into another self-aggrandizing reflection:

> But another reason, all the same, was enough to give, for me, a heraldic importance to the name Arturo: and that is that to destine me this name (even without knowing, I think, its titled symbols) had been, I discovered, my mother. Who, in herself, was no more than an illiterate girl; but more than a queen, for me.

Of course, the verb "destine" is rarely used, aside from the past participle "destined", and won't do in a final translation, but I put it in this literal version to suggest just how much the nar-rator is puffing things up. One of our two translators felt this long sentence (which, in spite of the period, actually continues in the relative clause "Who, in herself…") was really too much; it was overheated, he thought, and manically indirect. In fact, both translators have split it into three more standard segments. As if to show, though, that the overheating was precisely the point, Morante's next paragraph again begins with a splash of cold water. Translated literally, we have:

About her, in reality, I have always known little, almost nothing: since she died, at the age of not even eighteen years, in the very moment that I, her first son, was born.

Have we done anything to counter the objection that response to translator choices are "just subjective", and so beyond discussion? If we turn to the published translation (1959, by Isabel Quigly), we notice that our three paragraphs have been reduced to two; the boy's disappointment that King Arthur was only legend is now included in the first paragraph, while the second begins with the fact that it was his mother who chose the name. At the same time, the register in this translation shifts radically towards something colloquial and recognizably boyish: "ages ago there was some king called Arthur as well... I thought legends were kid's stuff... a sort of heraldic ring".

Here we have neither the rhetorical puffing-up of the boyish boast, nor the paragraph interruption that underlines its deflation. This observation is not subjective, any more than it is subjective to say that "phalanx" is a word generally used in the context of ancient Greece rather than ancient Britain. It's true, though, that we might find, in spite of these observations, that we *prefer* Quigly's version. There is no reasoning that can *make* us like or dislike something. But with the knowledge we now have of the original, we might also wonder how Quigly's different, more laconic voice can possibly be made to fit with the story that is going to be told. Just as, once it is pointed out, you might start to feel that Arthur's knights are not the three hundred Spartans.

Translating literature is not always more difficult than translating other texts – tourist brochures, technical manuals, art catalogues, sales contracts and the like. But it does have this distinguishing characteristic: its sense is not limited to a simple function of informing or persuading, but rather thrives on a superabundance of possible meanings, an openness to inter-pretation, an invitation to measure what is described against our experience. This is stimulating. The more we bring to it, the more it offers, with the result that later readings will be different from the first in a way that is hardly true of a product description or city guide.

Translators are people who read books for us. Tolstoy wrote in Russian, so someone must read him for us and then write down that reading in our language. Since the book will be fuller and richer the more experience a reader brings to it, we would want our translator, as he or she reads, to be aware of as much as possible, aware of cultural references, aware of lexical pat-terns, aware of geographical setting and historical moment. Aware, too, of our own language and its many resources. Far from being "just subjective", these differences will be a function of the different experiences these readers bring to the book, since none of us accumulates the same experience. Even then, of course, two expert translators will very likely produce two quite different versions. But if what we want is a translation of Tolstoy, rather than just something that sounds good enough sentence by sentence, it would seem preferable to have our reading done for us by people who can bring more, rather than less, to the work.

Does Literature Help Us Live?

Is literature wise? In the sense, does it help us to live? And if not, what exactly is it good for?

One way into that question might be to look at how great writers themselves have benefited. Or haven't. The situation is not immediately promising, since the list of writers who committed suicide, from Seneca the Younger to David Foster Wallace, would be long; Nerval, Hemingway, Plath, Pavese, Zweig, Mayakovsky and Woolf all spring to mind. But I suppose you could argue that there are situations where suicide is the wise decision, or that without literature these talented people might have gone much earlier. The list of those who have driven themselves to an unhappy death would likely be longer still. Dickens, Tolstoy, Joyce, Faulkner, Fitzgerald, Henry Green, Elsa Morante and Dylan Thomas arguably fall in that category. Not to mention those forever frustrated by insufficient recognition and other occupational hazards; the gloom of Giacomo Leopardi would appear to have been oceanic. It is not that there aren't cases of writers who have approached the end of their lives happily enough – Victor Hugo, Alberto Moravia, Natalia Ginzburg, Fyodor Dostoevsky of all unlikely candidates, even that great pessimist Thomas Hardy – simply that a few moments' reflection will suffice to convince us that being a fine writer does not necessarily mean being "skilful" in the Buddhist sense of acting in such a way as to foster serenity, joy, happiness.

Is there, then, something in the nature of the literary that renders the author, but perhaps also the reader, more vulnerable than most people to unhappiness, being troubled, or perhaps simply to the kind of emotional turbulence that writers as far apart as Shelley and Simenon seem invariably to have created around themselves? In short, could it be that there is something about our conception of the literary that not only does not help us to live, but actually makes things more difficult?

Generalization is treacherous, but let's posit that at the centre of most modern storytelling, in particular most literary story-telling, lies the struggling self, or selves, individuals seeking some kind of definition or stability in a world that appears hostile to such aspirations: life is precarious, tumultuous, fickle, and the self seeks in vain, or manages only with great effort, to put together a personal narrative that is, even briefly, satisfying. Of course, the story can end in various ways, or simply stop at some convenient grace point; happy endings are not entirely taboo, though certainly frowned on in the more elevated spheres of seri-ous literary fiction. And even when things do come to a pleasing conclusion, it is either shot through with irony or presented as merely a new beginning, with everything still to fight for.

"They went quietly down into the roaring streets, inseparable and blessed," Dickens tells us of Little Dorrit and Clennam after their five hundred pages of misery, "and as they passed along in sunshine and shade, the noisy and the eager, and the arrogant and the froward and the vain, fretted, and chafed, and made their usual uproar."

How promising is that?

In short, at the core of the literary experience, as it is generally construed and promoted, is the pathos of this unequal battle and of a self inevitably saddened – though perhaps galvanized too, or, in any event, tempered and hardened – by the systematic be-trayal of youth's great expectations. Life promises so much, but then slips through one's fingers. Leopardi offers the refrain of a thousand works of fiction, from Gustave Flaubert's *Sentimental*

Education to Muriel Spark's *The Prime of Miss Jean Brodie*, or any of a hundred Alice Munro stories, when he writes:

> Ah, how truly past you are,
> Dear companion of my innocence,
> My much lamented hope!
> Is this that world? Are these
> The joys, love, deeds, experience
> We talked so often of?

The experience of the literary, then, would seem to be seeing this bitter pill dressed up or administered in such a way that, at least in the telling, it becomes a pleasure. There is the excitement of drama, of complex and unstable situations; there is immersion in fine description, that heightened sense of engagement that comes with recognizing an accurate portrayal of things we know; and, of course, there is the satisfaction of seeing the desperate human condition brilliantly dissected. Sometimes, the more brilliantly pessimistic the dissection, the more stimulating the reading experience, the greater the sense of catastrophe, the more noble, profound and grand the writer who eloquently expresses it. Here is Chateaubriand:

> This impossibility of duration and continuity in human relations, the profound forgetfulness that follows us wherever we go, the invincible silence that fills our graves and stretches from there to our homes, puts me constantly in mind of our inexorable isolation. Any hand will do to give us the last glass of water we will ever need, when we lie sweating on our deathbed. Only let it not be a hand that we love! For how, without despair, can we let go of a hand we have covered with kisses, a hand that we would like to hold for ever to our heart?

What is on offer, then, is the consolation of intelligent form and seductive style, but enlisted to deliver a content that invariably smacks of defeat, or at best a temporary stay of execution. In this sense, our literature seems locked into a systemic antagonism with the crasser side of Western civilization, the brash confidence that all could be improved, controlled, resolved, if only we were better organized and our science more advanced. Literature determinedly confounds such unwarranted optimism; we must face the grim truth, it says, though always armed with the artist's ability to make the performance palatable.

"Works of [literary] genius," Leopardi observed, "have this intrinsic quality, that even when they capture exactly the nothingness of things, or vividly reveal and make us feel life's inevitable unhappiness, or express the most acute hopelessness... they are always a source of consolation and renewed enthusiasm."

But what if one were to suggest that literature exacerbates the very condition it then soothes, the way smoking a cigarette, say, increases the nervousness from which it offers a brief reprieve? This would have to be the position of someone who took, for example, a Buddhist approach to Western literature. With rare exceptions, such a person would surely observe, the literature of modern times exalts the self, the idea of self, the existence of self. Predicated on a hubris of individualism, literature shows the self forming in childhood, narrating itself into selfhood, as it were, in one *Bildungsroman* after another; then it shows the self struggling to maintain its supposed integrity and personhood in adult life. Where a character is conflicted, unable to decide between identities – and that would be the case of so many literary heroes from Hamlet to Stephen Dedalus – this is presented as torment and potential failure.

In short, if this belief in self, or in the construction of selfhood, is to be considered unwise, then literature, for all its magnificent achievements, becomes as much a part of the problem as the solution, an addiction that feeds the sufferings it consoles. One enjoys Kafka's *The Metamorphosis*, one admires Faulkner's *Absalom, Absalom!* or Bernhard's *Gargoyles*, but one comes away with a heightened sense of how much more literature will be required to console such a desperate human condition.

Any number of writers have sensed the trap involved in needing to offer ever more catastrophe and catharsis. If character is destiny and destiny disaster in Shakespeare's tragedies, that conceit becomes far more malleable and open to transformation in the late plays, as the bard prepares to bow out of writing altogether. In *The Winter's Tale* or *Cymbeline*, one senses, as in myth, the coexistence of various versions of the same story, even a detachment of moral qualities and consequent behaviour from personal identity. In those works, evil or compassion or envy is unfolding as an abstract entity, rather than such-and-such a person being evil, compassionate or envious. When Cymbeline or King Polixenes behave rashly, what we have is not the inevitable product of a fatal flaw in a tragic figure, as with Lear or Macbeth, but simply a failure to guard against aberration provoked by special circumstances. So all becomes reversible, and seemingly ruinous behaviour is set to right.

But who would not say that *King Lear* and *Macbeth* are closer to the core of our narrative tradition than *Cymbeline* or *The Winter's Tale*? Samuel Beckett, who repeatedly encourages readers to become aware of their expectations of fiction, making fun of their eagerness for "meaning" and identification, does all he can in his trilogy of novels, *Molloy*, *Malone Dies* and *The Unnamable*, to suggest the absence of anything that might be described as selfhood. Molloy, Moran, Malone, McMann, the Unnamable, are all, apparently, the same "person", but one who is quite unable to impose a coherent story or even a single name on their collective life – though they seem equally unable to stop trying to do so. "I wonder if I am not talking yet again about myself," worries Malone. "Shall I be incapable, to the end, of lying on any other subject? I feel the old dark gathering, the solitude preparing, by which I know myself, and the call of that ignorance which might be noble and is mere poltroonery." Even where there is no selfhood, the nostalgia for self and the compulsive search for selfhood remains the central subject and guarantees unhappiness. The Swiss writer Peter Stamm's most recent novel, *To the Back of Beyond*, in which a character simply splits in two, offering the tragic in one manifestation and the picaresque in the other, is another exploration of this territory.

Again, though, such novels are very much outsiders and, while admired, soon acquire the status of the dead end, the work that cannot influence writers in the mainstream tradition, as though to ditch the self would be to ditch literary fiction *tout court*. Perhaps, in a society so deeply invested in individualism, writers are inevitably drawn to a vision at once catastrophic and consoling, precisely because such a vision exalts the self. It's an approach that finds its most extravagant expression in works like Chateaubriand's *René* or Byron's *Childe Harold's Pilgrimage*, but is still powerfully present in novels as apparently different as *The Catcher in the Rye* or Saul Bellow's *Herzog*. Leopardi catches the grandeur, misery and comedy of it all in this note on a line from the *Aeneid*:

"*Moriemur inultæ, Sed moriamur, ait. Sic sic iuvat ire sub umbras.*" ["I shall die unavenged, but let me die" – Dido says – "like this, like this it's good to go down among the shades".]
Here Virgil wanted to get across... the pleasure the mind takes in dwelling on its downfall, its adversities, then picturing them for itself, not just intensely, but minutely, intimately, completely; in exaggerating them even, if it can (and if it can, it certainly will), in recognizing, or imagining, but definitely

in persuading itself and making absolutely sure it persuades itself, beyond any doubt, that these adversities are extreme, endless, boundless, irremediable, unstoppable, beyond any redress... in short in seeing and intensely feeling that its own personal tragedy is truly immense and perfect and as complete as it could be in all its parts.

"The pleasure the mind takes in dwelling on its downfall"... At this point, then, we may have our answer to what literature is good for. It is good, at least in a great majority of cases, for going on exactly as we always have, for keeping the market supplied.

Certainly, this was Tolstoy's feeling when he gave up writing fiction after *Anna Karenina*. There were more serious things to be getting on with. But he went back to it years later, to write the tormented *Kreutzer Sonata*, and years later again, to write the distraught and penitential *Resurrection*. For when the fiction drug is pure, and with Tolstoy it always was, inebriation is guaranteed. This is not an easy habit to break.

Acknowledgements

Many, many thanks to everybody who made this book what it is. First of all the team at the *New York Review of Books* – Hugh Eakin, Matt Seaton, Gabriel Winslow-Yost and Lucy McKeon – who helped me shape and also shorten these pieces. Their feedback was invaluable. Thanks also to Gregory Cowles for his input on the three pieces published with the *New York Times*. Then heartfelt gratitude to Alessandro Gallenzi and Elisabetta Minervini at Alma Books, who saw at once that these pieces were meant to be read together and would make sense as a book. Without them it wouldn't have got into print. And finally thanks to Christian Müller for his meticulous editing in the final stages. Books are a joint effort, the author can't do it alone. I have been lucky with my collaborators.

Note on the Texts

The essays in this collection first appeared online in the *New York Review of Books Daily* between 2014 and 2017, except for 'Book Fair Hype', 'After Brexit' and 'God's Smuggler', which were published in the *New York Times* in 2016 and 2017.